Rin Tin Tin

Most Faithfully
Rin-tin-tin
Lee Duncan
master and friend 1931

RIN TIN TIN

THE LIFE AND THE LEGEND

SUSAN ORLEAN

THORNDIKE PRESS
A part of Gale, Cengage Learning

Detroit • New York • San Francisco • New Haven, Conn • Waterville, Maine • London

GALE
CENGAGE Learning™

LIBRARY OF CONGRESS CATALOGING-IN-PUBLICATION DATA

Orlean, Susan.
   Rin Tin Tin : the life and the legend / by Susan Orlean.
     p. cm. — (Thorndike press large print biography.)
   Includes bibliographical references.
   ISBN-13: 978-1-4104-4344-1 (hardcover : lg. print)
   ISBN-10: 1-4104-4344-2 (hardcover : lg. print)
   1. Rin-Tin-Tin (Dog) 2. German shepherd dog—United
States—Biography. 3. Working dogs—United States—Biography. 4. Dogs
in motion pictures—History—20th century. 5. Dogs in the performing
arts—History—20th century. I. Title.
SF429.G37O75 2011b
636.737'6—dc23   2011033912

Published in 2011 by arrangement with Simon & Schuster, Inc.

For John and Austin, my people
and
For Molly, Cooper, and Ivy, my dogs

CONTENTS

Rin Tin Tin

FOREVER

He believed the dog was immortal. "There will always be a Rin Tin Tin," Lee Duncan said, time and time again, to reporters, to visitors, to fan magazines, to neighbors, to family, to friends. At first this must have sounded absurd — just wishful thinking about the creature that had eased his loneliness and made him famous around the world. And yet, just as Lee believed, there has always been a Rin Tin Tin. The second Rin Tin Tin was not the talent his father was, but still, he was Rin Tin Tin, carrying on what the first dog had begun. After Rin Tin Tin Jr. there was Rin Tin Tin III, and then another Rin Tin Tin after him, and then another, and then another: there has always been another. And Rin Tin Tin has always been more than a dog. He was an idea and an ideal — a hero who was also a friend, a fighter who was also a caretaker, a mute genius, a companionable loner. He was one dog and many dogs, a real animal and an invented character, a pet as well as an international celebrity. He was born in 1918 and he never died.

There were low moments and setbacks when Lee did doubt himself and Rin Tin Tin. The winter of 1952 was one such point. Lee was broke. He had washed out of Hollywood and was living in the blank, baked valley east of Los Angeles, surviving on his wife's job at an orange-packing plant while Rin Tin Tin survived on free kibble Lee received through an old sponsorship arrangement with Ken-L-Ration, the dog food company. The days were long. Most afternoons Lee retreated to a little annex off his barn that he called the Memory Room, where he shuffled through old newspaper clips and yellowing photographs of Rin Tin Tin's glory days, pulling the soft quilt of memory — of what really was and what he recalled and what he wished had been — over the bony edges of his life.

Twenty years earlier, the death of the first Rin Tin Tin had been so momentous that radio stations around the country interrupted programming to announce the news and then broadcast an hour-long tribute to the late, great dog. Rumors sprang up that

Rin Tin Tin's last moments, like his life, were something extraordinary — that he had died like a star, cradled in the pale, glamorous arms of actress Jean Harlow, who lived near Lee in Beverly Hills. But now everything was different. Even Ken-L-Ration was doubting him. "Your moving picture activities have not materialized as you expected," the company's executives scolded Lee in a letter warning that they were planning to cut off his supply of free dog food. Lee was stunned. He needed the dog food, but the rejection stung even more because he believed that his dog, Rin Tin Tin III, was destined to be a star, just as his grandfather had been. Lee wrote back to the company, pleading. He said that the dog had "his whole life before him" and new opportunities lined up. His father and grandfather had already been celebrated around the world in silent films, talkies, radio, vaudeville, comics, and books; this new Rin Tin Tin, Lee insisted, was ready to conquer television, "the coming medium," as he described it.

In truth, Lee had no contracts and no connections to the television business and doubts about its being anything more than a fad, but with the prospect of losing Ken-L-Ration hanging over him, he rushed to

13

find a producer interested in making a television show starring Rin Tin Tin. It couldn't be just anybody, though: Lee wanted someone who he felt really understood the dog and his profound attachment to him.

The winter went by with no luck; then spring, then summer. Then one September afternoon in 1953, a stuntman who knew Lee from his Hollywood days came out to visit along with a young production manager named Herbert "Bert" Leonard. The stuntman knew Lee was looking for a producer, and he also knew Bert wanted a project to produce. Even so, it was an unlikely match. Lee was a Westerner, an eccentric cowboy who was comfortable only with his dogs and horses; Bert was a young, loud New Yorker who gambled, smoked cigars while playing tennis, and loved attention, but had no interest in dogs. And yet their connection was lightning, and Bert decided he wanted to make a television show starring Rin Tin Tin.

At the time, Bert was managing the production of a low-budget thriller called *Slaves of Babylon;* during his lunch break the next day, he wrote up his idea for a show he called *The Adventures of Rin Tin Tin,* starring the dog and an orphaned boy who are adopted by a U.S. Cavalry troop in Arizona in the late 1800s, during the Apache wars. As Bert recalled later, Lee "went crazy for it." The story was fiction, but it captured something essential in Lee's relationship to the dog, and in the dog's nature — a quality of pure attachment, of bravery, of independence that was wrapped around a core of vulnerability. The show debuted three years later. It climbed in the ratings faster than any show in the history of television. Almost four decades after Lee first found Rin Tin Tin, the most famous dog in the world was born again. Lee had always been convinced that his dog was immortal. Now Bert was convinced, too. As he liked to say, "Rin Tin Tin just seems to go on forever."

In the first years of the twenty-first century, Daphne Hereford hitched her 1984 Cadillac El Dorado Biarritz convertible parade car to the back of a U-Haul truck and fishtailed out of her driveway in Texas, setting off on an eleven-month tour of the United States with three of her German shepherds: Gayle, Joanne, and Rin Tin Tin VIII, whose registered name was Rin Tin Tins Oooh-Ahhh but whom she generally referred to as the

Old Man. Gayle was pregnant and needed attention and Joanne was good company; the Old Man, though, was the big ticket. Daphne never went anywhere without the Old Man. At home, the other dogs spent most of their time in their kennels in the backyard; only the Old Man had house privileges. She planned to have him taxidermied when he died so she could always have him around.

The purpose of this cross-country trip was to present the Old Man at German shepherd shows and Hollywood memorabilia events around the country. It was not luxury travel. Daphne tolerated the meaner vagaries of life on the road, including, for example, the time when a friend she was staying with out west tried to kill her. She shrugs off the attempted murder along with all the other inconveniences of the journey. "I don't give up," she told me when I visited her in Texas not long ago. "I just don't give up."

Persistence is a family trait. Her grandmother, who had fallen in love with Rin Tin Tin when she saw his early movies, was so determined to have a Rin Tin Tin dog of her own that in 1956 she tracked down Lee Duncan and sent a letter pleading for a puppy. "I have wanted a Rin

Tin Tin dog all my life," she wrote, adding, before asking the price, "I am not one of those Rich Texans you hear about. Just a plain old country girl that was raised on a ranch." She said she hoped to begin "a living legacy of Rin Tin Tin dogs in Houston" and promised that if Lee would send a puppy to her in Houston, she would return the shipping crate to him, posthaste, parcel post. Lee, impressed by her determination, agreed to sell her a puppy "of excellent quality" sired by Rin Tin Tin IV.

When her grandmother died in 1988, Daphne took on the stewardship of that legacy. She also revived the Rin Tin Tin Fan Club and registered as many Rin Tin Tin trademarks as she could. All of her money went to the dogs, the fan club, and other dog-related projects. She lived in a little shotgun house in Latexo, Texas, and scrimped to keep her costs down. For Daphne, it was all about continuing the Rin Tin Tin line. The line led from the Old Man back through the generations, from dog to dog to dog, a knot here and there, but always continuing, back to the original dog, and, most important, back to the original notion — that something you truly love will never die.

■ ■ ■ ■

My most vivid memory of Rin Tin Tin is not of a live dog at all, but of a plastic one: a Rin Tin Tin figure about eight inches high, stoic, bright-eyed, the bud of his tongue draped over his bottom teeth. My grandfather kept this figurine on his desk blotter, maddeningly out of reach. Somewhat dour and formal, my grandfather, an accountant, was not very interested in, or natural with, children. Strangely enough, however, he was very fond of toys; in fact, he collected them, and displayed a few special ones in his office at home. The most exceptional of these was the Rin Tin Tin figurine, that special dog, the star of the television show I loved.

At that time, in the 1950s, Rin Tin Tin was everywhere, universal, almost something in the air. I was only four years old when the show began its initial run, so my memory of that period is only a faint outline. But my brother and sister watched the show with the dedication and regularity of churchgoers, so I'm sure I plunked down beside them. When you're as young as I was at the time, you just soak something like that up and it becomes part of you, so

I feel I have always known of Rin Tin Tin, as if he was introduced to me by osmosis. He became part of my consciousness, like a nursery lullaby you can sing without realizing how you came to know it. In the buzzing white noise of my babyhood, a boy on a television was always shouting "Yo, Rinty," a bugle was always blowing, and a big dog was always bounding across the screen to save the day.

That is why the first dog I ever wanted was a German shepherd, and why I kept wanting one well past the point at which it had been made amply clear that I was never going to get one — my mother, unfortunately, was afraid of dogs. Like so many childhood passions, it eventually receded but never died. I came across the name "Rin Tin Tin" a few years ago, while reading about animals in Hollywood. It was a name I had not heard or thought about for decades, but a shock of recognition surged through me and made me sit up straight, as if I had brushed against a hot stove.

And instantly I remembered that figurine, and remembered yearning for it. My desire for it had remained unrequited. My grandfather allowed us to hold one or two of his toys on occasion, but never Rin Tin Tin. I didn't understand why this was the one treasure we could never touch; it wasn't more delicate than the other toys, and it didn't have any finicky mechanism. There was no explanation; it was simply not ours to have.

There was something spellbinding about our visits to that office — my grandfather looming above us, his hand hovering over the desk blotter to choose the toy he would allow us to hold, our eyes following his hand as it paused at this toy and that toy, each time drifting close to Rin Tin Tin but passing it by again, lifting our hopes and dropping them; then his hand grasping and passing to us some other forgettable toy and waving us out of the room. Time tumbled on, as it does, and people changed, as they do, but that dog figurine was always constant, always beckoning, always the same. When I was reminded of Rin Tin Tin after decades of forgetting all about him, the first thing I thought of, with a deep, sharp pang, was that mysterious and eternal figurine.

FOUNDLINGS

1.

Rin Tin Tin was born on a battlefield in eastern France in September 1918. The exact date isn't certain, because no one who was present during the birth ever reported on it, but when Lee found the puppies on September 15, 1918, they were blind and bald and still nursing. They were probably just a few days old.

The Meuse Valley of France in 1918 was a terrible place to be born. In most other circumstances, the valley — plush and undulating, checkered with dairy farms — would have been inviting, but it rolls to the German border, and in 1918 it was the hot center of World War I. As the German artillery advanced westward, the villages in the Meuse were pounded to a muddy pulp. The troops faced off in trenches, where the fighting was slow, relentless, and brutal. Barbed wire was strung across hundreds of miles. Much of the combat was hand-to-hand. Weapons were crude. Blistering, poisonous chlorine and mustard gas had recently been introduced in battle for the first time. Casualties were almost medieval. There were so many victims with severe facial injuries that a group of them formed an organization called La Union des Blessés de la Face — the Union of the Smashed Faces. Death was everywhere. By 1918, when Rin Tin Tin was born, there were more than 1 million war orphans in France.

Unlike the Rin Tin Tin I knew as a kid, the puppy in this litter who grew up to be a movie star was dark-coated and slim-nosed, with unexpectedly dainty feet and the resigned and solemn air of an existentialist. In his most popular portrait — shot in the 1920s, copied by the tens of thousands, and signed "Most Faithfully, Rin Tin Tin" in Lee's spiky script — his jaw is set and his eyes are cast downward, as if he was thinking about something very sad. Even when he was photographed doing something playful like, say, waterskiing or sunbathing or riding a horse or getting a manicure or snowshoeing with starlets or drinking a glass of milk with a group of children who were also drinking milk, he had a way of looking pensive, preoccupied, as if there were a weight in his soul.

2.

Leland Duncan was a country boy, a third-generation Californian. One of his grandmothers was a Cherokee, and one grandfather had come west with the Mormon pioneer Brigham Young and then settled in the still-empty stretches of southern California. The family ranched, farmed, scratched out some kind of living, made their way. They were not fancy. Lee's mother, Elizabeth, fell in love when she was sixteen. Little is known of her beau other than that his name was Grant Duncan, and he was a dreamer. Even though Grant's family was better off than Elizabeth's, her parents didn't like him, and they were furious when she married him in 1891.

Lee was born in 1893, when Elizabeth was just eighteen. She pictured a bright future for him: she named him after California railroad magnate Leland Stanford. Three years later, Elizabeth gave birth to a girl, Marjorie. Two years after that, when Lee was five, the dreamy Grant Duncan took off and was never heard from again. In time, when Lee became a Hollywood figure, Grant's disappearance was transformed by the alchemy of press agentry; instead of having abandoned his wife and children, he had suffered a "tragic early death due to a burst appendix." Lee never corrected that account, nor did he elaborate on it.

Lee was a great keeper of notes and letters and memos and documents, which are now archived in the Riverside Metropolitan Museum. In those thousands of pages, which include a detailed memoir — a rough draft for the autobiography Lee planned to write and the movie he hoped would be made about his life — there is only one reference to his father, and even that is almost an aside. Lee writes that he "lost Father" around the same time that Elizabeth's brother died from a rattlesnake bite. Lee then notes that his mother took her horse for a long, hard ride to shake off the grief of losing her brother. Lee describes the horse in great detail, but there is not another word about his father.

Uneducated, unskilled, and on her own with two young children, estranged from her parents and unaided by other relatives, Elizabeth gathered up Lee and Marjorie, took the train from Los Angeles to Oakland, and applied to leave them at the Fred Finch

Children's Home, an orphanage in the East Bay Hills.

This was 1898. A decade earlier, the United States had been in a period of growth and comfortable decorousness, but in 1893 several major businesses had collapsed, setting off a financial panic, and the country had cartwheeled into a depression. Banks were failing; railroads were going bankrupt. There was a cholera outbreak; a smallpox outbreak; a miserable and suffocating closeness in city slums. For children, it was a particularly harsh time. Thousands lived on their own, having lost their parents to disease, and thousands more were cast out by families who couldn't afford to keep them. In New York City, gangs of abandoned children lived on the streets. Eventually, more than two hundred thousand children from the New York area were sent west on "orphan trains," which dropped them off along the route to be taken in by pioneer families, sometimes as foster children, and sometimes as near slaves.

The Fred Finch Children's Home was a Methodist institution, solid and earnest. Its founders were proud of the home's cleanliness and order, especially compared to the dank, germy orphanages in bigger cities. An

27

early brochure boasted that in its first five years of operation, not a single one of the Fred Finch children had died.

Like most orphanages of the time, Fred Finch was a refuge not just for the truly orphaned but also for children who needed care while their parents struggled through a period of adversity or until the children were fourteen years old, when state payments for their upkeep ended. The orphanage operated as a peculiar sort of pawnshop. Parents could reclaim their children when circumstances improved — unless, in the meantime, the children had been adopted by other couples, who could shop the orphanage inventory and ask to take a child home if one happened to catch their eye.

Elizabeth filled out an application to leave Lee and Marjorie at Fred Finch, answering the questions tersely:

Reputation and sobriety of parents? *Good.*

If either or both parents have deserted the child, state when. *Father deserted January 8, 1897.*

Will the child inherit anything from its parents' estate or insurance? If so, how much? *Nothing that I know of.*

Is the father dead? *I do not know.*

The orphanage physician examined Lee and

Marjorie, and then Elizabeth signed the papers and said goodbye. "How [Mother] kissed us, left us on the porch and walked down that long lane to the car line will be a picture I shall never forget," Lee later wrote in his memoir. "The days that followed were very lonely and sad and when night came, it seemed as though my bed was falling into some dark well or canyon."

Over the next three years, many people who visited Fred Finch looked at cute, curly-haired Marjorie and came close to adopting her, but only one family gave serious thought to adopting Lee, pausing to look him over as if he were a stray at an animal shelter. Then they decided that Lee's ears were too big and moved on to examine other children.

Lee and Marjorie lived at the orphanage for three years. In the span of a child's life, that's a long time: Lee was six years old, a child, when he arrived and nine when he left, a real boy. He was never, technically, an orphan, since his mother was alive, but in a sense, he came of age in the orphanage. The experience shaped him; for the rest of his life, he was always deeply alone, always had the aloneness to retreat to, as if it were a room in his house. The only companion in his loneliness he would ever find would be his dog, and his attachment to animals grew to be deeper than his attachment to any person.

Surprisingly, once he left Fred Finch, Lee didn't choose to forget the place and the years he lived there. He seemed to look on it not as a nightmare he had survived but as a sorrowful time that had been redeemed. When Rin Tin Tin was bringing him all the money and fame in the world, Lee took every opportunity to mention publicly that he had lived in an orphanage when he was young. He carried a copy of his Fred Finch admission papers with him at all times, till the day he died. When he did publicity tours with Rin Tin Tin, his first stop was always the local orphanage. This kind of visit was a convention for many public figures, but for Lee it was like going home. He visited Fred Finch often; he became a celebrity there. In 1934, the children at the home staged a play based on his life. After the performance, a staff member wrote to Lee, "Boys and girls are beginning to hold their heads a little higher — to say with a note of pride, 'I came from the home, too — same home as Mr. Lee Duncan!' You have raised us to a pedestal by your coming."

Fred Finch is on the rise of a hill in Oakland, in the shadow of a huge Mormon temple, and is now called the Fred Finch Youth Center. One day not long ago, I stopped by hoping to visit the dormitory where Lee felt himself falling into a dark well. But most of what had existed when Lee and Marjorie lived there is gone: many of the original buildings burned down years ago, and others were torn down in the 1960s because they had gotten shabby. The new buildings are bland and boxy, the usual institutional structures, and the campus resembles a midpriced office park. The residence building, where the children lived, is now an administrative office; a bedroom that could have been Lee's is now the accounting department. I strolled across the campus and then, at the last minute, ducked into another of the remaining original buildings. I wandered down a long corridor with glossy green walls and went around a corner. Hanging there, in front of me, was a large framed picture of Lee on one of his many visits to Fred Finch with Rin Tin Tin, smiling down at a crowd of eager little kids.

Was it by chance or by design or by some mix of the two that the fatherless and motherless were drawn to Rin Tin Tin? Lee never knew his father, and had no parents at all for three critical years of his life. Bert Leonard had the edgy, fists-up manner of a

31

stray, and he had only a passing relationship with his father, who always managed to be missing when Bert needed him. Daphne Hereford was abandoned by her mother; she was raised by her grandmother and spent most of her time with her grandmother's dogs. Rin Tin Tin came to be loved by millions of people around the world. Many of them had intact families and no hole in their happiness. But he meant something special to people who had a persistent absence in their lives: he was, ultimately, the true companion for the companionless.

3.

In 1901, Elizabeth reconciled with her parents. At the time, they were managing a ranch outside San Diego, and they offered to take her and the children in. On that news, Elizabeth went to Fred Finch to reclaim Lee and Marjorie, who had spent their years at the orphanage not knowing whether that day would ever come. Elizabeth bundled the children onto the train and headed south.

"Then came the ride back to the country, the life I love best of all," Lee wrote. In a single day, he was whisked from Fred Finch, where he lived in close quarters with three hundred children, to a ranch where the closest neighbors lived nine miles away. Lee's only friend there was a stick horse he rode day and night. His grandfather had several dogs, but Lee wasn't permitted to even touch them, let alone treat them as companions. They were ranch dogs, used to herd livestock, and his grandfather, a severe and unyielding figure, told Lee their training would be ruined if he played with them. Lee was only allowed to "admire them from a distance."

Eventually Lee was given a lamb as a pet. He adored the lamb, taught him tricks, took him everywhere — he even slept with the lamb, whenever he managed to sneak him into the house. One day, when Lee wasn't paying attention, the lamb ate Lee's grandfather's favorite rose bush. The man was enraged. He had the lamb slaughtered. "It was then that he killed something inside of me," Lee wrote in his memoir. "It took many years to outgrow that hurt."

Several years later, Lee finally got his first dog, a little terrier he named Jack. He quickly discovered the pleasure of training him, and the two of them spent hours together every day in a corral behind the house, practicing their routine. Lee realized, right away, that he had a talent for it. He always attributed his talent more to diligence than to genius, more to patience and practice than to anything else, but he knew that he had a special capacity for working with dogs.

One day, Elizabeth announced that she and the children were leaving the ranch. It is unclear what prompted the decision, but she took Lee and Marjorie to Los Angeles and moved in with an uncle of Grant Duncan's — the husband who had deserted her — which suggests that she might have fallen out with her parents. She told Lee they would have to leave his dog, Jack, behind until they had settled in but promised they would send for him as soon as they could. Lee was physically sick with longing for the dog and spent ten days in bed. Elizabeth finally told him that Jack would never be joining them. He had been given to some friends of hers; she told Lee she had decided it was best if he didn't visit him. Losing Jack was one of the worst experiences of his life, but Lee promised his mother he would put it out of his mind. "From that time on," he declared, "Jack was just a memory." He never saw Jack again.

Elizabeth eventually married a man named Oscar Sampson, and the family moved from

Los Angeles to Burbank, probably into Sampson's home. Lee lived with his mother and sister well into adulthood and wrote extensively in his memoir about their life together, but he never once mentioned Sampson. He also never mentioned that Elizabeth and Oscar Sampson had a daughter. It was as if Lee was determined to stay orphaned forever — as if he was more comfortable with, or at least accustomed to, being a solitary, fatherless boy.

He found his pleasure everywhere other than with people. He loved being alone, outside. One of Elizabeth's cousins was the foreman of a colossal 350,000-acre ranch near Los Angeles, and Lee went there as often as he could, spending days in the wilderness alone, fishing and hunting and hiking. During high school he got a job in the gun department at Bernal Dyas Sporting Goods, and after he dropped out of school he worked at the store full-time. He had no particular idea of what he would do with himself, but he knew he wanted to work outdoors. He thought about becoming a forest ranger or a fire lookout, and he wanted to learn how to fly a plane because he thought it might advance either of those plans.

Whatever reason Elizabeth had for getting

rid of Jack seems to have evaporated by this time, and Lee got a new dog, which he named Firefly. This wasn't another mongrel ranch dog like Jack: Firefly was a purebred Airedale, with a star-studded pedigree. Owning a purebred dog in the early 1900s was unusual, and the showing and breeding of pedigree dogs was an upper-class sport, nearly as exclusive as racehorse breeding. For a lower-middle-class kid like Lee, it was a surprising pursuit. He started taking Firefly to dog shows, and once the dog became a champion, Lee started breeding her and selling the puppies. He was devoted to the dog. When he joined the army in 1917, hoping he would get free flying lessons out of it, he left Firefly behind with great regret.

The first Americans in World War I were rich, educated pilots who signed up even before the United States officially joined the Allied effort. Most of them flew with a French squadron called Lafayette Escadrille. The squadron was a stylish outfit that had a pair of lion cubs named Whiskey and Soda as its mascots. The pilots often brought Whiskey and Soda along when they flew sorties. There were other squadron pets, too. Blair Thaw, heir to a train and boat fortune, never took off without his big Irish terrier on board and loved to demonstrate how he had trained the dog to refuse food if Thaw told him that the kaiser had sent it. Blair's brother William, who was the first American to fly a mission in the war, usually had his pet skunk in the copilot's seat.

In spite of their antics, the Lafayette Escadrille pilots were capable and accomplished; they flew scores of successful missions and amassed dozens of medals, including the Croix de Guerre. They were also killed at a staggering rate. But they projected something dashing and indomitable, and they became popular subjects of the short, biweekly newsreels that were shown in theaters before featured films. The pilots' animals were ideal sidekicks, making the whole thing appear casual, almost sporting — as if aerial combat were a prelude to a good game of fetch. Even when the news from Europe was discouraging, a newsreel featuring a handsome young man skimming through the sky with a round-eyed lion cub beside him in the cockpit made the grim war almost seem gay.

The newsreels, with their jazzy, insouciant tone, must have tantalized kids like Lee Duncan, who had never seen anything so glamorous. When the United States finally entered the war, these were the kids who fumbled their way into the armed forces right out of high school or off the farm, and rode slow boats across the ocean to watch the world being harshly remade.

4.

At the time, the United States had fewer than two hundred thousand battle-ready troops, so training for newly enlisted men like Lee was hasty. He went through a two-week boot camp in Texas. Then, along with several thousand recruits and several hundred horses, he shipped out to Europe on a slow-moving decommissioned British troop carrier. The crossing to Europe was seventeen days of rough seas. Most of the men were desperately seasick. Three died of disease. Lee's most vivid recollection of the trip, though, was of the terrible noise made by the horses, miserable and sick in their stalls below decks.

They landed at Glasgow and were then loaded on a train for England. At first, Lee was utterly lost. In his memoir, he gamely described the experience as interesting. "Even the food is novel," he wrote, noting that it was the first time he had ever drunk tea or been served rabbit with its ears still attached. Everything in England astonished him. When I first read his memoir, I was surprised by how surprised he was, until I remembered that in 1917 most Americans had no idea what other countries looked like — and similarly, most Europeans had never seen the United States.

Lee was assigned to the 135th Aero Squadron. He was a low-ranking gunnery corporal, although in time, his Hollywood biography and his own gentle embellishments made him out to be an officer — sometimes a lieutenant, often a captain — or an aviator. His squadron had nineteen soldiers and a plane called *What the Hell Bill.* The troops believed that *What the Hell Bill* was a lucky charm, although, as it turned out, this was hardly true: most of the squadron's officers were eventually killed in combat. Lee had enlisted hoping to fly, but he was earthbound. Thanks to his job at Bernal Dyas, he was a crack gun mechanic, so he was assigned to service the artillery. For weeks after arriving in England, the squadron was on hold, waiting for their orders to head to the front. On furloughs, Lee didn't explore London or flirt with local girls; he spent his time traveling around the English countryside, looking for a well-bred dog to bring home.

The countryside, though, was quiet; all the dogs were gone. Lee later learned that because of food shortages, many people had gotten rid of their pets, and many others had donated their dogs to the British Army to use in the war.

It is estimated that 16 million animals were deployed in World War I. Their presence alongside the equipment of warfare suggests a surreal fusion of clumsy antiquity and vicious modernity. Many species were involved. Britain's Imperial Camel Corps boasted thousands of ill-tempered camels. The cavalry used close to a million riding horses. Heavy draft horses pulled artillery and guns. Thousands of mules drew carts or packed loads. Hundreds of thousands of homing pigeons carried messages. Oxen dragged the heaviest equipment wagons. Dogs were everywhere. Germany, where the first military dog training school in the world was established in 1884, had 30,000 dogs on active duty, and the British and French armies had at least 20,000, of which 7,000 were pets donated by private citizens. (If a dog was deemed a washout in training, the British put a tag around its neck saying USELESS. Most of these dogs were taken out and shot.) In fact, every country in the war used dogs except for the United States. By the time the U.S. military came to appreciate their value, it was too late to develop an American canine corps, so when necessary, the United States borrowed dogs from the French and British armies.

Dogs worked in every imaginable capacity, and some that were unimaginable. Many served as messengers, carrying notes between troops across contested ground. It was a dangerous job that was assigned to the lowest-ranked soldiers if no dogs were available. (Adolf Hitler was a messenger in the kaiser's army.) Red Cross dogs, also known as "sanitary" or "mercy" dogs, worked in the field after battles ended, roaming among the casualties with saddlebags of medical supplies. If a soldier was injured but conscious, he could call a dog over and help himself to bandages or water; if he was mortally wounded, he could embrace the dog for comfort while he died. Other dogs were trained to assist medics. Once fighting stopped, these animals, known as cadaver dogs, were sent out to survey the field. Dogs can distinguish by scent whether someone is alive or dead, and the cadaver dogs were taught to indicate, by barking or pulling a piece of a soldier's clothing, which bodies on a battlefield still had life in them. When there were hundreds or thousands of bodies littered on a field, the dogs' survey saved the medics a great deal of time.

Every type of dog had a role. Big dogs pulled ordnance and ammunition on carts; little dogs — "ratters" — cleared rodents out of the trenches. Aggressive dogs were used as sentries and on patrol. The unluckiest dogs were called "demolition wolves" — they were suicide bombers, released into enemy territory with explosives strapped to their bodies. Probably the most warmly welcomed were the cigarette dogs: terriers that carried saddlebags full of cigarettes, which they were trained to distribute among the troops.

The British Army's official dog was the Airedale, tall and agile, useful in nearly every capacity; in England there had been a call to the public to donate their Airedales to the army, which is why Lee couldn't find one to bring home. The Belgian army had several breeds of huge working dogs. Accustomed to pulling milk carts in peacetime, these dogs were easily reassigned to haul machine guns during the war. Sled dogs, retrievers, collies, and bulldogs were also used. Mixed breeds, if they were strong and smart — and preferably dark-colored, so they were harder to spot at night — were put to work. Any dog, as long as it was not shy or stupid, had a chance to take part in the war.

Stories circulated of dogs that performed extraordinary feats. There was Prince, of the North Staffordshire Regiment, who walked two hundred miles from his home in Hammersmith, England, to find his master in a trench in Armentières, France; Sergeant-Major Mac, a mongrel who was able to distinguish between enemy and Allied aircraft by sound and served as an early-warning system for the 449th British Siege Battery; Crump, a Brussels griffon who was a pack-a-day smoker and accompanied a British general on active service until the Armistice. Stubby the Hero Dog, a moth-eaten stray, was the mascot of the U.S. Army's 102nd Infantry and stood with the troops through seventeen major battles. After the war, Stubby shook hands with Presidents Woodrow Wilson, Warren Harding, and Calvin Coolidge; when he died he was stuffed and mounted and put in the Smithsonian on display.

The first time most people in the world saw a German shepherd dog was in the war, and it caused an immediate sensation. A cavalry officer named Max Emil Friedrich von Stephanitz had developed the breed in Germany in 1899, just fifteen years before the war. Von Stephanitz was a German nobleman with a tentative-looking jaw and a bold black moustache, and a great interest in dogs. Just as he was about to be promoted in the army, he made the strategic mistake of marrying an actress. By the standards of priggish nineteenth-century Germany, a woman in theater was practically a prostitute; the scandal of his marriage forced von Stephanitz to resign his commission. He seemed to enjoy the fact that unemployment afforded him more time to spend at dog shows. At that point, there were many different shepherd-like breeds in Germany, but not a single standardized type. Von Stephanitz had a Germanic enthusiasm for genetics and had studied briefly at a veterinary college. He was convinced that if he carefully managed bloodlines he could establish a distinct and superior type of dog that could become the national breed of Germany. He preferred muscular dogs with erect ears rather than fuzzy dogs with floppy ears, and as he wrote in his book *The German Shepherd Dog,* he liked dogs that demonstrated "attentiveness, unshockability, tractability, watchfulness, reliability, and incorruptibility together with courage, fighting tenacity, and hardness." This new breed, von Stephanitz imagined, would be a worker, good at managing flocks and guarding farms: smart, athletic, and loyal to the bone. Most important, it would have a unique capacity for bonding with human beings.

In 1899, after months of searching throughout Germany, von Stephanitz found a dog that had the look and temperament he had in mind. The dog was named Hektor. According to von Stephanitz, he was "one live wire . . . his character was on a par with his exterior qualities . . . the straightforward nature of a gentleman with a boundless zest for living." From the sound of it, Hektor was, to put it politely, an untrained creature. "When left to himself," von Stephanitz admitted, "he is the maddest rascal, the wildest ruffian and incorrigible provoker of strife; never idle, always on the go; well disposed to harmless people, but no cringer, mad about children and always in love."

Von Stephanitz changed Hektor's name to Horand and began breeding him with suitable mates, hoping to advance what he called his "grand design." As soon as there was a sufficient number of Horand's puppies that matched his standard for the breed, von Stephanitz founded the Verein für Deutsche Schäferhunde — commonly known as simply SV, the German Shepherd Dog Club — and established benchmarks for the breed such as height, weight, color, bone structure, and coat.

Von Stephanitz's new breed proved popular; Horand's puppies were snapped up and the club grew quickly. Von Stephanitz maintained strict control, insisting on approving which dogs were mated, having all new litters of German shepherds inspected by the club's "breed wardens," and even deciding how many puppies a breeder could keep of any new litters. The American Kennel Club first recognized German shepherd dogs as a breed in 1908 and registered a female named Queen of Switzerland that year. For years, German shepherds were rare and expensive in the United States: a male German shepherd at the 1913 Westminster Kennel Club show sold for $10,000, the equivalent of $215,000 today. In Germany, though, there were enough dogs that met von Stephanitz's breed standards by 1914 that he approached the German high command and suggested adopting German shepherds as the country's official army dog.

Dogs were already highly valued by the German military; they were classified by the army as "important auxiliaries." The *New York Times* reported that the first military dog training school, opened in Berlin in 1884, had made "wonderful progress" in preparing animals to assist on the battlefield. Most of the dogs used in the German army were a ragtag assortment of shepherd types. Von Stephanitz dreamed of a unified, standardized German dog army, the sons and daughters and nieces and nephews of Horand. At first the military ignored his proposal. Von Stephanitz then donated a number of his German shepherds to local police departments, where they quickly proved their worth. The military noticed and reconsidered, and soon hundreds and then thousands of these new German shepherd dogs joined the ranks.

5.

After months of waiting, Lee's squadron was transferred from England to France and was headquartered near Toul, a Gothic town on the Moselle River that had once been sacked by Attila the Hun. Toul had so far been untouched by the war, even though it was just fifty miles from the stone-ringed citadel town of Verdun, where a deadly battle had been fought just two years earlier.

Verdun was a war prize: it was an important midpoint on the "sacred road," as the main supply route from Paris to the battlefront was called. The Germans and French had squared off at Verdun for almost a year in a clash that alternated between ferocity and numbing dullness. Sixty million artillery shells were fired, pocking the hills and battering the fields until Verdun was a mire of mud. Between the assaults, nothing moved, nothing happened. The soldiers sat in bored terror in their trenches. Many used their idle hours to make "trench art" — tiny animal figurines sculpted out of spent bullets, war scenes carved on shell casings, little cars and trucks whittled out of bits of bone or wood. Somehow, being in an ugly place inspired them to make things that were beautiful or playful. Eleven months into the conflict, the French finally pushed forward and the Germans pulled back, abandoning field guns, artillery, vehicles, and animals in the pudding of the Verdun battlefield. By then, more than half a million soldiers had been injured and more than a quarter of a million had been killed.

One of the heroes of the Battle of Verdun was Satan, a mongrel with gray fur and a small, thick body. It is hard to know what Satan's face looked like because the only photograph of him that still exists shows him wearing a gas mask, which obscures all but the base of his ears. During the battle, a contingent of French troops had been sent forward but soon disappeared in the haze of fighting. Satan was dispatched to look for the lost troops. Picking his way through enemy lines, Satan was shot twice, but he kept going. He located the men and ran toward them. According to the soldiers, he seemed to materialize out of the smoke of the battlefield. Because he was wearing his gas mask and a backpack, some mistook him for a small angel with large wings.

In Toul, the Americans waited anxiously to be called to the front, where the fatalities were mounting. They had been welcomed in the village as potential liberators, as well as a reliable source of chocolate and chewing gum, and in the afternoons, neighborhood children hung out at the army mess, looking for handouts or curiosities. The soldiers liked their company. One nine-year-old boy, who had been orphaned in an air raid, was taken in as the squadron's mascot. The soldiers made the boy his own American uniform and taught him to speak a little English. He lived on the base and helped out in the kitchen.

Then one day the French authorities took

the boy away from the squadron and sent him to an orphanage, and the soldiers never saw him again. "We all missed him," Duncan wrote in his memoir, "but I think our Mess Sergeant missed him most of all. To forget his little chum, the sergeant went in to Toul and tried to drown his sorrow in cognac."

6.

In September 1918, General John Pershing launched the Saint-Mihiel offensive, one of the first major American assaults in the war. It was an attempt to push the Germans east out of the Meuse Valley. The Germans were dug in, and the Allied advance was agonizing. The air was thick with driving rain and the ground was churned into hip-deep mud. Lee was assigned to the armory department, but so many pilots were being killed or injured that even soldiers in his low position were told they might be placed on flying status when the biggest push of the offensive began.

Lee's account of this dark time is soldierly and understated. In his memoir he lists which pilot flew which mission and who did and didn't come back. The more detailed accounting is reserved for the types of planes and equipment used. If this wasn't precisely what he envisioned when he enlisted in southern California the previous year, there is no mention of that fact. What Lee did recall, though — vividly, obsessively — was the morning of September 15, when he was sent to inspect the ruins of a German encampment in Fluiry, northwest of Toul, to determine if it would make a suitable flying field. Fluiry was a tiny farm town with a punishing history. It had been destroyed twice previously in wars, had been rebuilt, and now was ruined again. In World War I it had already changed hands several times. When Lee was sent to do the inspection, the Germans had just retreated, leaving the broken town behind.

Lee implies in his memoir that he went to Fluiry alone, although it is surprising that a soldier would be sent near the front lines unaccompanied. He might have been with a few other soldiers, or he might have traveled there with George Bryant, the captain of another squadron, whom Lee had come to know. It is hard — impossible, really — to know. By his description, he strolled around the field in Fluiry, taking stock of the place and looking for the battlefield mementos the troops most prized — small engine parts, called Bosch Magnetos, from the Germans' tough Fokker planes. He noticed a long, low concrete building at the edge of the field. Because he was familiar with dogs, he knew immediately that the building was a kennel, probably built by the Germans for their canine troops.

He stooped down and looked inside the building. When his eyes adjusted to the dark, he saw a hellish image of slaughter: twenty or more dogs, killed by artillery shells. He stepped into the kennel and made his way among the bodies. They were clearly army dogs; one had a messenger-pigeon cage strapped to its back, and two of the pigeons were still alive. Lee released the pigeons. In the stillness, he heard whimpering. He followed the sound to the back of the kennel. There, in the farthest corner of this shattered, deathly place, was a frantic German shepherd female with a litter of five puppies.

It took him an hour — a "hard struggle," in his words — to wrangle the agitated female into his vehicle. Once he had her secured, he scooped up the puppies and drove back to the base. For a moment, anyway, it probably felt as if the war had faded away. He filled an empty oil barrel with straw and set it on its side as a doghouse. "And then," he noted in his diary, "the little family started light housekeeping." He knew he couldn't manage all the dogs, so after he shared the news of his discovery, he gave the mother dog to George Bryant and three of the puppies to various other soldiers. He kept the two prettiest, a male and a female, for himself.

From the moment he found these puppies, Lee considered himself a lucky man. He believed he was lucky despite the absence of his father, the rock-ribbed loneliness of his childhood, the tough years in the orphanage, the adored pets lost to him. For the rest of his life, he marveled at his good fortune in finding the puppies, turning the story over and over again and again like a shiny stone, watching it catch the light.

He thought about that luck when it came to naming the puppies. At that time, the most popular good-luck charm was a pair of dolls, a boy and a girl, made of yarn or silk, about as long as a finger, crude as stick figures, with a dab for a nose, a dash for a mouth, shapeless little arms and legs, and sad eyes "like periods made by the point of a pencil over which the writer had paused sorrowfully," according to one soldier. The dolls were named Rin Tin Tin and Nanette, in honor of a pair of young lovers who had survived a bombing in a Parisian railway station at the start of the war. They were lucky, and would bring luck; as an ad for the dolls proclaimed, "Avec nous rien à craindre" — With us, you have nothing to fear. Nanette was a common girl's name, but the boy's name, Rin Tin Tin, was unusual; no one could even settle on how to spell or punctuate it. Sometimes it was Rintintin, sometimes Rin Tin Tin, and sometimes even Ran-Tan-Tan. And no one could explain where it originated. It didn't seem to be a diminutive, because no proper name came close to sounding like Rin Tin Tin. It was less like a name than a tongue-clicking sound, a rhythm, perhaps even the chorus of a children's song: Rin Tin Tin, Rin Tin Tin, Rin Tin Tin.

Many French girls made the Rin Tin Tin and Nanette dolls by hand and gave them away, and at least one French charity sold them to raise money for an orphanage. American soldiers became eager customers. Everyone in Lee's squadron carried a rabbit's foot, or painted a lucky insignia on their plane, or had a girl's name scrawled on the interior of the cockpit. When Rin Tin Tin and Nanette dolls became a fad, soldiers began to wear them on chains around their necks or dangle them from their gun barrels or helmets. Lee had bought his Rin

Tin Tin and Nanette charms from a little girl in Toul, and he wore them for the rest of his life. The lucky puppies, he decided, would be given these lucky names, Rin Tin Tin and Nanette.

The pace of the war was relentless. In addition, a flu epidemic was burning through the troops like a fuse. Lee was relieved to have the puppies to distract him. "Each day, I found them more interesting," he wrote. "They were keeping my mind off the hectic days we were going through." Lee's squadron was reassigned to a field in Colombey-les-Belles, several hours north of Toul. Captain Bryant and the puppies' mother, Betty, were staying in Toul. The puppies were still nursing, so Lee had to decide whether to leave them with Betty or take them to Colombey-les-Belles. He decided he couldn't bear to be without them, but he could think of only one solution to keep them fed. Until the puppies were weaned, he flew back to Toul every day by wheedling his way onto one of the squadron's planes, an offense that could have warranted a court-martial.

Lee was hopelessly devoted to the puppies and wanted to learn everything he could about this new breed of dog. It turned out that one of the prisoners of war at the camp at Colombey-les-Belles was a German sergeant who was fluent in English and also happened to be the son of the man who had trained the dogs that had been kenneled at Fluiry — at least that is what Lee would have us believe, although the coincidence seems improbable. They talked for hours about German shepherds, prisoner and captor, absorbed in their obsession, while the war rolled on.

In November 1918, Lee finally had a chance to fly, but on his first mission, he was shot in the arm. He was hospitalized for months. The puppies came with him. When an orderly complained about having dogs in the hospital, Lee set up a kennel for them outside in a toolshed. By the time he was well enough to rejoin his unit in Bordeaux, the puppies had grown big and rambunctious, and some of the soldiers were not charmed by their antics. Lee, already a loner, never taking part in the squadron's frequent drinking and carousing, moved with the puppies to an old barn near the barracks. He had always loved sleeping in the barn at his grandfather's ranch, but the barn in Bordeaux was nothing like that clean, well-tended property; it was a mouse house, a wreck. Still, Lee was happier away from the rest of the men, alone with his charges. They were old enough to start training. He used a squeaky rubber doll to keep their attention, and he let them play with it as a reward when they behaved. He loved both puppies, but he thought Nanette was the outstanding one of the two, a little brighter than her brother. He hated to be away from them. When he was granted a nine-day leave to visit Paris he entrusted the puppies to one of the other soldiers but found he couldn't enjoy himself without them and returned to camp after only one day.

7.

He planned on bringing them home, although most animals in the war never left it. Transporting animals back to the States, particularly horses and mules, was too expensive; retraining war dogs to be anything other than war dogs was thought to be impossible. The French military destroyed the majority of its dogs as the war skidded to a close. The British, German, Italian, and Russian military likely did the same. American military horses and mules were sold to the French, who butchered most of them.

In July 1919, after the Armistice, Lee's

squadron was transferred to Brest, France, where the men waited for their orders. It was a tense, chaotic time; there were thousands of soldiers in Brest, longing to go home, and yet no one knew when they would be leaving. At last, the word came: Lee's squadron was sailing on the *F. J. Luckenbach* to New York; they were given just a few hours to prepare. Lee gathered his gear and his puppies and was preparing to board the ship when an officer stopped him, saying he needed permission from the Army Remount Service to bring any animals on board. He warned Lee that ship captains had the authority to throw any animals overboard that didn't have official clearance, and they often exercised it. Lee left the embarkation area and made his way through the crowd to the Remount Service. He needed permission immediately, but the Remount officer waved him away, saying he didn't have time for Lee's case when he had thousands of animals to account for and dispose of.

More than two thousand soldiers were leaving for home that day, each one with some complication, some need; no one had time for Lee, or for anything beyond the exigencies of the moment. In the disorder at the end of the war — the weariness, the scramble to leave, the mountains of equipment to be sorted, the unsettling diffusion of focus after five years of dire, burning purpose, the scores of urgent unfolding and competing dramas, the romances to uncouple, the friends to reconnect, the travel plans to arrange — there was Lee Duncan, war-worn, standing still in this tumult of activity, cradling his two war orphans, as he liked to call them, vying for someone to help him, being elbowed aside, realizing he was very close to once again losing something he loved and cared about. It would have been easiest to find some French youngster and hand the puppies over, but he couldn't bring himself to do so. The puppies had come to mean too much to him. "I felt there was something about their lives that reminded me of my own life," Lee wrote. "They had crept right into a lonesome place in my life and had become a part of me."

He finally got the puppies on the boat. His captain, Otto Sandman, intervened and helped Lee find a more sympathetic officer at the Remount Service, who issued the necessary papers. Lee was ecstatic; he told Sandman that if he ever bred the dogs, he would send him a puppy. At last, he boarded the ship. He had his gear, a few war trophies — his Bosch Magnetos, two small dueling pistols given to him by an old lady in Toul who had done his laundry during the war, a propeller, and a clock taken from a German Fokker plane — and his puppies, Rin Tin Tin and Nanette.

Rin Tin Tin's life turned out to be extraordinary, not just because things went his way but because so often they came close to going the other way. At his birth, he had survived a bombing that had killed many other dogs; then he had been found by someone who was eager to take care of him; he could so easily have been left behind in France, but he wasn't. Lee saw no accident in any of this. He believed that the dog was destined for greatness, and he was lucky to be his human guide and companion.

8.

I went to the Meuse Valley not long ago and spent a week wandering around Toul and Verdun and Fluiry to see where Rin Tin Tin was born. I don't usually visit the birthplace of celebrities and stars, and have never understood why so many people do. I assume it is because they think it might supply some clue about who the person was and who they became, or maybe the desire is actually more primitive — an urge to absorb something in the air, as if the place itself breathed out the deep essence of the person, the way a volcano vents the deep essence of the earth. Maybe it also provides the idea of a beginning, proof that something large and fully realized was once a pinpoint of an event. Seeing a beginning allows you to retract time like a measuring tape. That was something I wanted to experience about Rin Tin Tin, especially because I was still adjusting to the idea that he had been a real dog and not just a character, which was all I had ever known him to be. Once I stumbled into his real story, I wanted every bit of evidence that he had been born, and lived, and died.

Before I went to France, I thought it wise to find Fluiry on a map, so I would know where I was headed. I could find no such place. I searched for it on Google and Mapquest and finally on a real paper map, but no matter how closely I examined the snarl of little thready French roads, all those primary and secondary routes with their hash of letters and numbers and the long, multi-hyphenated names of tiny towns, I couldn't find it. The war had redrawn the map of the region: many villages, including the red-roofed market towns of Beaumont, Bezonvaux, and Ornes, had been so wrecked by the German assault that they were consigned to history, never to be rebuilt; the government proclaimed that these villages had "died for France." A 1919 French law granted each of the ghost villages a town committee and a president, similar to a town council and a mayor. But Fluiry wasn't on the list, so I decided to just go to the Meuse Valley and try my luck.

It was late summer, when the light was liquid and everything green was etched with gold. I took a train to Nancy, an elegant old city of fountains and figurine shops, and then drove to Toul, a few kilometers away, assuming that someone in Toul could direct me from there. It was midafternoon, midweek, midmonth. Toul was as quiet as a soundstage: every fixture of life was in place but every door was locked, every window shuttered. Finally, I happened on a café near a small town square with a dribbling fountain. A half-dozen people were having wine and coffee around a small round table; they had the brash, happy drunkenness of employees who had just been unexpectedly given the afternoon off. All of them were smoking so furiously that it looked as if they were sitting around a small campfire. I sat at a table nearby and ordered a coffee. After a minute I gathered my nerve and my high school French and leaned over to ask if any of them knew how to get to Fluiry.

They sucked their breath almost as one, and then they frowned at me. "Fluiry?" one of them repeated.

"Yes, Fluiry," I said, trying to go lightly on the *r* — not easy for an Ohioan, but I tried.

"Fluiry. Fluiry?"

"Yes, Fluiry," I said. I had a copy of Lee's notes with me. I held out the pages and read the part where he had written, "I had been sent to Fluiry on the morning of the fifteenth."

At first, they shook their heads. My heart skipped. No one spoke. The fountain dribbled. At last, one of the smokers put his cigarette down and beamed at me. "Oh," he said, triumphantly, "you mean *Flirey!*"

Another one gasped. "Oh, oui, oui! *Flirey!*" I could discern no difference at all in what they were saying but they were now congratulating themselves as if they'd cracked an Aztec code. Then they all lit new cigarettes and poured wine and went on with their afternoon recess.

"Excuse me," I said, after a moment, enunciating as carefully as I could. "Do you know how to get to *Flirey?*"

The road to Flirey rose and dipped along

a ridge, the soft fields falling away in every direction, the huge churches perched here and there, looming and gloomy and dark. Just outside of Toul I passed a hippie couple walking on the shoulder of the road carrying a million bags and packs and baskets and boxes — they looked more like a parade float than actual people. A raggedy dog ambled along with them; hard to tell what he was at first, but when I glanced back at them in my rearview mirror, I could see that the dog had the high forehead and erect ears of a German shepherd. A minute after I passed the hippie couple, I slowed for a leathery old farmer walking with his dog. It was also a German shepherd, glossy and muscular, lashing the farmer's legs with his thick tail as they strode along.

I knew that seeing these dogs was merely coincidence — that since I'd begun thinking about Rin Tin Tin, I was seeing him everywhere, and this after so many years of feeling like I never saw German shepherds anymore. It was as if the sheer force of thinking about the dog had made him materialize, as if I had been seeding the clouds with memories of Rin Tin Tin until it rained.

I had Bruce Springsteen on a German radio

station, the road skimming along beside quiet fields and quiet houses and the occasional cow, and then, suddenly, I was in Flirey.

It was nothing much, a cluster of fawn brown houses, a monument honoring General Pershing's army, a schoolyard, a stop sign. At the center of town there was an informational plaque explaining Flirey's history of ruination and its ever-changing name. As if to try to outrun its misfortune, the town had renamed itself time and again — Fleury, Fleury-aux-Bois, Fluirey, Fluiry — which is why it had been so hard to find on maps.

I drove down an alley off the main road. The village houses went on for a short distance, and then the alley narrowed and the houses petered out. Off to my right was an open expanse, empty except for a rusty soccer goal, a life-sized plastic clown bobbing gently on a rusty spring, and one large white sheep, his mouth pressed firmly to the ground, chopping at the grass around the soccer goal. Even if this was the right place, the field Lee had been sent to inspect, the remains of that kennel probably would have since sunk beneath ninety years of accumulated soil and gravel and grass. I sat for a while, watching the sheep work his way

65

industriously around the soccer goal, trying to imagine what it had been like in 1918, which was of course unimaginable, and waiting for someone walking by to lead me to a spot and say, "This happened here," as if that alone would make it come alive again.

But no one appeared other than two schoolkids, who skittered like mice across the alley and into a dark doorway, moving so lightly that they didn't even leave a wake of disturbed molecules behind. This field, a smooth green square in a small town, might have been the starting point, where the puppy was found, and from here everything else happened, history and stories unspooling, lives changing, from a point that had long since disappeared. When the sheep finally finished his assault on the grass and raised his head, I started the car and headed for Verdun.

I had come to see where Rin Tin Tin was born, but what you see in the Meuse Valley, besides clusters of houses and nice old farms and a patchwork of fields, is many, many cemeteries. The dead are all soldiers from World War I. I passed a German cemetery at Andilly with 33,000 graves; a Franco-British cemetery at Choloy-Ménillot with many thousands more. The Douaumont Ossuary at Verdun, a terrifying gray building shaped like a jumbo jet plunging nose-first into the ground, holds the remains of 130,000 unidentified soldiers, the jumbled bones of French and German boys laid to rest according to where they were found on the battlefield, their remains commingled and then parceled out, like an annotated map of the dead. On the outskirts of Flirey, I pulled over onto the side of the road just to stretch my legs. When I got out of the car and looked around, I realized I had parked in front of yet another cemetery, the Necropolis Nationale, a pie-shaped plot cut into a mossy hillside with 4,379 French soldiers' graves. After reading some of the tombstones, I realized that many of the soldiers had died on the same day in 1918.

A few miles past the necropolis, I drove by an ornate iron gate trimmed with gold medallions. It was so striking and singular in the middle of these farm fields that I doubled back to look at it, thinking it might be a grand estate or a country club. It turned out to be the St. Mihiel American Cemetery, a burial ground operated by the American Battle Monuments Commission, which oversees American military cemeteries in foreign countries. There are eight American military cemeteries in Europe. St.

Mihiel is the third largest: forty acres, four thousand dead. The cemetery director, a stout, cheerful man named Bobby Bell, came out of his office to greet me when I walked in. He told me he had worked at a number of the American cemeteries in Europe — two others in France, one in England, and one in the Netherlands. He said he liked St. Mihiel most of all, and he showed me around with as much enthusiasm as if he were trying to sell me a plot.

The constant presence of death I was encountering while searching for Rin Tin Tin's birthplace was starting to depress me, but the cemetery at St. Mihiel was actually one of the most beautiful places I've ever been. The crosses on the graves were a luminous white, lined up with an almost Moroccan symmetry against the geometry of freshly mowed grass and sharply sheared boxwood hedges and soldierly rows of linden trees. The names on the graves had another sort of symmetry, matching boys with their home states: Howard Lewis of Colorado; Vincenzo Brandolini of Connecticut; Jens Larsen of Iowa; Pinckney Rouse of North Carolina; Stanley Stubensz of Michigan. It was a mathematical sensation, walking up and down the green rows, the late light throwing long lines across the flat field, two graves per stride, fifty strides per row. The steady repetition was like a drumbeat, hypnotizing. I walked on and on, reading name after name, soothed by the rhythm of my steps, the soft spongy ground yielding under my feet, and by the flashing white of the crosses as I passed them, the whoosh of the wind tossing the linden trees' leaves with exaggerated drama, the way little girls toss their hair. At last I stopped at the end of a row, in front of a statue of a young army officer in a field uniform, trench helmet in hand. Above the figure was engraved "Il dort loin des siens dans la douce terre de France" — *He sleeps far from his family in the gentle land of France.* Beneath that, on the pedestal, it said:

BLESSED ARE THEY THAT
HAVE THE HOME LONGING
FOR THEY SHALL GO HOME

9.

As I drove away in the dusky light, I kept seeing the tailored rows of graves, those tiny repositories of stories that are hardly remembered, all those sad and broken boys resting in the velvet lawn of St. Mihiel, forever. Almost one hundred years of resting there, enough time to be forgotten, the lives that continued after theirs ended having now filled up the space that opened up when they died, so their absence now has been lacquered over, smoothed out, almost invisible.

What lasts? What lingers? What is snagged by the brambles of time, and what slips through and disappears? What leaves only a little dent in the world, the soft sunken green grave, the scribble on a scrap of paper, the memory that is bleached by time and then vanishes bit by bit each day?

Could it be that we fill out our lives, experience all that we experience, and then simply leave this world and are forgotten? I can't bear thinking that existence is so insubstantial, a stone thrown in a pond that leaves no ripple. Maybe all that we do in life is just a race against this idea of disappearing. Having children, making money, doing good, being in love, building something, discovering something, inventing something, learning something, collecting something, knowing something: these are the pursuits that make us feel like our lives aren't flimsy, that they build up into stories that are about something achieved, grown, found, built, loved, or even lost.

Thanks to Lee Duncan, Rin Tin Tin left a

great deal behind — in, among other places, the municipal museum in Riverside, California. When I first visited there, three years before my trip to Flirey, I was startled to discover no fewer than fourteen boxes of Lee Duncan's papers and Rin Tin Tin memorabilia, meticulously organized and indexed and mostly untouched. It was like coming upon a gift that had been selected for me and then sat waiting almost half a century for me to come by and open it.

That day at St. Mihiel, I found myself thinking about why I had been drawn to this particular story, at this moment, when I could have chosen any story to pursue. I knew that I loved the narrative of Rin Tin Tin because it contained so many stories within it: it was a tale of lost families, and of identity, and also of the way we live with animals; it was a story of luck, both good and bad, and the half turns that life takes all the time. It was a story of war as well as a story of amusement. It was an account of how we create heroes and what we want from them. It laid out, through the story of Rin Tin Tin, the whole range of devotion — to ideas and to a companion — as well as the pure, half-magical devotion an animal can have to a person.

It was also the story of an extraordinary

journey — across land and sea, in war and in peacetime, from poverty to wealth and back again, from obscurity to fame — and, from there, into the murky world of the once famous and almost obscure. It was also a journey through time. For me, the story of Rin Tin Tin let me cast a line into the pool of my childhood memories, an undertaking that felt more urgent every day I walked farther away from the edge of that pool. I began the story of Rin Tin Tin soon after my father had died and my son had been born; the idea of continuity was suddenly very real to me. Reeling Rin Tin Tin into the present would not only revive his story but also perhaps clarify my own — the story of who I am and how I happened to become the person I seem to be.

In truth, though, this pursuit had begun not with a story or an idea but with a feeling. I had come upon a mention of Rin Tin Tin quite by accident while researching another story, and my reaction was so strong that it made me feel as though I had been waiting for decades just to be reminded of him again. And after my visit to St. Mihiel, a monument to what might otherwise crumble to nothing, I began to understand that what drew me to Rin Tin Tin most of all was his permanence — how he had managed to linger in the minds of so many people for so long, when so much else shines for a moment only and then finally fades away. He was something you could dream about. He could leap twelve feet, and he could leap through time.

1.

It took fifteen days to cross the Atlantic. The troops were then taken to a reentry camp, where they were debriefed and deloused. Many society women worked as camp hostesses, welcoming back the troops and tending to minor needs. Lee and his shipmates were sent to the reentry camp in Hempstead, Long Island; one of the hostesses there was Mrs. Leo Wanner, the deputy sheriff of Nassau County and also, coincidentally, a breeder of German shepherds. A few months before Lee's ship landed, one of the buildings at Wanner's kennel, Meadowbrook, had burned down. Seven of her dogs were killed, including her champion, Filax, whom she had loaned to the Belgian army and who had come back to Long Island after he was wounded.

Wanner met Lee while she was greeting soldiers at the camp, and of course they discovered their mutual affection for German shepherds. The troops were to be interned at the camp for ten days, and Lee had nowhere to keep his puppies. Wanner offered to take care of them until he was discharged. When Lee was ready to head home to California, however, he received word from Meadowbrook that Nanette had developed pneumonia and was too weak for the long train ride to California. Lee reluctantly agreed to leave her at Meadowbrook, on the promise that the kennel manager would ship her west as soon as she improved. In the meantime, Wanner offered Lee a Meadowbrook puppy to keep Rin Tin Tin company on the train ride home.

In his memoir, Lee wrote that the Meadowbrook kennel manager was "none other than the famous B.B.B. of Hollywood and picture fame." I could never track down a Hollywood dog trainer with those initials, but Lee was obviously impressed by whoever B.B.B. was, and this might have been the first moment the idea of training a dog for the movies started to form in his mind.

Rin Tin Tin — Rinty, as Lee called him — was a bossy young dog, and when he was introduced to the new puppy from Meadowbrook, he bit her on the ear and left her with a permanent scar. In spite of this rough introduction, she became his companion and eventually his mate. Rinty's sister Nanette died shortly after Lee left Long Island, so Lee decided to name the new puppy Nanette II in her memory. When Rin Tin Tin became an international star, Nanette was often referred to as his wife.

The train ride back to California was tonic. Marching bands blared a welcome at many of the stops, crowds greeted the soldiers, Red Cross girls served ice cream. Lee fed his ice cream to Rin Tin Tin, and the dog developed a passion for it that he retained for the rest of his life.

Lee was heading home, but he wasn't sure where he was going. He was twenty-eight years old and still looked fresh and rugged, like a young cowboy, with a narrow frame and hardly any hips. He had a broad forehead, an aquiline nose, bright dark eyes, a flirtatious arch in his eyebrows, and a toothy smile. His hair had turned white at some point in his teenage years and he began to wear it longish and slicked straight back so that it looked like a silver cap, a bright shock against his skin. With the horror of the war now behind him, his only plan was to return to his job in the gun department at Bernal Dyas. What he wanted was to sweep back all the time that had passed since he left for France and find life just as he had left it.

But of course nothing, really, was the same. California — the whole country, in fact — had changed since he'd left for the war. Bernal Dyas Sporting Goods had changed: the store had moved to a new location, and the gun department was now in the basement. It was a beautiful basement with a scale-model log cabin, a shooting range, and artificial trout pools for practice casting. Even so, Lee felt suffocated below ground. He found it disturbing to be around guns and ammunition. He spent as much time in the mountains as he could, hiking and swimming, but his distaste for guns was so strong that he stopped hunting, something he had done since he was a boy. At the store, business in the gun department had fallen off; Lee believed this was due to the war and the way it had peeled away the romance of shooting. "Every time I looked at a gun," he told an interviewer many years later, "I remembered the buddies who didn't come back."

Perhaps worst of all, Lee's dog Firefly had died while he was away — news his mother delivered to him only after he got home.

Then, a few days after settling in at home, Rin Tin Tin developed distemper, and for three weeks the dog was so sick that Lee wasn't sure he would survive. Lee doted on him and fed him a home remedy of raw egg white in cherry wine, which he was convinced saved Rin Tin Tin's life.

Single and unmoored, he whiled away a year working at the store and playing with his dogs. Then the war came back to him. He developed a twitch in his left hand and a spasm on the left side of his face. He began having nightmares. He couldn't stand being inside. He wrote in his memoir, "Things were so changed from the old days. I was restless and couldn't get my feet on the ground, as it were." His mother, who worked as a housekeeper, and his sister, who gave piano lessons, worried about him; they wanted him to settle down and hoped he might tease out a promotion at work and feel more contented. Instead, Lee asked the store for a leave of absence. He decided the cure was to look for a job outdoors — any job, the harder the better. He worked for several months on the crew building the Chalk Hill section of the highway running from Los Angeles to San Francisco. When the road was finished, he returned uneasily to the Dyas gun department.

Meanwhile, just a few miles away, in Hollywood, the new industry of moviemaking was thriving. The first studio had opened in 1911, and by 1919 more than 80 percent of the movies being made in the world were coming out of Hollywood. Lee had a friend in the business, a barrel-chested comic named Eugene Pallette who was building a career as a character actor. By the time Lee came back from the war, Pallette had already appeared in almost one hundred films, including *Texas Bill's Last Ride, Birth of a Nation, Gretchen the Greenhorn,* and *Tarzan of the Apes.* Lee and Pallette began taking Rin Tin Tin on trips in the Sierras; while Pallette hunted, Lee taught Rinty tricks. His plan for Rin Tin Tin was quite modest: he wanted to breed him and Nanette, sell a few puppies, and maybe make a name for himself and Rin Tin Tin at dog shows.

2.

Lee was not the only soldier to have brought home a dog, and he was one of many to come home with stories praising the German shepherds they'd seen in battle. As a result, the popularity of the breed in the United States after World War I grew quickly and somewhat heedlessly. Everyone wanted one of these remarkable dogs, and the rush to produce German shepherd puppies was already creating genetic problems such as weak hips and bad eyesight. The Shepherd Dog Club of America, trying to slow the deterioration of the breed, hired experts from Germany to tour the United States and conduct a "breed survey," analyzing pedigrees and making recommendations to improve the breed's genetics. Lee got to know other German shepherd fanciers in Los Angeles, and in 1922 he and a few others founded the Shepherd Dog Club of California. They scheduled their first show for the upcoming season in Pasadena.

Rinty was three years old. He had lost his puppy fluffiness; his coat was lustrous and dark, nearly black, with gold marbling on his legs and chin and chest. His tail was as bushy as a squirrel's. He wasn't overly tall or overly broad, his chest wasn't especially deep, his legs weren't unusually muscular or long, but he was powerful and nimble, as light on his feet as a mountain goat. His ears were comically large, tulip-shaped, and set far apart on a wide skull. His face was more arresting than beautiful, his expression worried and pitying and generous: instead of a look of doggy excitement it was something more tender, a little sorrowful, as if he was viewing with charity and resignation the whole enterprise of living and striving and hoping.

The dog show in Pasadena did not go as planned. Rinty demonstrated his athleticism but also his hot temper. He snapped and barked at the judges and was nearly unmanageable, all of which Lee ascribed to his "lack of ring technique" and being "so full of life and vigor." The trip ended terribly. After the show, while Lee was walking Rinty, a newspaper delivery truck passed them on the street, and a worker pitched a heavy bundle of papers off the back of the truck. The bundle slammed into the dog, knocking him over. His left front leg was broken in four places.

It took nine months to heal. For those nine months Lee lived in dread that the dog's toes would rot off or the bones would heal crookedly (he had made the cast himself, out of plaster of paris), or that the dog would become wincing and shy as a result of the accident. Rinty had already been inseparable from Lee, but his injury made him even more so; the first day Lee left him to go to work, the dog moaned so loudly that the neighbors thought there had been a death in the Duncan family. When

Lee finally removed the cast, he could barely stand to watch as Rinty took his first steps. But the dog healed so well that within a month he was ready to jump and run again, and Lee decided to enter him in a big German shepherd show at the Ambassador Hotel in Los Angeles.

An acquaintance of Lee's named Charley Jones, whose daughters took piano lessons from Marjorie Duncan, asked if he could come with Lee to the show. He had just developed a type of slow-motion camera, and a dog show, with all its activity, seemed a good opportunity for trying it out. Lee agreed, so Jones set up his camera to film Rinty and some of the other dogs performing that day.

In his memoir, Lee made no mention of how Rin Tin Tin did in the conformation competition. What mattered — and what would come to matter more than Lee could possibly imagine — was what took place during the "working dog" part of the show. Rin Tin Tin and a female shepherd named Marie were tied for first place and had to compete in a jump-off. The jump, a wall made of wooden planks, was set at eleven and a half feet. Both dogs cleared it. The wall was raised three inches. The judge and show officials gathered beside the jump for a close look. Marie took her turn, flying up and over, but hit the top plank with her back feet. Rin Tin Tin then squared off for his leap. "Charley Jones had his camera on Rinty as he made his jump and as he came down on the other side," Lee wrote, "and Rinty jumped over the head of the judge and several others." The dog had cleared an obstacle of almost twelve feet. It was an amazing jump for any dog, especially one who was only eighty-five pounds. Jones was delighted with his new camera and the film he had shot. Lee assumed Jones was just conducting a casual experiment and seemed to pay it little mind. He was more excited about the mentions Rinty got in the Los Angeles newspapers. He decided then to start a scrapbook, "never dreaming," as he wrote, "that some day Rinty would be in all the newspapers all over the world."

But something about Rin Tin Tin being filmed must have stuck with Lee, because in the weeks following the show, he was seized by a new desire to get Rin Tin Tin into Hollywood. "I was so excited over the motion picture idea that I found myself thinking of it night and day," he wrote. "I wanted to talk pictures instead of guns."

Lee was an avid reader of *Physical Culture*,

a magazine founded in 1899 that preached self-improvement and self-reliance, with features like "I Had Appendicitis and Cured It Myself" and "Learn How to Breathe and Laugh at T.B." The ads in the magazine were for products that offered to help develop a better version of yourself: body-building systems (*If a Jelly Fish Could Slap a Rat in the Face he would do it. But he can't. He has no arms. Neither does he have a backbone. How much worse off is a man who was given a good backbone and a pair of arms — and won't use them*); beauty helpers such as the Genuine Patented Nose Adjuster (*Special sizes for Children. A Perfect Nose for You*); or cosmetics (*Gertrude Follis left home an Ugly Duckling. Now New York Artists Pay to Paint her Likeness and Her New Beauty Was Won in Three Months*); and etiquette books that promised to teach behavior and leave you "free from all embarrassment."

After the war, the magazine expanded its mission to include the idea of wealth. Getting rich, it suggested, was the ultimate form of self-improvement, especially if it was the result of doing something you enjoyed. The article that advanced this theory, and caught Lee's attention, was called "Why Not Make Your Hobby Pay?"

This is familiar thinking now, but in the

1920s, it was surprising. Work had always been just work, and it had never promised to be fulfilling, or even satisfying — nor did it generally have anything to do with the hobbies you liked or the idea of fulfilling some personal vision. If you were fortunate, you had a job and you would prosper — perhaps even become wealthy. Happiness was seen as something that came from *being* rich, rather than from what you did in order to become rich. But the war had blurred that line of thought. There was the exhilaration of peace, the buzz of new factories, the energy of new prosperity. So many of the new things to buy — especially things like cars and radios and movie tickets — seemed to promise that you could aspire to do anything, go anywhere. You could actually strive to be happy, and it suddenly seemed reasonable to expect satisfaction in your work. The magazine urged readers to share stories of how they had made money from their hobbies and offered a prize for the best and most inspiring example.

What Lee enjoyed was his dog. If you are to take his memoir at face value, he had few friends, no interest in girls, and no hobbies that didn't include the dog. He also happened to think that Rin Tin Tin was showing "signs of genius." After reading "Why

Not Make Your Hobby Pay?" in 1921, and feeling the influence of Hollywood, right over the hill from home, he decided to do just that: he would write a screenplay starring Rinty. He wanted to win the magazine contest, but he also started to imagine that he could go the next step — convince a studio to make a movie based on a story he wrote, starring his dog.

3.

In the 1920s, movies were a constant in almost everyone's life. One out of two Americans saw a movie every week. Everyone wanted to write a screenplay, and there were scores of "systems" marketed to help the amateur. According to an ad for one of them, the Irving System, "Millions of People Can Write Stories and Photoplays and Don't Know It!!" Advertisements for the Elinor Glyn System were more spiritual, asking, "Don't You Believe the Creator Gave You a Story-Writing Faculty, Just As He Did the Greatest Writer?"

Lee did believe he had that "story-writing faculty" and he had a story idea, inspired by a folktale about a prince and his beloved dog. According to the tale, Prince Llewellyn was hunting wolves on his estate one morning when he realized that his constant companion, his dog Gelert, was missing. Llewellyn rode home and went into his son's bedroom because he thought the dog might be resting there with the boy. He found the room in shambles, the bed drenched with blood, the dog cowering in the corner. The prince took this to mean that the dog had killed his son, and enraged, he pulled out his hunting knife and stabbed the dog. As the dog was dying, Llewellyn noticed a flash of movement beside the bed; there he found the child unharmed, lying beside the body of a timber wolf, which Gelert had obviously killed to protect the boy. Llewellyn realized his terrible mistake, but it was too late to save the dog. Gelert's final act, before succumbing, was to lick the prince's hand, forgiving him for his fatal misjudgment.

Lee titled his screenplay *Where the North Begins.* Instead of a prince, his main character was a fur trapper; the dog is a stray that has been raised by wolves. The trapper, Dupre, comes to trust the dog because he helps him fight off a crooked trading-post owner and his henchman. But then Dupre is told that he must destroy the dog because it has killed a child. He reluctantly agrees, but the dog escapes and rejoins the wolf pack.

Later, when Dupre learns that the accusation was false, he goes into the woods to find the dog. Instead of hating Dupre for betraying him, the dog holds no grudge, and they are reunited as loyal companions.

As different as the setting was, Lee's story kept the themes of the Llewellyn legend intact: the intimacy between a man and a dog; the dog's virtue and his mute acceptance of being wrongly accused; the blinding effect of human rage; a dog's capacity for forgiveness and absolution; the human need to assign blame; the dog's generous, Christ-like martyrdom. For someone like Lee, whose father had abandoned him, a story about a father so devoted to his child that he would kill for him may have been an exquisite fantasy.

The structure of the Llewellyn story and Lee's version of it are interesting not only for what is included but for what is left out. The fight between the dog and the wolf is not described in the folktale at all; the story is about misjudgment and regret and forgiveness, rather than the spectacle of the fight. There is no bloody battle in which the dog triumphs, yet he is clearly a hero. He is not a conventional action hero, elevated by strength and valor. What ennobles the dog is his compassion — for the child, who is in danger, but also for the prince, who has erred. The dog absolves Llewellyn even as Llewellyn kills him.

In *Where the North Begins,* the pivotal violence also takes place offscreen. Once again the dog is steadfast and loyal, accepts being unjustly accused, and ultimately forgives his master. The dog embodies a rich, mythic sort of heroism, an empathy that is broader and deeper and more pure than what an ordinary human would be capable of. This is the quality that eventually lifted Rin Tin Tin from the world of novelty into something classical.

Since films in 1921 had no sound track and no dialogue, everything had to be conveyed by action or facial expression. The only language was the small amount of text on the intertitle cards, which amounted to just a few dozen words. A dog was at no disadvantage to a human in a silent film; both species had the same set of tools for telling a story — action, expression, gesture. In fact, an animal acting without words looked natural and didn't fall into panto-mime and exaggeration the way human actors in silent film often did. Before writing his screenplay, Lee studied Rinty's facial expressions and tried to think how they could be used in a movie. He became convinced that Rinty could be taught to act a part — not only to carry out a story through action, but "to register emotions and portray a real character with its individual loves, loyalties, and hates."

Just before Lee finished the script he received a letter from an executive at Novagraph, a newsreel company, informing him that it had purchased Charley Jones's film of Rinty jumping the wall at the dog show to use in a newsreel. There was a check inside the letter for $350 — a huge amount of money for Lee, about three months' salary at his Bernal Dyas job. The executive mentioned that the clip was already one of Novagraph's most popular and would be playing soon at a theater in Los Angeles.

Lee was so astonished that he refused to cash the check for weeks. He was afraid it was a mistake and he would get a second letter demanding the money back. But Charley Jones assured him it was real. Once the fact of it sank in, Lee made the decision to commit himself to getting Rin Tin Tin into the movies.

The day Lee finished the draft of *Where the North Begins,* he asked for another leave of absence from Bernal Dyas. His mother was dismayed, and with some good reason:

Hollywood in the 1920s could be a dark place. Narcotics were common; directors and producers were a motley group that included tramps, medicine-show barkers, lumberjacks, and swindlers. Marjorie also worried that having Lee participate in such a tawdry business — especially working with a dog — would disgrace her and ruin her fledgling music school. Lee refused to change his mind in spite of the pleas from his mother and sister. "They told me how that afternoon one of the neighbors had said, 'Why, the idea of him trying to make a living off of his dog!' " Lee wrote. "Mother and Marjorie had a big cry."

4.

Dogs have been in movies ever since there have been movies. If you take into account Eadweard Muybridge's "The Horse in Motion," a series of sequential photographs that was produced in 1882 and is considered the forerunner of film, animals were part of the medium from the start. The first dog featured in a film was in Auguste and Louis Lumière's *Workers Leaving the Lumière Factory,* made in 1895. The dog, who is uncredited, comes waggling into the frame to greet the workers as they walk out of a factory gate. The first instance of a dog performing as a fictional character was in the 1905 British film *Rescued by Rover.* The film is a landmark on several accounts: It was the first film to star a dog and it is the earliest example of a movie conceived as a narrative. The entire film is only six minutes long, but it has a real story with a cinematic arc that moves from exposition to crisis to resolution, told through a series of related and continuous shots rather than just being a pastiche of moving images. It was also the first known instance of a film using paid, professional actors, and the first and last time — according to the self-effacing British Film Institute — when British cinema "unquestionably led the world."

Rescued by Rover was produced by Cecil Milton Hepworth, who went on to direct and produce more than four hundred films, including *The Egg-Laying Man, Baby's Toilet, How It Feels to Be Run Over,* and *Explosion of a Motor Car.* Rover, in *Rescued by Rover,* was played by Hepworth's pet collie, Blair. The film opens with Rover out for a walk with his owner's baby and the baby's nanny. The nanny is an irresponsible flirt and is so busy making eyes at a soldier on the street that she doesn't even notice a beggar woman sidling up to the stroller and grabbing the baby. The beggar runs off, and Rover and the nanny run home to report the terrible news to the baby's parents, played by Hepworth and his wife.

In the end, of course, the baby is rescued by Rover. The dog, using amazing powers of reasoning, deduces that the beggar probably lives in the poor section of town, so he races there, searches until he locates her, races back home, and convinces the distraught parents to follow him to the beggar's hideaway, where at last father, mother, and baby are joyfully reunited. What's interesting is that the only character in the movie who knows the whole story — who sees as much as the camera does — is Rover.

Rescued by Rover was a low-budget enterprise — it cost $37 to produce — but it made Hepworth a rich man. It was so popular that it was played constantly; the repeated screenings wore out the original negatives, so Hepworth actually made the whole film over again, shot by shot. Those negatives wore out as well, and Hepworth had to make the movie for a third time. Its success also had collateral impact: "Rover," an unusual dog name before the film was made, suddenly became the most popular one in the country, and animal films became a rage.

Hepworth produced some of these animal films; he made a version of *Black Beauty* and then featured his collie, Blair, again in a 1907 film called *Dumb Sagacity*. Blair/Rover became enough of a star that when he died, his passing was announced with great solemnity in the company newsletter. "The Hepworth Manufacturing Company have just suffered quite a severe loss in the death of their famous old dog Rover," the newsletter stated. "This faithful animal had been Mr. Hepworth's constant companion even before the Hepworth Company had been founded, and was the general pet of the studio at Walton-on-Thames. He was the first animal to play an independent part in a cinematograph film, and was the hero of many pictures. . . . Many others besides the Hepworth Company will deplore the death of this old favourite." Blair's success as Rover had come to overshadow his real identity; he wasn't even called Blair in his obituary.

After Rover's success, dozens of other filmmakers began working with animals. In many cases, the results were long, mostly unedited spools of documentary footage — lions lolling in zoos; elephants marching in parades; bullfights; horse races; boxing matches between cats. A meek British schoolteacher named Perry Smith made a number of films starring wild and domestic animals, including *Tiny Honey Gatherers, Snakes and Their Habits, Peculiar Pets,* and *Fun in a Bear Pit.* His magnum opus was a time-lapse film about mold, which he shot at home; the mold got out of control and contaminated his entire house.

Many studios kept animals on hand to use in films. Mack Sennett collected the largest Hollywood menagerie, which included Teddy, a Great Dane who could drive a train; Josephine, a monkey who could drive a car; and a trained chicken named Susie. An independent animal trainer rented out a troupe of monkey actors, known as the Dippity-Do-Dads, that appeared in many films. Universal Films decided it needed a dog star equal to Rover and held open casting. The job went to a mutt named Brownie who eventually starred in twenty-six films. Charlie Chaplin wanted a dog sidekick, too; he auditioned a dachshund, a Pomeranian, a poodle, and a bull terrier but wasn't satisfied with any of them. His studio took out an ad, declaring, "Chaplin Wants a Dog with Lots of Comedy Sense." He eventually found the dog he wanted, a sad-eyed piebald mongrel, at the City of Los Angeles pound.

Laurence Trimble had been involved with animal films since their earliest days. An outdoorsman and an oddball, Trimble grew up in a small town in Maine and moved to New York in the early 1900s to try his hand as a writer. He found work as a freelancer for local papers. He often brought along his dog, Jean, a black-and-white collie, when he was reporting. One day, he and Jean were at Vitagraph Studios to write a story about the movie in production, which starred Vitagraph's biggest attraction, the petite, doleful Florence Turner. One of the scenes called for a dog. Apparently the dog that had been brought in for the job failed to perform adequately and Trimble, who was watching the proceedings, suggested giving Jean a chance. The director agreed. Jean played the part perfectly. The studio offered the dog a contract on the spot and threw in a screenwriting contract for Trimble just for good measure.

Of course, this story is almost laughably implausible, and yet it is the same sort of story that is repeated throughout Hollywood history, used to explain the innocent, almost accidental but also seemingly fated moment when life marvelously changes course. It paves over the bumpy road of tiny, unplanned steps you might have taken to advance from being a small-town kid from Maine with a pet collie to being a movie director with a famous dog — steps that are so many and so hard to retrace that it is natural for the story to blur into a fairy tale. And movies seem so dreamlike and enchanted that everything associated with them seems just as dreamlike and enchanted — including the moment you are transformed from a mortal creature in the real world, who will age and bleed and then die, into a splash of light on a movie screen, who will last forever and never change.

However they really did get their break, Jean — whose signature talent was an ability to untie knots — soon appeared regularly alongside Turner, and Trimble advanced from his screenwriting job to directing. The dozens of features he directed starring Florence Turner and Jean were so successful that Trimble was earning the equivalent of about $50,000 a week. But he was moody and restless. He and his wife, the screenwriter Jane Murfin, wanted more control over their films, as did Turner. In 1913, the three of them moved to England and set up as an independent studio. The experiment failed and they returned to California three years later. Meanwhile, Trimble started making peculiar short movies; one, for example, showed nothing but the actors' hands and feet. When he needed twenty-four wolves for a film, he bought the wolves from a wildlife supplier in California and shipped them to Canada. Rather than training them in the conventional manner, he moved into their den and lived alongside them for months, sleeping in a hole in the enclosure, as the wolves did, and eating off the ground with them. Perhaps unsurprisingly, his personal life was unsettled; he and Murfin fought all the time.

In 1916, Jean died. Trimble and Murfin decided they wanted to develop another dog actor, but one that could be more of a dramatic actor than Jean was, and would stand out among other dogs in Hollywood, who were usually in comic roles. They were familiar with German shepherds; the dogs were starting to show up in the United States from Europe, and the alert and somewhat grave aspect of a German shepherd face appealed to them. In 1920, Murfin and Trimble traveled around the United States looking for the right German shepherd for their plan and then looked in Europe when they didn't find the ideal dog at home. By one account, they found their dog, Etzel von Oeringen, in Berlin; by other accounts they found Etzel in White Plains, New York, through a breeder who had just imported him from Germany.

Etzel was three years old when Trimble and Murfin first saw him, and even though he was a beautiful animal, he was not lovable. He was a driven, aggressive military guard dog who, Trimble later said, "had never played with a child, had never known the fun of retrieving a ball or a stick; had never been petted; in short, had never been a dog." Trimble changed the dog's name from Etzel to Strongheart and shipped him to Murfin's mansion on Ivarene Avenue, up the hill from Gower Gulch, a section of Hollywood where actors dressed in cowboy costumes gathered every day, hoping to be cast as extras in a western.

Strongheart's first film, *The Silent Call,* released in 1921, is about an animal that is half wolf, one-quarter coyote, and one-quarter dog, and his struggle to choose which part of his nature — predatory or protective — he will favor. Flash, as the wolf-coyote-dog is known, lives on a ranch herding and guarding the livestock. As the film opens, Flash has been wrongly accused of killing sheep and chased off the ranch. Flash is distraught but resigned to his fate and eventually finds companionship in the wilderness with a female wolf.

Back at the ranch, a drama is unfolding, and Flash learns of the troubles. He must decide whether to stay with his wolf mate and live as a wild animal or go back to the ranch to help his former master, and perhaps win his way back into his master's graces. He has paid the cost of being misjudged and misunderstood; now he struggles with the conflict, possibly irreconcilable, between what is wild and what is tame in his character.

Ads for *The Silent Call* urged audiences to "See the Wonder-Dog of All Dramas — Strongheart, the Killer — More Human than Human!" The reviews of the film were more qualified, criticizing it as too derivative of Jack London, but Strongheart's performance was praised. The *New York Times* called him "a magnificent creature, and an excellent photographic subject, and an interesting performer. He is not one of your tiresome trick dogs, but an apparently independent animal." The reviewer added that even when the story dragged, "Strongheart's scenes are exceptionally well made and entirely enjoyable." Many reviewers singled out a scene near the end of the film, when Flash rejoins his mate. The female wolf has just given birth, and an explosion has trapped her and the pups in their cave. When Flash — Strongheart — discovers this, he throws himself to the ground and weeps. It was reported that Strongheart actually produced real tears in the scene. This is physically impossible — dogs don't cry tears — but was accepted as truth and brought Strongheart great acclaim. Audiences were entranced. The film was a hit and reportedly grossed $1 million, an extraordinary amount in 1921. Strongheart's noble, contemplative face was an electrifying contrast to the most popular American dogs at the time — Boston terriers, Airedales, collies, beagles, cocker spaniels, and bulldogs. Just one year after the film was released — and undoubtedly as a result of it — German shepherds became the most popular breed in the United States.

A profile of Strongheart in *Photoplay Magazine* took his skills as an actor seriously. "While other screen canines appear only in comedy, Strongheart is making a drama. And so his position is entirely unique. . . . When he thought his puppies were killed in the movie he cried with an apparent depth of suffering that only a human is supposed to be capable of." Strongheart was "a dramatic dog, an emotional actor . . . and now he takes his place among the premier dogs of the screen."

Strongheart, "the most intelligent dog that ever lived," according to the magazine, made a triumphant publicity tour around the country, accompanied by his mate — a slim, silver-coated German shepherd named Lady Jule. His next film, *Brawn of the North,* was a "snow," as the genre of silent films shot in wintery locations was known. Again, the theme of the movie was the dog's struggle to discover his true nature: Is he tame, allied with his human caretakers? Or is he wild, at home with the wolves?

An ad for the film promised nothing but melodrama:

Hold your breath a hundred times on Strongheart's trail of thrills — follow his tracks up to the snowlands. Great drama there — of a woman driven into marriage in self-defense, finding love at last for the man; love, too, for the giant dog; and a woman's greatest love for the child that was born in the snows. Then she lost them all when the wolves swooped out of the night. And — the end of this great drama — well, it just can't be described. By all means see it! Fighting a famine-mad wolf pack, guarding a child against the slinking circle, listening for the cry of a demented mother, but only hearing a she-wolf's mating call.

From the beginning of Strongheart's success, Murfin and Trimble were applauded as the shrewd acting coaches who had shaped him into a star. They would have undoubtedly inspired Lee while he was working on his screenplay for Rinty and trying to imagine a career in Hollywood. The *New York Times* ran an interview with Murfin called "Writing for a Dog Star," in which she credited some of Strongheart's authenticity to scripts that required him only to do what was natural. In a good animal film, Murfin explained, "you cannot let your dog give your baby a bath, for instance, no matter how funny, because dogs don't give babies baths under any conceivable circumstances." Lee seems to have taken Murfin's advice to heart.

Besides praising Strongheart's films in its reviews, the *Times* published at least two more feature stories about him — one, written by Trimble, about how he trained Strongheart, and another in which Strongheart himself visited the newsroom and was "interviewed." The paper viewed Strongheart not as a novelty but as an important new figure in cinema. "He has a fine head, on which a worried intelligence is written, especially in the different looks he gives with his eyes," the story in the *Times* explained. Another writer described the dog as "the essence of tragedy."

After having made only six films — all of them huge successes — Strongheart fell against a lamp on a movie set. The burn on his leg grew cancerous and he died in 1929. Today he is mostly forgotten. All of his movies except for *The Return of Boston Blackie* have been lost — like many silent films they were treated offhandedly, either cut up to be reused as stock footage or simply left to crumble in their cans by studios that have long since gone out of business.

What remains of Strongheart's flash of fame is a brand of dog food that is still manufactured under his name and two books, *Letters to Strongheart* and *Kinship with All Life,* written by J. Allen Boone, a friend of Trimble and Murfin. Boone was a correspondent for the *Washington Post,* an occasional film producer, and a distant cousin of Daniel Boone. He developed a unified theory about humans and animals that he called Totality. For a while, he cultivated a friendship with a housefly he named Freddie, whom he conversed with "not in a condemning way but as a fellow being"; Freddie reciprocated by visiting Boone at his shaving mirror every morning at 7:00 a.m., allowing Boone to pet him and answering to his name.

Boone took care of Strongheart for a year while Murfin and Trimble were tending to business in New York. At first, he had been reluctant. "The difficulty was Strongheart himself," Boone wrote. "He was too mysterious, too self-contained, too capable." Eventually, Boone felt that Strongheart had accepted him. Their relationship grew deep. Strongheart slept in Boone's bed every night, and Boone came to believe that Strongheart was there to teach him "new meanings of happiness . . . of devotion . . . of honor . . . of individuality . . . of loyalty . . . of sincerity . . . of love . . . of life . . . of God." When Strongheart died — or "disappeared from the earth scene and human visibility" — Boone started writing him letters. He addressed each one "To Strongheart/Eternal Playground/Out Yonder," and used them to tell Strongheart "things that are in my mind and heart about us, things too intimate and deep to discuss with most human beings."

Boone was irked each time someone referred to Strongheart as "dead." He had just "changed his world," Boone explained. "From this vantage point, I want to tell you once again why I am insisting that you *are* a great dog, instead of *were* one . . . the popular belief has you listed as a 'dead dog' and me as a 'living human.' Well, let's see about it." Each letter ended with Boone's confident salute, "I'll be seein' you." According to Boone, Strongheart was more than a dog and more than an actor: he was a transformational being. "He emancipated millions of men, women, and children from monotonous and unsatisfying behavior patterns," Boone wrote. "He took away for the time being their friction and discontent. . . . He had what they wanted, what they needed. I doubt if anyone ever turned away from him unsatisfied or unnourished." Were people fascinated by Strongheart because he was well trained and a good performer? No, Boone explained, it was far more magical than that. "What they were really doing," he wrote, "was looking through a moving transparency on four legs, and seeing a much better universe than the one they had been living in."

Boone's beliefs were extreme, but something did make these movies soar. *The Return of Boston Blackie,* Strongheart's last film, was shot in 1927. The story follows Boston Blackie, a bad guy who has just been released from prison and has resolved to become a good guy. His old criminal pals pressure him to make one more score, but his dog, Strongheart, acts as his moral guardian and helps him stay on the right path. It is Blackie — not his dog — who is tugged between two worlds — his wild, criminal side and his tame, reformed side; the dog is unconditionally good. Like many silent films, *The Return of Boston Blackie* is sometimes broad and overly schematic, but it is also fast-paced and engaging. Strongheart is a big, gorgeous dog with a sharp economy of movement and a look of concerned attention on his face, and he is commanding and charismatic as he growls at Denver Dan, chases after Necklace Nellie, busts out of a trap, and leaps out of a plane. At those moments, as J. Allen Boone would agree, it is as if he is still here in this world and never went away.

5.

Not long ago, I was introduced to Willie and Louise Benitez, who live in Murfin's old house in the Hollywood Hills. The house has a red tile roof, dormer windows, and a small yard that tumbles down a series of terraces to the street. It is a charming place, almost elfin, with a tangle of jacaranda trees shading it; the Benitezes' dog, Beauty, was dozing in the one spot of sun in the yard when I arrived.

Neither of the Benitezes had ever heard of Strongheart before they bought the house. When they first moved in, a few neighbors told them that the house had belonged to Rin Tin Tin, but when they researched it, they discovered the mistake and found the house's connection to Strongheart. Since then, they have been trying to collect as much Strongheart memorabilia as they can, although there is little of it to be found. Louise showed me what she had managed to dig up: some newspaper clippings and snapshots; a photograph of Strongheart with several koalas sitting on his back, taken in an animal sanctuary in Australia; and a copy of *Screen Almanac,* featuring a picture of Strongheart with Lady Jule in the bridal suite of a Manhattan hotel.

I had been under the impression that Murfin lived in a mansion. She was a very successful screenwriter, and after her divorce from Trimble she married a prominent actor, Donald Crisp. She was a woman of means. Every description of her house made it sound a lot grander than the Benitezes' stucco cottage. I didn't know how to ask about this discrepancy without sounding insulting. Then I remembered an interview in which Trimble said that Murfin's house was on Ivarene, which was a block away from the Benitezes' house. I mentioned this to Louise. She looked at me for a moment and then started to laugh. "This wasn't Murfin's house!" she exclaimed. "This was the doghouse! This was Strongheart's house! Murfin's house was up the hill!"

She pulled out a photograph of an elegant white house with a formal driveway and an imposing front entryway, set on a hill with no other house in sight. Murfin's nearest neighbor, well out of view, had been Roy Rogers. The photograph must have been taken when Murfin and Trimble were having a party, because the house was lit up and there were black Ford Model As and Chrysler Maxwells parked all along the road. Murfin's property had extended from the mansion down the long hillside to the Benitezes' cottage. The mansion is gone now, and something else has been built in its place, but the doghouse, which is as grand as a doghouse could possibly be, remains. As I was leaving, Louise told me that she hoped to write a children's book about their unusual circumstances. She said she was planning to call it *I Live in the Doghouse.*

6.

Why were animals so popular in film, especially so early in the history of movies? It was partly a matter of convenience: animals were available, didn't need to be paid, and could be directed and manipulated easily. Additionally, people are fond of animals, enjoy looking at them, and experience little of the self-consciousness they might have when viewing other people — the "otherness" of animals makes them easy to watch.

As cultural critic John Berger has written in his essay "Why Look at Animals?" the advent of film corresponded with our becoming modern and was an important part of what spurred us toward that. Film took what was seemingly inviolable — the irreversible nature of time and the impossibility of revisiting a moment — and defied it. No one thought that a movie was real life or that time was indeed reversing, but the gauzy, timeless time within a film and the ability to create something that seemed to contain a refracted bit of reality is powerful even now, in spite of how accustomed we are to it, and was shockingly powerful when people first experienced it. More than many modern developments, film set us apart from the natural world, with its rules that cannot be altered.

The invention of cinema came at the moment when animals were starting to recede from a central role in human civilization; from that moment forward, they began to be sentimental — a soft memento of another time, consolation for the cost of modernity. The ability to feel emotion about animals came to be a marker for being human just as humans began living apart from them, and it remains that way today. In the science fiction movie *Blade Runner,* the only way to tell whether an individual is a natural-born human or a machine-made replica of a human is to measure that individual's reaction to a description of animals suffering; a real person experiences sadness and discomfort, whereas a replicant experiences nothing. Movies about animals brought together these two divergent endpoints — the new man-made world that film symbolized and could conjure and even control, and the lost world of our life with animals.

The irony is that people began regarding animals differently at the same time they were becoming more like them. At the beginning of the twentieth century, huge numbers of people began leaving farms and the countryside, pulled like iron filings by the magnetic draw of cities, looking for the "modern" life, and for jobs. In 1920, for the first time in our history, most Americans lived in cities — often detached from their families, packed into tenements that must have seemed like stockyards, harnessed to factory jobs that were as monotonous and depersonalizing as the kind of work previously reserved for beasts. Lee, for instance, reacted to "modern city living" as if he were a dog confined in a cage. People began dreaming about animals because animals reminded them of a more tender time. But they also may have cared about animals more because they saw more clearly into their lives.

7.

Rin Tin Tin moved into the dreamtime of film with the ease of a natural. Charley Jones noticed the dog's magnetism and used him in several other short films for Novagraph in 1921, doing everything from riding a steeplechase horse to driving an aquaplane to diving off a thirty-foot pier. Jones also used Lee in one of the films, having him work a punching bag with the lightweight boxer Leach Cross, for which Lee got $250.

That same year, Lee married a wealthy socialite named Charlotte Anderson, who owned a fancy stable and a champion horse named Nobleman. Most likely, they first met at a dog or horse show — their social worlds would not have overlapped otherwise. The marriage is curious. Lee was good-looking and always described as a likeable man, but when he and Anderson met, he was living with his mother and spent all of his time with his dog. It's hard to imagine him presenting an alluring package to a woman like Anderson, a sophisticated, worldly divorcée who was quite a bit older than Lee. It's even harder to picture Lee having a romantic life — he made no mention of it, or of Anderson, in his memoir.

Lee's devotion, before and after the wedding, was to the dog, and it was about to pay off. When he wasn't training Rinty to follow directions — which he did for hours every day — he took him to "Poverty Row" in Hollywood, where the studios were located. They walked up and down the street, knocking on doors, trying to interest someone in using Rinty in a film. This wasn't as implausible as it might sound: the movie business in 1922 was still nearly homemade, and bit players were often plucked from the crowds that gathered at the studio gates. Moreover, ever since Strongheart's spectacular and profitable appearance in *Silent Call* in 1921, German shepherds were as sought after as blond starlets. Lee probably brushed past other hopeful young men with their own trained German shepherds as he went from door to door.

At first, Lee got nowhere. "I was told they were not interested in my dog or my story," he wrote about his visit to one of the studios. "To them I was just another dog trainer with his dog." Then, unexpectedly, he got a break: he secured a small part for Rinty in a melodrama called *Man from Hell's River*. Rinty — who is not in the cast list but is mentioned in the *Variety* review as "Rin Tan" — plays a sled dog belonging to a Canadian Mountie.

Unfortunately, as with seventeen of Rin Tin Tin's twenty-three silent films, no copy of *Man from Hell's River* exists today. All we have is the movie's "shot list," which was a guide for the film editor who cut and pasted the footage together. Parts of it read like a kind of silent-film found poetry:

Long shot dog on tree stump
Long shot wolf
Long shot prairie
Long shot dog runs and exits
Long shot deer
Long shot dog
Medium shot girl
Close-up shot little monkey

And then, at the end:

Med shot dog and puppies
Med close-up more puppies
Med shot people and dogs

Two months after this debut, Rinty was cast in another film, a run-of-the-mill "snow" called *My Dad*. It, too, was a small part, but it marked a significant step: for the first time, he was given a film credit. In the cast list, he appeared thus:

Rin-Tin-Tin . . . . Played by himself

In his wanderings on Poverty Row, Lee finally got through the door at Warner Bros. — on what pretense, he never explains, and no record exists to detail it. One of the smallest studios in Hollywood, Warner Bros.

was founded by the four Warner brothers who came to Hollywood from New Castle, Pennsylvania, and set up shop in a drafty barn on Sunset Boulevard. The day Lee managed to get in the door Harry Warner was directing a scene that included a wolf. The animal being used had been borrowed from the Los Angeles Zoo and was not performing well. Lee's version of what followed is another Hollywood fable: he liked to tell people that he rubbed dirt into Rinty's fur to make him look like a wolf, and convinced Warner to give Rinty a chance to try the scene. Rinty performed brilliantly, and thus the dog's eight-year relationship with Warner Bros. began. However it happened — and chances are it wasn't quite as Lee described it — Harry Warner liked what he saw in the dog, and he also agreed to look at Lee's script for *Where the North Begins.* He promised to let Lee know within thirty days if he would make him an offer for either the dog or the script.

While Lee awaited word from Warner Bros., he got another small part for Rinty in a film directed by William Desmond. The shooting took ten days. When it finished, Lee got a letter from Warner Bros. with the answer he had hardly dared to imagine. The studio wanted to buy his screenplay for

Where the North Begins and cast Rin Tin Tin in the lead.

Lee was so excited that he hardly heard what he would be paid, although he would have accepted any offer. Production on *Where the North Begins* began almost immediately, with Chester Franklin, an accomplished director, in charge. Claire Adams, Walter McGrail, and Pat Hartigan — silent-film stalwarts — were cast opposite Rinty. The film was shot in the High Sierras and followed Lee's screenplay almost exactly as he wrote it. "It didn't seem like work," he wrote. "Even Rinty was bubbling over with happiness out in the woods and snow." Rinty sometimes bubbled too much, chasing foxes into snowdrifts, and in one case attacking a porcupine, which filled his movie-star face with quills. Otherwise, Lee was proud of the dog's performance, which included a twelve-foot jump — three inches higher than his show-winning jump in Los Angeles — and scenes in which he was required to fight wolves. "Rinty loved a fight with man or beast," Lee wrote, referring obliquely to Rinty's famously short temper. At least in the fight scenes, both Rinty and the wolves wore light muzzles so that none of the animals risked getting hurt.

The movie premiered at a small theater in Glendale, a few blocks from where Lee had lived with his mother and sister. At the end of the film, the audience applauded for what felt to Lee like hours. Then Lee and Rinty took the stage. At first Lee was terrified. In the past, anytime he had needed to speak in front of a group, his stage fright had been so paralyzing that he had had trouble uttering a word. But with Rin Tin Tin at his side he found his voice. "I felt that everyone was watching *him* and not me," he explained. He saw himself there just to serve the dog and explain him to the public. It was the role Lee would play for the next thirty-eight years.

To advertise the film, Warner Bros. distributed promotional material to theater owners that included prewritten ads and publicity stunts, as well as feature stories that could be offered to local newspapers. The features were meant to make the filming of the movie seem almost as dramatic as the movie:

HUNGRY WOLVES
SURROUND CAMP
Movie Actors in Panic When
Pack Bays at Them
GREAT RISK OF LIFE IN

THE MOVIE'S NO BED OF ROSES
Chester Franklin, Director, Tells
Hard-Luck Story of Blizzard

Other story suggestions were less dramatic. One piece about actor Claire Adams and her fondness for clothing was headlined "Knows Canadian Garb from Alpha to Omega." The publicity stunts, which studio marketing people referred to as "exploitation," included suggestions that theater owners "get a crate and inside it put a puppy or a litter of them" for the lobby ("You will be sure to get a crowd"); place signs in a military recruiting office saying, "WHERE THE NORTH BEGINS AT [BLANK] THEATRE *is a thrilling picture of red-blooded ADVENTURE. Your adventure will begin when you join the marines and see the world*"; or, as one stunt titled "Holding Up Pedestrians" proposed, "Get a man to walk along the principal streets of the city stopping pedestrians and asking them the question, 'Where Does the North Begin?' and upon their answering (or even not answering) he can . . . tell them it begins at your playhouse."

"Here is a cracking good film for almost any audience," *Variety* declared when *Where the North Begins* was released nationwide. "A film packed full of the old heroic stuff and having as its leading character a dog actor, 'Rin-Tin-Tin.' . . . It has the conventional hero and the conventional heroine, but Rin-Tin-Tin is the show. A good many close-ups are given the dog and in all of them he holds the attention of the audience closely for a good many facial expressions are gained of him." In closing, the reviewer added, "The dog, incidentally, is a police dog and a good actor." Another review praised Rinty's eyes, saying they conveyed something "tragic, fierce, sad and . . . a nobility and degree of loyalty not credible in a person."

The *New York Times* was more ambivalent, comparing Rin Tin Tin to the prevailing German shepherd champion, Strongheart: "Rin-Tin-Tin has splendid eyes and ears . . . but this dog engages in a pantomimic struggle that is not always impressive, at least not as realistic as the work of Strongheart." *Motion Picture Magazine*'s story "The Rival of Strongheart" went further, noting that Rin Tin Tin "is now competing with Strongheart for the canine celluloid honors."

According to *Variety,* the film caught on "like wildfire." It quickly earned $352,000, a big success. Still, it wasn't quite at the level of Strongheart's *Silent Call,* which had broken attendance records in Los Angeles when it was shown eight times a day for thirteen weeks.

8.

Strongheart was setting the pace, but after starring in just one movie, Rin Tin Tin was already a celebrity. It had happened so fast, really; soon after *Where the North Begins* was released, thousands of fan letters for Rin Tin Tin arrived at Warner Bros. each week. The movie was playing all over the country, and — as was typical with popular films — most theaters extended its run as long as people kept showing up. A film as popular as *Where the North Begins* might stay in a theater for months, playing several times a day. Fans might come to see it a half-dozen times. Television didn't exist and movies were still such a new form of entertainment that a hit film was a spectacle, a national event that everyone wanted to view.

Inspired by Strongheart and now Rin Tin Tin, German shepherds took over Hollywood. Wolfheart and Braveheart; Wolfang and Duke; Fang, Fangs, Flash, and Flame; Thunder, Lightning, Lightnin', and Lightnin' Girl; Ace the Wonder Dog, Captain the King of Dogs, and Kazan the Dog Marvel; Rex, Pearl, Thorne, and Saccha; Silver Wolf, Silver Streak, Silver King, and King; Fearless, Leader, Tarzan, and Napoleon; Champion, Dynamite, Klondike, and Lobo; Zoro, Ranger, Smoke, and Smokey; White Fawn, Grey Shadow, Zandra, and Cyclone; Grief, Chinook, and Peter the Great. More than fifty of them were working in Hollywood during that period, playing serious, heroic figures in films that, like them, are now mostly lost or forgotten: *A Flame in the Sky, Courage of the North, The Silent Code, Avenging Fangs, Fangs of Destiny, Wild Justice.*

The dogs in these films were always heroes, and in real life dog heroes were also having their day, making news with genuine accomplishments. In 1925, for instance, a sled dog named Balto led a team carrying diphtheria antitoxin to Nome, Alaska, saving the town from epidemic; the dog team was celebrated around the world. Just three years later, there was another occasion for celebrating dogs' selfless service to humankind, when the nation's first seeing-eye dog, Buddy, began guiding a young blind man named Morris Frank.

Dogs, in fact, were perfect heroes: unknowable but accessible, driven but egoless, strong but tragic, limited by their muteness and animal vulnerability. Humans played heroes in films, too, but they were more complicated to admire because they were so particular — too much like us or too much unlike us or too much like someone we knew. Dogs, on the other hand, have the talent of seeming to understand and care about humans in spite of not being human and perhaps are better at it because of that difference. They are compassionate without being competitive, and there is nothing in their valor that threatens us, no demand for reciprocity. As Lee knew very well, a dog can make you feel complete without ever expecting much in return.

Even as this sea of German shepherds rose around him, Rin Tin Tin was singled out. He was praised by everyone from director Sergei Eisenstein, who posed for a picture with him, to poet Carl Sandberg, who was working as a film critic for the Chicago *Daily News.* "A beautiful animal, he has the power of expression in his every movement that makes him one of the leading pantomimists of the screen," Sandberg wrote, adding that Rinty was "phenomenal" and "thrillingly intelligent." Warner Bros. got fifty thousand requests for pictures of Rinty, which were signed with a paw print as well as that spidery handwriting of Lee's, saying "Most faithfully, Rin Tin Tin."

From the start, Rin Tin Tin was admired as an actor but also seen as a real dog, a genetic model; everyone, it seemed, wanted a piece of him. As soon as Nanette started having puppies, Lee began distributing them — especially to some of Rin Tin Tin's most celebrated fans. Greta Garbo and Jean Harlow each owned a Rin Tin Tin pup, as did W. K. Kellogg, the cereal magnate, and a number of directors and other movie stars. (President Herbert Hoover didn't own a direct Rin Tin Tin descendant, but he did have a German shepherd.) Some of the puppies went far afield. The Japanese government was so impressed with Rin Tin Tin that it directed its consul in California to begin buying as many Rin Tin Tin puppies as possible; the puppies were then shipped to Japan and raised with the hope of breeding them.

Warner Bros. was, of course, delighted by Rin Tin Tin's success. Even Jack Warner, the youngest of the brothers, who had been leery of animal stars ever since a monkey actor bit him, appreciated what Rin Tin Tin was doing for the studio. The first box office returns had been unbelievable, Warner told a reporter, and the studio wanted to "cash in" while Rin Tin Tin was "hot."

Before starting production on the next Rinty film, *Find Your Man,* the studio sent Lee and the dog on a four-month promotional tour around the country. They appeared at hospitals and schools and orphanages, gave interviews, and visited animal shelters. When describing a visit to one shelter, Lee sounded as if he was telling the story of his own childhood through Rin Tin Tin. "Perhaps if I could have understood, I might have heard Rinty telling these other less fortunate dogs [in the shelter] of how his mother failed in her terrific struggle to keep her little family together. Or, how he as a little war orphan had found a kindred spirit in his master and friend, also a half-orphan." Of course, Rin Tin Tin's mother had actually succeeded in keeping her little family together in the bombed-out dog shelter, against extraordinary odds. It was Lee's mother who had, at least for a time, failed in her terrific struggle.

In the evening, Lee and Rinty went to the theater, and after a showing of *Where the North Begins,* they came onstage. Lee usually began by explaining how he had trained Rinty. "There are persons who have said I must have been very cruel to Rinty in order to get him to act in the pictures," especially in the scenes where the dog is shown "groveling in the dust, shrinking away, his tail between his legs," which Rinty did not only in *Where the North Begins* but in almost every film that followed — all of his movies seem to have included a moment in which Rinty is shamed or punished or reproved. Lee would then demonstrate to the theater audience how he worked with the dog, saying it was best to use a low voice "with a tone of entreaty." He didn't believe in bribing Rin Tin Tin with food or excessive praise; he rewarded him by letting him play with the squeaky rubber doll he had first given to Rinty when he was a puppy. At this point in the show, Lee would run Rinty through some of his tricks — his pathetic belly crawling, his ability to stand stock-still for minutes on end, his range of expressions from anger to delight to dread.

A writer named Francis Rule was at one of those performances, and he described it in detail. He said Lee began by calling Rinty onstage, and then, for laughs, scolded when the dog stretched and yawned and flopped to the ground. "There then followed one of the most interesting exhibitions I have ever witnessed," Rule wrote. As Lee led Rinty through a series of acting exercises, "there was between that dog and his master as perfect an understanding as could possibly exist between two living beings. [Duncan] scarcely touched him during the entire proceedings — he stood about eight feet away and simply gave directions. And it fairly took your breath away to watch that dog respond, his ears up unless told to put them down and his eyes intently glued on his master. There was something almost uncanny about it."

Everywhere Lee and Rinty appeared, the dog was treated like a dignitary. In New York, Mayor Jimmy Walker gave him a key to the city. In Portland, Oregon, he was welcomed as "a distinguished canine visitor" and met at the train station by the city's school superintendent, the chief of police, and the head of the local Humane Society; then he made a statesmanlike pilgrimage to the grave of Bobby the Oregon Wonder Dog, a local legend who was said to have walked from Indiana to Oregon to reconnect with his owners. During the ceremony, according to news reports, "Rin Tin Tin with his own teeth placed the flowers on Bobby's grave and then in a moment's silence laid his head on the cross marking the resting place of the dog who gave his life to give the world another stirring example of a dog's devotion and faithfulness to his master." The next day, at the Music Box Theatre, Rinty was presented with the Abraham Lincoln humanitarian award and medal for distinguished service.

He stirred something in people. "The thing he possesses is the thing which few actors or actresses possess and that no dog on stage or screen today possesses, the power to realistically portray feeling or emotion," one fan wrote to Lee, adding, "Yes, he is a *human* dog, for in the picture *Where the North Begins,* has he not shown that he was human — human in the real big sense of the word? Truly, Rin Tin Tin is without an equal. I have seen a number of dog pictures on the screen. They have been true dogs and good ones, but in none, with the exception of Rin Tin Tin in *Where the North Begins* have I been able to feel that the only difference between man and beast is perhaps in the way we walk."

Another fan wrote, "Rin Tin Tin registers more range of emotion than any other dog actor known to the screen has attained. He shows in his expression and acting such deep, human, contrasting feelings as trust and distrust, sorrow and joy, jealousy and love, hatred and devotion. These qualities, and his wonderful ability to carry his audience with him in sympathy, mark him as the greatest dog actor of the screen today."

For Lee, this leap from the basement of the sporting goods store to the stage of the Orpheum Theater in Chicago and the three-room suite at Boston's Copley Plaza Hotel and the three-year contract with Warner Bros. was dizzying. It was as if, after a long night, he had awoken into a new life. With his Warner Bros. salary and the $60,000 he made on *Where the North Begins,* he set up a trust fund for his mother and bought new appliances for her kitchen. He also bought three lots in Beverly Hills, adjacent to the Los Angeles Country Club. He planned to build three structures: a house for Elizabeth, a house for himself, and a kennel for Rin Tin Tin.

Not surprisingly, he became a target for swindlers and opportunists. In Chicago, he was accused of having contributed to the delinquency of a teenage girl. It was a fumbling attempt at blackmail and he had a sound alibi — he was with executives from a dog food company at the time of the alleged assault — so the case was dropped, but it made him aware of his vulnerability. In Boston, a woman carrying a Chihuahua stopped to admire the movie star. Rinty bit

130

the Chihuahua. The aggrieved owner, with the help of a local lawyer, puffed up her damages to include not just the veterinary bill to stitch the Chihuahua's ear but also the cost of repairing her coat, buying new silk stockings, and having some dental work. (After a year of negotiation, the woman settled for $25.) As Lee wrote in his memoir, he was learning what it meant to be famous, for good and for ill.

In 1924 the studio began shooting *Find Your Man.* It was directed by Mal St. Clair and written by a "downy-cheeked youngster who looked as though he had just had the bands removed from his teeth so he could go to the high school prom," according to Jack Warner. This youngster was Darryl Zanuck, the son of a professional gambler and the wayward daughter of a wealthy Nebraska hotel owner, both of whom abandoned him by the time he was thirteen. He came to Hollywood when he was seventeen. Zanuck's first job was writing ads for Yuccatone Hair Restorer. Zanuck's slogan, "You've Never Seen a Bald Indian," helped make Yuccatone a success — until bottles of the hair tonic fermented and exploded in twenty-five different drugstores and the company was driven out of business. Zanuck left advertising for a job as a gag writer for Charlie Chaplin and slapstick director Mack Sennett. He met Mal St. Clair through Sennett. St. Clair had directed dogs in several of his films. The two decided to pair up and write a star vehicle for Rin Tin Tin.

The movie Zanuck had in mind was set during the war and portrayed Rin Tin Tin as a Red Cross dog. The main human character is Paul Andrews, a disillusioned war vet "who has found that the 'welcome home' stories he had heard are merely fables." Once Zanuck had finished a draft, he and St. Clair acted out the plot for Harry Warner, with Zanuck taking the part of the dog. Warner loved it, and the studio started production almost immediately. Billed as "Wholesome Melodrama at Its Very Best" and starring "Rin Tin Tin the Wonder Dog," the movie became a "box office rocket," in Jack Warner's words.

Zanuck always acknowledged that Rin Tin Tin was his ticket into Warner Bros., but he later told interviewers that he hated the dog and hated writing for him. Even so, he wrote five more scripts for Rinty. All of the films were great successes. By the time he was twenty-five, Zanuck was running the studio.

9.

Of all of the canine film stars, Peter the Great was perhaps the one German shepherd besides Strongheart who had a chance to equal Rin Tin Tin's success. Peter had been imported from Germany in 1920 by two brothers, Edward and Arlis Faust, who, inspired by Strongheart, had spent months searching for a cinematic shepherd — just as Lee was trying to make his way into Hollywood. The Fausts' search turned up Peter, a natural talent who could crawl like a cat and supposedly walk backward up a ladder, but was best known for what was said to be his extraordinary intelligence. In an odd and emotional little book that she wrote about the dog in 1945, author Clara Foglesong described Peter the Great's aptitude as superhuman. "Exhaustive tests demonstrated a mental capacity almost beyond belief," Foglesong wrote. "His intellectual faculties were various and of the highest order of the great. He was exacting and practical. All who came in contact with him agreed that he was a genius second to none."

Genius or not, Peter was a good actor. Besides starring in his own movies, which included *Silent Accuser* and *Sign of the Claw,* he doubled for both Strongheart and another German shepherd actor named Thunder, performing stunts they were not able to pull off. The *Los Angeles Times* declared Peter "so appealing that human players might well be jealous of his ability." According to Foglesong, Peter was also a prohibitionist. "If there was one thing he objected to more than another, it was to see his masters indulge in the use of intoxicating beverages," she wrote. "His only interest was in seeing that neither Edward nor Arlis indulged in the fiery liquor."

In at least one instance, Peter the Great failed at this task with tragic results. That day, a Mr. Richardson and his wife dropped by to visit Edward Faust. Mrs. Richardson insisted on petting Peter, even though he had growled at her and seemed to dislike her. The Richardsons quarreled about the dog, and the woman ended up storming out of the house. Faust and Richardson began drinking. Another friend came by, and after more drinking the three men decided to go look for the missing Mrs. Richardson. With Peter in the backseat, they drove to the home of Fred Cyriacks, a rich North Hollywood real estate developer, because they thought Mrs. Richardson might be with him. According to Faust's testimony, the men rang the bell and Cyriacks came to the door. Richardson asked if his wife was inside. Cyriaks glared at him, said nothing, and then smacked Faust in the face. Then Cyriacks ordered his dog, which happened to be a German shepherd, to attack them. Cyriacks also grabbed a .30-gauge Winchester rifle. Seeing the dog and the rifle, Faust and Richardson ran back to the car and started to drive away. Cyriacks fired at the departing car, hitting the spare tire, the third man's hat, and Peter the Great. The dog died in a hospital three days later, reportedly with his paws in the hands of Edward Faust.

Faust sued Cyriacks for $100,000 — his estimate of Peter's value — and $25,000 in additional damages. Directors and producers attested to the dog's value and Faust won the case; the award of $125,000 was at the time one of the largest in history. Cyriacks appealed the award, claiming the dog was worth only $250. The appellate court agreed with Cyriacks, saying the amount of the award had been "based on fanciful speculation." Faust eventually settled for an undisclosed amount — whatever the amount, it was meager reimbursement for a dog that had been, by Foglesong's description, "endowed with courage without van-

135

ity, power without savagery, tenderness without deceit."

10.

No one wanted to miss seeing a Rin Tin Tin movie. *Lighthouse by the Sea,* written by Zanuck and released in 1924, concerned a pretty girl and her father, who was a blind lighthouse keeper. (The American Film Institute tags the movie with the keywords "Filial relations. Blindness. Bootlegging. Lighthouses. Maine. Shipwrecks. Dogs.") Warner Bros. held screenings for the sightless, complete with a narrator on stage who described the action and read the intertitle cards, which included, "He's so tough I have to feed him manhole covers for biscuits! This pup can whip his weight in alligators — believe me!" and "I thought you said that flea incubator could fight!"

Rinty's films were so profitable that Warner Bros. paid him almost eight times as much as it paid its human actors; even at that, Rin Tin Tin was a bargain. "The dog," Jack Warner told one reporter, "is literally a bonanza." Around the Warner Bros. lot he was called "the mortgage lifter" because every time the studio was in financial straits it released a Rin Tin Tin movie and the income from it set things right again. Lee, responsible for this bonanza dog, was given every privilege by the studio: a car and driver brought him to the set every day, and he had an office on the Warner Bros. lot, where he sifted through fan mail and little mementos that arrived for Rin Tin Tin.

His sudden new wealth dazzled him. He had never imagined this part of the equation — he had only imagined the satisfaction of making Rin Tin Tin a star. In his eight years at Warner Bros. he earned the equivalent of $5 million. He started buying fancy clothes and cars. He had copies of his Rin Tin Tin and Nanette charms made in solid gold, and one pair made up in gold and cloisonné, which he carried with him every day. He began construction on the lots he'd bought in Beverly Hills. Club View Drive is not the most expensive street in Beverly Hills, but it is solid and prosperous, a badge of accomplishment. Today, the house Lee built is gone and it's hard to know much about it because he never described it — in his memoir, he talked only about the kennel he built for his dogs.

After finishing his house and the kennel, he built a house next door for his mother. Then he bought a house in North Hollywood for his sister, Marjorie. His biggest splurge was on a beach house for himself in a gated section of Malibu, where his neighbors were Hollywood stars. He invested some of his money and put some in the bank. He was no longer the leggy young soldier, but he was still as trim as a tennis player. With his slicked-back silver hair, high cheekbones, strong nose, and his newfound affection for sharp clothes, he looked at home in Hollywood. Even though he was married to Charlotte Anderson at the time, he hardly mentioned her in his memoir. He wrote only about life on the set and his publicity tours with the dog.

No matter how much money he spent, there always seemed to be more coming in. Chappel Bros. introduced Ken-L-Ration, the first commercial canned dog food, in 1923. Phillip Chappel was so eager to have Rin Tin Tin as its spokesperson that with Lee watching he ate a can of the dog food to demonstrate its tastiness. Lee was convinced. Rinty was featured in ads for Chappel Bros.' Ken-L-Ration, Ken-L-Biskit, and Pup-E-Crumbles brands, with the slogan "My Favorite Food, Most Faithfully, Rin Tin Tin." It was the first of many endorsement deals that made Lee an even richer man.

Rin Tin Tin's athleticism first got him onto a movie screen, but it was his acting that made him a star. "Rin-Tin-Tin shows himself to be as effective a canine actor as ever," *Variety* wrote of the 1925 movie *Tracked in Snow Country*. "The humans in the cast have very little to do." One of Rin Tin Tin's most admired performances was in the 1926 film *The Night Cry*. In the film, Rinty belongs to a young sheep rancher named John Martin. Some lambs on neighboring ranches are killed and Rinty is suspected of being responsible. The other ranchers confront Martin and tell him he has to destroy the dog.

Meanwhile, Rinty is miles away pursuing the real sheep killer — a giant condor (played by the only giant condor in captivity at that time, a cold-eyed, hunchbacked creature named Bozo). Rinty is injured while chasing the condor and stumbles home. As he enters the Martins' house, he gazes at the family with the tentative, humble eagerness that only a dog can convey; his expression also conveys the pride he feels in having chased the condor away, and his faith that Martin will take care of him and help him heal. But Martin, who is in the house with his wife and infant daughter, freezes at the sight of Rinty. For a moment, no one moves and nothing happens, but the subtle shift in Martin's and Rinty's expressions is remarkable. It is as if you can see the man wavering between his love of his dog, his obligation to his neighbors, his concern for the dog's injury, his dismay at the idea of the dog as a sheep killer, and his refusal to believe that his trustworthy companion could be so disloyal. At the same time, as Rin Tin Tin approaches his master in a broken and broken-hearted shuffle, you can see him working through his own set of dissonant feelings — love of his owner, his need for help, the confusion over a rejection he doesn't understand, and, finally, defeat. It may seem absurd to claim that Rin Tin Tin was a good actor, but after you see this scene, it's hard to deny.

Rinty's physical feats were also magical. In various films, he gnaws through wooden doors, unties knots, climbs trees, vaults over huge chasms, saves someone from drowning by dropping a lifeline to him, feeds a lamb with a baby bottle, lights a wick and rekindles the light in a lighthouse, treads water for at least ten minutes, presses the lever on a police box to unhook the receiver and then barks for help, fights countless wolves and bad dogs and bad guys on land and in water. He crashes through dozens of plateglass windows, which were actually made of sugar; he was allowed to eat the sweet shards after the scenes were filmed. Sometimes his actions were simply too incredible for the critics' taste. In the 1927 film *Tracked by the Police,* Rin Tin Tin operates a crane to rescue the female lead and also halts a flood by operating the mechanism of a dam; the *New York Times* griped, "His exploits in determining the levers that close the locks seem like asking almost too much of any animal."

By contemporary standards, the movies are melodramatic — every situation in them dire, every story arc as obvious as daylight. But they engage you anyway. It is almost like watching slow-motion choreography; the actions and reactions are rhythmically coupled and then unwound just as elegantly. What seems most old-fashioned about the movies is the way Rin Tin Tin figures in the story: without irony, he is treated as an equal player. He is not a pet or a utility animal but rather another fully realized character with his own storyline. Maybe what marks these films as relics from a long-gone period is that sincerity, the earnestness that imagines a dog outwitting a dozen gangsters against a score that might mix Dvořák, Tchaikovsky, and thirty-two bars of "What Do You Mean, You Lost Your Dog?"

In these silent films, Rin Tin Tin was always the hero, but like any hero, he encounters the struggles of the hero's journey. He was always tested — usually by being wrongly accused or doubted or mistrusted. Many of the films, including *Where the North Begins, The Night Cry,* and *Clash of the Wolves,* revisit Lee's favorite story of Prince Llewellyn. But unlike that story, the films didn't end with the dog's death. Rather, Rinty always prevailed over the evildoer, proving himself and his loyalty — being recognized for, and redeemed by, his strength of character.

A hero who is questioned and then is able to answer is more compelling than a figure who is so powerful that he is never doubted. The war had made that even more real. Even though many men performed heroically in World War I, many of them, like Lee, were terrified, shell-shocked, numbed, or simply not able to be as brave as they thought they might be, but they managed to make it through. In these movies, Rin Tin Tin was just that sort of character: a hero built from little bits, some bent and some broken, who still manages to gather himself together and fly.

Of the six Rin Tin Tin silent films still in existence, the most memorable is *Clash of the Wolves,* which was released in 1925. Rin Tin Tin plays a half-dog, half-wolf named Lobo, who is living in the wild as the leader of a wolf pack. The film begins with a disturbing scene of a forest fire, which drives Lobo and his pack, including Nanette and their pups, from their forest home to the desert ranchlands, where they are forced to prey on cattle to survive. The ranchers hate the wolves, and especially Lobo; a bounty of $100 is offered as a reward for his hide. In the meantime, a young mineral prospector named Dave arrives in town. A claim jumper who lusts after Dave's mineral discovery (and Dave's girlfriend, Mae) soon schemes against him. Mae happens to be the daughter of the rancher who is most determined to kill Lobo and who also, for some reason, doesn't like Dave.

The wolves, led by Lobo, attack a steer, and the ranchers set out after them. The chase is fast and frightening, and when Rin Tin Tin weaves through the horses' churning legs it looks like he's about to be trampled. He runs faster and for longer than

143

seems possible. He outruns the horses, his body flattened and stretched as he bullets along the desert floor, and if you didn't see the little puffs of dust when his feet touch the ground, you'd swear he was floating. He scrambles up a tree — a stunt so startling that I had to replay it a few times to believe it. Can dogs climb trees? Evidently. At least certain dogs can. And they can climb down, too, and then tear along a rock ridge, and then come to a halt at the narrow crest of the ridge. The other side of the gorge is miles away. Rin Tin Tin stops, pivots; you feel him calculating his options; then he crouches and leaps, and the half second before he lands safely feels very long and fraught. His feet touch ground and he scrambles on, but a moment later he somersaults off the edge of another cliff, slamming through the branches of a cactus, collapsing in a heap, with a cactus needle skewered through the pad of his foot.

The action is thrilling, and it would have been even more exciting on a huge screen, in an elegant movie palace, with hundreds of people cheering and the orchestra pounding out the score. But the best part of the movie is the quieter section, after Rin Tin Tin falls. He limps home, stopping every few steps to lick his injured paw; his bearing is so abject and afflicted that it is easy to understand why Lee felt the need to explain he was just acting. Rin Tin Tin hobbles into his den and collapses next to Nanette, in terrible pain.

Do the wolves of his pack gather around and help pull the cactus thorn out of their leader's paw? No, they don't. In an earlier scene in the movie, one of the wolves is injured and the pack musters around him. At first, it looks like they are coming to his aid, but suddenly, their action seems more agitated than soothing, and just then an intertitle card flashes up, saying simply "Law of the Pack. Death to the wounded wolf." This establishes the fact that the other wolves will kill Rin Tin Tin if they realize he's injured. Rinty and Nanette try to work on the cactus needle in his paw surreptitiously. But the pack (which is played by an assortment of German shepherds, huskies, coyotes, and wolves) senses that something is wrong. Finally, one of them approaches, a black look on his face, ready to attack. Rinty draws himself up and snarls. The two animals freeze, and then, very subtly, Rinty snarls again, almost sotto voce, as if he were saying, "I don't care what you think you know about my condition. I am still the leader here." The murderous wolf backs off.

The rest of the plot is a crosshatch of misperception and treachery. Rinty, fearing he will still be killed by his pack and attract harm to Nanette and their pups, decides to leave so that he might die alone; his wobbling, wincing departure is masterful acting. The humans in the movie, all flawed to varying degrees by either greed or naïveté or prejudice or stupidity — except for Mae, who is played by June Marlowe — stumble around double-crossing one another. Dave comes upon Rinty as he is on his death walk. Knowing there is a $100 bounty for the animal, he pulls out his gun, but then gives in to his sympathy for the suffering animal and removes the cactus thorn. (Actor Charles Farrell must have been a brave man; Rinty was required to snap and snarl at him in the scene when Farrell is tending to his paw, and there are a few snaps when Rinty looks like he's not kidding.)

Dave's decision to save Lobo is of great consequence because, of course, according to the perfect circular arc of life within a film, Lobo ends up saving Dave's life. He chooses to be a dog — a guardian — and protect Dave, rather than give in to his wolf impulse to be a killer.

The film doesn't just set good against bad;

it raises the questions of natural versus domesticated, and needs versus wants, and even the triumph of subtle thinking over unilateralism, since the characters who can ignore a narrow rule and make an independent decision (as Dave does with Lobo) prevail. Even wolfishness, in the movie, isn't a simple evil. The forest fire in the opening scene establishes that the wolves are reluctant cattle killers; they are forced into it not because they are vicious but because they have been driven from their home and have no other option.

The film has its share of silliness — a scene in which Rinty wears a fake beard as a disguise to avoid being identified as Lobo, for example — and the human acting, to the modern eye, is stilted. But *Clash of the Wolves* made me understand why so many millions of people fell in love with Rin Tin Tin and were moved by the way he wordlessly embodied many of the questions and conflicts and challenges that come with being alive.

11.

By the middle of the 1920s, the movie business had grown into one of the ten biggest industries in the United States. Almost 100 million movie tickets were sold each week, to a population of only 115 million. Warner Bros., thanks largely to Rin Tin Tin, was prospering. In 1928 the studio was worth $16 million; just two years later, $200 million. It still had the reputation of being a bit mingy and second-rate compared to Paramount or MGM, but it was expanding and innovating. It launched a chain of movie palaces, with orchestras and elaborate, thematic decor — Arabian nights in one theater, Egyptian days or Beaux Arts Paris in another — and, best of all, air-conditioning, which was rare in public buildings and even rarer in private homes.

The year 1927 was busy for Lee and Rinty: they shot four films, back to back, and during any break in the production schedule, they were on the road doing stage appearances. Lee hardly had a life at home. In the middle of that year, Charlotte Anderson filed for divorce. She said she didn't like Rin Tin Tin and didn't like competing with him. In the proceedings, Charlotte testified that Lee didn't love her or her horses. "All he cared for was Rin Tin Tin," she told the *Los Angeles Times,* in an article about the trial headlined "Dog Film Star May Be an Orphan." The story continued, "Evidently, Rin Tin Tin's company was so much pleasure to Duncan that he considered Mrs. Duncan's presence rather secondary." Rinty was named as a corespondent in the divorce, a role usually reserved for mistresses.

The divorce came at what was otherwise a high point for Lee. That year, Rin Tin Tin was designated the most popular performer in the United States, and his four films— *A Dog of the Regiment, Jaws of Steel, Tracked by the Police,* and *Hills of Kentucky* — were box office hits as well as critical successes. The Academy Awards were presented for the first time, and Rinty received the most votes for Best Actor. But members of the Academy, anxious to establish the new awards as serious and important, decided that giving an Oscar to a dog did not serve that end, so the votes were recalculated, and the award was diverted to Emil Jannings, for his performances in both *The Way of All Flesh* and *The Last Command.*

Even without winning the Oscar, Rinty was in the news all the time. He was variously referred to as Rin, Rinty, Rin Tin Tin, and, more often, the hyphenated Rin-Tin-Tin. He was frequently given an honorific — the King of Pets, the Famous Police Dog of the Movies, the Dog Wonder, the Wonder Dog of the Screen, the Wonder Dog of All

Creation, the Mastermind Dog, the Marvelous Dog of the Movies, and America's Greatest Movie Dog. By 1927, he was clearly surpassing Strongheart. A review of Rin Tin Tin's film *A Race for Life* even began with the haunting question, "Strongheart who?"

In his way, Rin Tin Tin had come to represent something essentially American. He wasn't born in the United States, and neither were his parents, but those facts only made him more quintessentially American: he was an immigrant in a country of immigrants. He was everything Americans wanted to think they were — brave, enterprising, bold, and most of all, individual. In a dog, even more than in a human, individuality is exceptional; after all, dogs are pack animals, and many of Rinty's plots revolved around him making choices between pack mentality and individual judgment, an almost impossible feat for a dog.

In the 1920s, this was still a new country, still something of an experiment, trying out the notion that a society could reconcile private desires and ambitions with the demands of community. The American identity was still pliable, still taking shape. Many Americans had left ancient cultures of permanence and constraints and ethnic identities to join a society where identities were exploded and recombined — who can know how many different religions and backgrounds were represented in audiences at Rinty's films in New York City or Chicago or Los Angeles? People watching *Clash of the Wolves* might not have talked after the movie about how Rinty played out the founding principles of the nation, but his popularity came from the emotions he inspired, including pride in the dog's stubborn, resilient, complex character and an appreciation of his struggles — not just with the bad guys, but with himself.

At the same time, he was absolutely universal. Rin Tin Tin's movies went all over the world. Silent films were easy to distribute internationally. There was no dialogue to dub or need for subtitles — only the intertitle cards had to be replaced. In 1927, Jack Warner attended a dinner in Vienna and was seated next to a countess. He introduced himself as a producer. The countess asked which actors he worked with. Warner mentioned such luminaries as John Barrymore, but the countess seemed unimpressed. Warner was exasperated. Finally he said that he produced all of Rin Tin Tin's films. From that moment on, Warner recalled, "the name 'Jack Warner' meant something in Vienna."

The fact that the films were distributed around the world had some unanticipated benefits. In 1975, nitrate projection prints of *Clash of the Wolves, Jaws of Steel,* and *The Night Cry* were found in South Africa. Warner Bros. had distributed the films to South Africa in the 1920s, and these copies were apparently not sent back at the appointed time. Until these films were found, it was believed that there were no copies of *Clash of the Wolves* left in existence — like 80 percent of all silent films ever produced, it was thought to be just another one that vanished, with not a single copy to be found anywhere, including the studio vaults.

The National Film Preservation Foundation has restored the South African print of *Clash of the Wolves,* and the new copy of the film is beautiful. The tones, in black and white, are rich and deep; the black almost looks like velvet. You can also understand how Rin Tin Tin — with his dark eyes and dark face — was hard to light properly for a black-and-white film, and why, in the next generation of dogs, Lee looked for a light-colored animal who would be easier to see. Still, this Rin Tin Tin, the first, is a wonder. He's not a particularly pretty dog, but he is magnetic and engaging. His performance always looks natural — a credit to Lee's training. One advantage of silent films was that Lee could direct the dog by voice command, but still, Rinty's capacity for learning had to be exceptional. So many of the scenes involve long takes of the dog performing a complicated sequence of actions. Even with voice commands, it's amazing that you could train a dog to do all that.

Before I looked through the Warner Bros. archives, which included ledgers recording the studio's international sales, it had never occurred to me that films of this era — a time when most people in the world never traveled beyond their hometown — were distributed overseas. But they were. People all over the world were getting a look — a filmy, imaginary look, but still a look — at life in the United States. It must have been electrifying. To people in the crowded old cities in Europe and beyond, the spaciousness of those scenes in the American West in particular, with their endless horizon line and infinite sky, must have seemed like a glimpse of eternity.

My grandfather grew up in Hungary but came to the United States in his twenties, eventually settling in Ohio. His family was well established in Hungary, but something had spurred him to leave and try to make his own way alone. It was a pivotal choice, one that ended up being a matter of life and death. The figurine of Rin Tin Tin that he kept on his desk was such a puzzle to me, but the one thing I took for granted was that he had it because he knew of and enjoyed the Rin Tin Tin television show, since as a kid I had no idea that Rin Tin Tin existed in any form except for his presence on television. I saw the figurine as some evidence that my starchy, old-fashioned, European grandfather had become American, going so far as to embrace the popular culture of this new place. But as I unwound the story of Rin Tin Tin I began to see the dog on his desk in a different way. Although the plastic figurine was definitely merchandise from the television show, I now think that my grandfather's fascination with Rin Tin Tin began much earlier in his life. I believe the fascination took hold in some dark little theater in eastern Hungary when he first saw Rinty race across the screen in one of these 1920s melodramas — the huge western landscape stretching in the background, the sky like an unfurling banner — and that the dog's image, with its great promise, even had

154

something to do with his finding the courage to leave home.

12.

Throughout the 1920s, Rin Tin Tin was photographed constantly. Besides his studio headshot, which catches Rinty's moody gaze in three-quarters profile, his most popular picture was one of him posing with Nanette on a large rock by a lake. He was frequently photographed with celebrities — Ed Sullivan, Jackie Cooper, Myrna Loy, director Mervyn LeRoy, showgirl Evelyn Knapp — and with prominent citizens, such as members of the Beverly Hills police department or mayors of various large cities. Lee appears in some of these pictures, but more often he does not.

In some photographs, Rin Tin Tin posed doing human things. He pretended to sign for a ticket at an airline counter, operate a movie camera, receive a manicure, and work as a hotel clerk. He was photographed playing golf, snowshoeing, waterskiing, and swinging in a hammock. In one popular picture he sits in William McGann's director's chair — it has WILLIAM MCGANN stenciled across the back; McGann is seated next to him in a director's chair that says

RIN TIN TIN. Another photo, from a Ken-L-Ration ad, shows Rinty with Nanette and two of their puppies. The two adult dogs are sitting upright in chairs at a kitchen table, as if they are about to eat a meal, and the puppies are sitting on their parents' dinner plates; in the center of the table is a gigantic can of Ken-L-Ration.

Much was made of the grand style in which Rin Tin Tin supposedly lived. He snacked on steak served to him in silver bowls while classical music played over his kennel's sound system, or so the press releases from Warner Bros. claimed. His puppies had their own lavishly appointed kindergarten. The screens over the kennel windows were made of copper, or perhaps bronze. By some accounts, he wore a diamond collar. None of this is likely to be true; Lee loved the dog and made sure the kennel was comfortable, but he never lost the rancher's view that a dog was a dog was a dog. At the same time, it is true that Rin Tin Tin's name and phone number were listed in the Los Angeles phone book, and that he had an open invitation to the Warner Bros. commissary and was welcomed there like a star. He got his own salary, separate from Lee's salary as his trainer, and he earned more than most of his costars; in

Lighthouse by the Sea, for instance, he was paid $1,000 per week, while the lead human actor, William Collier Jr., was paid only $150.

The press treated Rin Tin Tin like a celebrity, writing and gossiping about him, without irony, never acknowledging that he was, after all, just a dog. "Famous Movie Dog in City; Thrills Kiddies" was the headline in a Wisconsin newspaper during one of his publicity tours. The story went on: "Rin Tin Tin, wife, occupy a doggy suite at hotel but canine actors left babies in West because of heat." A 1927 issue of *Movie Magazine* — which included a lineup of stories such as "When Will We Really Have Talking Movies?" "Are Actors People?" and "Is the World Tired of Children?" — ran a four-page feature called "The Rin-Tin-Tins," about Rin Tin Tin and Nanette's family life. "Nanette, like so many of the stars, is going to combine motherhood with a career," the writer noted. "The puppies are coming along beautifully, so she will play with Rin-Tin-Tin again in 'Trapped by the Police.' " Even Rin Tin Tin stand-ins were regarded as celebrities. The *New York Times* ran an obituary for Ginger, a German shepherd that performed under the name Lightning, with the headline, "Double for

Rin Tin Tin Is Dead."

Lee enjoyed the fact that he could now live well, but he never seemed to want or welcome attention for himself. He was a true Hollywood spouse, happy for the access it gave him, and for the money he earned, but he was most comfortable in a somewhat secondary role as a helpmate to a star rather than a star himself. There was more for him to manage all the time, which is perhaps another reason why he seemed to have no social life. In fact, when he finally mentions in his memoir that he had "met" a girl, while shooting on location, it comes as almost a shock.

Even after he and the girl, Eva Linden, got engaged, he was far more preoccupied with Rinty than with any other part of his life. They had what seemed to be endless publicity tours and movies and endorsement deals, and there was now even a Rin Tin Tin radio show, *The Wonder Dog.* Rinty did some of the barking on the show, but a human actor named Bob Barker did most of it. In truth, the dog's connection to the show was more abstract than actual. He rarely even figured in the plots except at the very end; in that sense, he was already beginning his transformation from a real dog into an idea and a character. The radio plots were wild. One episode was "a thrilling story of a heroic dog and a milkman, who upset the carefully laid plans of a criminal breaking into the house of the manager of the milk company." Another, called "A Trip to Mars," was described as "a story in which an inventor and scientist and his party, who have been shot to Mars in a giant torpedo, are saved from death at the hands of giant men by the heroic action of the inventor's faithful dog."

In 1926, Rin Tin Tin appeared on an experimental television station in New York City called W2XCR. Around that same time, he also became a character in books. One of the first, *The Little Folks' Story of Rin-Tin-Tin,* was published in 1927. In contrast to his masculine movie persona, the book casts Rinty as a doting nanny left to care for four children while their parents are out of town. As the parents are preparing to leave, Mother instructs Rin Tin Tin to "be sure to feed Baby Carol, to see that she has her naps." Rinty is also expected to cook for the kids; one of the chapters is titled "Rin Tin Tin Makes Sure That Lunch Is Satisfactory."

I often wonder what Rin Tin Tin was really like as a dog — not as a movie dog or a radio dog or a book dog or a television dog, but just as a dog. We know he liked to chase squirrels and skunks and foxes. He liked to run. He was muscular, not cuddly and soft. In his films, he looks so keyed up that he sometimes appears high-strung, but he was comfortable in crowds and in unfamiliar places. Maybe that intensity was just his attention to Lee and the anticipation of his next instructions.

He wasn't very friendly. The only person he was especially interested in was Lee. Von Stephanitz, who founded the breed, believed that German shepherds should bond only with their master; he considered excessive and promiscuous friendliness to be a weakness in a dog. Lee, taking this advice, raised Rin Tin Tin in the most cosseted fashion, rarely letting anyone else handle him. Actors who worked with Rin Tin Tin complained that he was mean and temperamental and that his only good quality was that he didn't drink. He was rumored to have bitten Jack Warner as well as several of his costars. But cinematographers were impressed by his patience: because of his dark coat, he had to be lit carefully so he was visible in these black-and-white films, and often had to stand still for long stretches while the lights were set for scenes.

His reputation for viciousness may have been nothing more than some contrarian Hollywood mythmaking. Maybe he played his fight scenes too enthusiastically (they do look realistic), and maybe he was not friendly, but a dog with a genuinely bad temper would be impossible to manage on a film set around a large crew or in the sorts of places that Rinty visited frequently, such as hospitals and orphanages. If Rin Tin Tin really *was* nasty, he was an even better actor than he was given credit for, since all of his movies included at least one scene in which he had to appear affectionate, toward either his master or his mate, or often with his puppies.

Or was the dog who appeared affectionate a different dog? Was there more than one dog being presented as Rin Tin Tin? Lee stated many times over the years that Rin Tin Tin was the only dog to appear in his movies, and that no doubles were used. He was adamant about it. But in a 1965 interview with the *Los Angeles Herald-Examiner,* Jack Warner said, "I guess there is no harm now in revealing what was secret information for so many years around the lot. It had occurred to us, when we realized Rinty's earning capacity, that our investment would be lost if anything happened to him. Therefore, with Duncan's consent, we agreed to breed and train a kennel full of doubles that could be used if our hero were ill or injured or even killed in some of the dangerous stunts we planned. Eventually we had 18 Rin Tin Tins and we used them all. Each animal was a specialist. One was used for attack scenes, another was trained to jump twelve-foot walls, a third was a gentle house dog, and so on."

Was this true? It stands to reason that other dogs would have been used when Rin Tin Tin was tired, or had to do something dangerous — he was too valuable to risk injury — or to perform a stunt he wasn't able to do, especially as he got older, just as there are almost always stunt doubles for human stars in films. Rin Tin Tin starred in twenty-two silents and seven talkies in just eight years, a breakneck pace, and he was not a young dog during most of that time. It would have been easy to use another dog to fill in for him in scenes that weren't close-ups, especially any in which he was doing something any well-trained German shepherd could do, like running or jumping. The fact is that dogs of the same breed do look a lot alike.

Only nine of those early films still exist, so we are able to assess just a small sample of his work. The dog starring in those nine silent films appears to be the same dog in the close-ups. In the long shots, the dog really could be any dog, since all you see is a German shepherd–shaped blur. In a few fight scenes, it looks as if a stuffed model is used.

Jack Warner didn't have any cause to say there were eighteen Rin Tin Tins if there was only one. Lee had more reason to deny that other dogs were used in the movies: maintaining that Rinty never had a double was a point of pride for him. It was a question of both the dog's identity and his own. He had one star, his war orphan pup, and that is what he wanted the world to see.

Over time, the story of Rin Tin Tin did end up forming a continuous multiple-strand loop of identity both bona fide and assumed — real individuals playing invented characters, and invented characters meant to represent real individuals played by other individuals chosen because they suited the role. Rin Tin Tin grew from being one dog to being a sort of franchise. And as his fame grew, Rin Tin Tin became, in a way, less particular — less specifically this one single dog — and more conceptual, the archetypal dog hero. I think that's why the first question I was asked whenever I told someone I was writing about Rin Tin Tin was always, "Was there really just one?"

14.

At Warner Bros., it was Sam Warner who thought it would be a good idea to have people talk in a movie. At his urging, the studio bought the rights to Vitagraph, a system for adding music to film, and he believed that it could be developed to add spoken dialogue to film, too. His hunch, which was shared by a number of other Hollywood executives, was correct. In October 1927, Warner Bros. released *The Jazz Singer,* and actor Al Jolson's ad-libbing was such a sensation that it changed the movie business forever. Unfortunately, Sam Warner, who had been so certain that the future of film included sound, died of a cerebral hemorrhage the day before the film premiered. As he predicted, talkies took over from silents quickly and completely, wiping them away, altering the entire industry, eliminating whole categories of jobs and an entire generation of actors who couldn't or wouldn't make the transition. Only ten years after *The Jazz Singer* was released, no more silent films were being made.

Did Lee see the changes on the horizon? On one hand, he and Rinty had never been busier. In 1927 Rinty made *Tracked by the Police, Dog of the Regiment, Jaws of Steel,* and *Hills of Kentucky* (which featured one of his puppies, Rin Tin Tin Jr., in a small role). In 1928, he starred in *A Race for Life, Rinty of the Desert,* and *Land of the Silver Fox,* and, in 1929, *The Million Dollar Collar.* Lee's contract with Warner Bros. was up for renewal the following year, but it must have seemed like a sure thing. After all, thirteen different films starring Rinty were playing at theaters across the country.

And yet, there were warnings. In May 1929, recognizing the new standard set by *The Jazz Singer,* the studio cast Rinty in a movie that was billed as "five percent dialog" — in other words, an awkward hybrid of a silent and a talkie. The *Variety* reviewer sniffed that the film, *Frozen River,* featured "a lot of badly synchronized barking." In an interesting bit of backtracking, the movie was then rereleased as a silent, with the sound track removed. Later that year, Rin Tin Tin's twenty-second film, *Tiger Rose,* premiered in a vast, 2,600-seat movie

165

palace, but at least one review treated it as if it was an artifact of a former time, calling it "strongly suggestive of the old Warner programmers," but pointing out that Rinty seemed like a "much less prominent doggie than in the days when mutts were glorified by Hollywood." The review was eerily prescient. "Rinty . . . has been scissored almost out of the picture," the reviewer added. "He now merely peeps through his paws and gets patted a couple of times. No more saving the express train or racing miles for the United States Marines."

That December, a Warner Bros. executive instructed a lawyer to draft a letter to Lee. Its purpose was to inform him that his contract was being canceled: the studio did not plan to make any more movies with Rin Tin Tin. "It has been decided that since the talking pictures have come into their own, particularly with this organization," the letter stated, "that the making of any animal pictures, such as we have in the past with Rin Tin Tin, is not in keeping with the policy that has been adopted by us for talking pictures, very obviously, of course, because dogs don't talk."

Lee was on Sound Stage One of the Warner Bros. studio lot when he was handed the envelope containing the letter and his termination papers. A studio executive standing nearby overheard Lee tell the messenger delivering the envelope that he had been expecting bad news. He walked to a spot where he thought he was out of sight, and read the letter. Then without any fanfare, he packed up his Warner Bros. office, retrieved his dog, and went home.

He left behind an oil portrait of Rin Tin Tin that hung in the Warner Bros. Hall of Fame — the first dog portrait to have enjoyed that honor at the studio. But he took all the other mementos that had accumulated in his office over the years: the drawings of Rin Tin Tin that had been sent to him by fans; the bas-relief plaques they had made for him; the carvings in redwood and gumwood; and the statuettes of ebony, ivory, clay, paste, soapstone, chalk, and Plasticine — all the awkward, handmade, heartfelt representations of the dog who had once been his personal war trophy and pet but had been shape-shifted and amplified and projected on the boundless scope of a public dream. Rin Tin Tin had always been Lee's private story about the possibility that love could be constant. This setback was real, but the dog was now something communal, a shared story about courage and endurance. He flickered past on a screen but he was fixed in immortality.

HEROES

1.

Was the advent of sound the real reason that Warner Bros. canceled Rinty's contract? Only three years before, Rin Tin Tin had been the biggest box office star in the country. The decision to abandon him seems precipitous. But sound was more than just an added dimension in a movie; it made movies totally different. In silent film, an animal could seem omniscient and often wiser than human beings. With dialogue, the difference in stature between a mute dog and a talking actor was insurmountable. A dog might jump twelve feet and convey, through looks and action, its capacity for empathy, but no dog, not even a wonder dog like Rin Tin Tin, had more than a few syllables to say.

Dogs found a place in the early talkies,

but most of the time they were cast in supporting roles or as comic sidekicks rather than in the dramatic roles they had played in the silents of the early 1920s. In 1929, MGM released *Hot Dog* and *College Hounds,* two short films directed by comedy veterans Zion Myers and Jules White that starred fifty dogs dressed in human costumes. There were no human beings in the films. The dogs acted out plots lifted from recent MGM films and seemed to speak, thanks to the magic of human voice-overs matched roughly to the movement of the dogs' mouths. These Dogville shorts were such a hit that Myers and White made six more, starting with *All Quiet on the Canine Front* and ending with *Dogway Melody,* a takeoff on *Broadway Melody,* which had elaborate musical numbers and a dance performed by a dog in blackface makeup.

The Dogville movies are engrossingly bizarre. They were meant to be light comedy, but their plots are sometimes uncomfortably adult, involving war, murder, infidelity, and attempted rape. Some of the dogs in the series became well known, especially Jiggs, a mutt with a pushed-in nose who was supposedly able to really talk, although his vocabulary was limited to "Mama," "Papa," and "hamburger." But none of the Dogville dogs became a star in their own right.

In 1929, when the first Dogville shorts were released, the world was on its heels, looking for some comedy. The stock market had collapsed in October, and the U.S. economy was spinning into deflation. Lee was hit hard. Soon after his Warner Bros. contract was canceled, his bank failed, just days after he had deposited $24,000 — possibly one of his last Warner Bros. paychecks — in his account. He needed money, so he decided to take some out of a laundry business he had invested in a few years earlier. He discovered then that the investment was a scam; there was no laundry business and no money. His business advisor, who had arranged the investment, committed suicide soon after.

In his memoir, Lee gamely describes the end of his eight-year relationship with Warner Bros. as "a much-needed vacation." He decided to use the time to do what had always felt most satisfying to him: he took his dog to the mountains and spent a few weeks alone with him.

Rinty was now twelve years old. He was fit but he was stiff, and there were flecks of gray around his muzzle; he was an old dog.

His contemporary, Strongheart, had died that year. After Trimble and Murfin divorced, Strongheart bounced from studio to studio, with none of them promoting him consistently; at the time of his death he was already fading from view. He had been a beautiful dog, Lee wrote, and then added, "Why he did not make more pictures, I do not know."

Lee knew a trip to the mountains would be demanding, and that the walking might be too much for Rinty, so he built a sort of sedan chair for him, with a canvas roof to block the sun, and mounted it on the back of one of his pack mules so that the dog could ride through the mountains like a rajah. Lee and Rin Tin Tin had made many such visits to the Sierras before the movies, before the money. They were back where they had started, just a boy and a dog in the mountains, as if nothing much had changed.

Lee was thirty-nine, still what we would consider a fairly young man, but for the dog — for all dogs — time dashes forward at a speed we humans can hardly perceive, until the day we realize that the puppy is no longer a puppy and has outpaced us. And yet a part of us lags behind, still seeing that old dog as a young dog even when he is standing at life's finish line. On this trip to the Sierras, in their slow advance across the mountain range, Lee hiking beside the mule while Rin Tin Tin rested in his travel bed, the arc of their extraordinary time together was almost complete.

This trip was also their purest moment together as companions. "I think it was on these trips that I really came so close to Rin-tin-tin," Lee wrote. "Although all his life he had lived close to me, out on this trip it seemed just the opposite — *I* was living close to *him.*"

2.

As it turned out, Rinty was not done with the movie business. In 1930, Mascot Pictures, an upstart studio that made movies and serials, offered Lee and Rinty a contract. The pay was less than Rin Tin Tin had earned at Warner Bros., and the status was several notches down, but Lee accepted and he and Rin Tin Tin went to work on *The Lone Defender.*

A cowboy story told in twelve short episodes, *The Lone Defender* starred June Marlowe, who had appeared with Rinty in many silent films, including *Clash of the Wolves* and *Find Your Man.* It was a sound picture, so at some point between their idyll in the Sierras and principal photography on the film, Lee must have retrained the dog to follow hand signals, since he couldn't direct him with voice commands anymore. In some scenes — or perhaps most scenes, according to skeptics — Lee used a stand-in to spare Rinty from the most demanding tricks.

The Lone Defender received disparaging reviews, and the scenes of cowboys on horses galloping across the plains are so long and boring that they look like an equine aerobics class. But audiences loved it anyway. In fact, *The Lone Defender* was so popular that many theaters ran it during regular showtimes, rather than on Fridays and Saturdays, when serials were usually shown.

Mascot quickly signed Rin Tin Tin for sequels, which turned out to be just as popular. Each episode ended with a cliff-hanger. The wait for the next installment of the serial was a delicious agony. One of the serials was shown at a 1932 meeting of the Colonial-Tribune Mickey Mouse Club No. 111 near Chicago. At the end of the show, the Mouseketeers found the suspense almost unbearable. "The picture ended at the most critical moment," the club secretary wrote, "leaving the children unable to suppress the disappointment that showed on their faces, though anxious enough to attend the next meeting and see the startling outcome of these adventures."

The Mascot serials brought another, younger audience into Rin Tin Tin's thrall — a demographic that included Bert Leonard and Daphne Hereford's grandmother, who first decided she needed a Rin Tin Tin puppy of her own after seeing the Mascot serials in a theater in Texas. My father saw them when he was a kid in Cleveland. I once asked him if he had ever seen *The Lone Defender,* and he was taken aback, as if it was no question at all. "Of course," he said. "Everyone saw them. *Everyone.*"

Then, out of the blue, Lee decided to take Rin Tin Tin on the vaudeville circuit. He wrote in his memoir that Rinty had conquered silent film and talkies, and that he wanted to see if they could master vaudeville as well. The real reason still seems mysterious. Vaudeville tours were grueling, hardly the ideal experience for an aging dog. Lee was still engaged to his "girl," Eva Linden, but he didn't seem to have been in any particular hurry to get married. The appeal of the vaudeville circuit might have been that it allowed Lee to do what he liked best

— spend time with Rinty — while sharing him with thousands of people who felt almost as strongly about the dog as Lee did.

"We would like very much to represent your act in this territory," a representative of the John Billsbury Agency Vaudeville Attractions wrote to Lee in 1930. Other vaudeville agents solicited him, too, and once he came to an arrangement with one of them, he and Rin Tin Tin started a nine-month national tour. The promotional material for the tour had the pitched, exaggerated tone of carnival barking. Even if he had been kicked off the Warner Bros. lot, Rin Tin Tin was still a star, and there was no superlative too grand for him. Here is one press release:

The dog that all the world loves . . . Rin Tin Tin, the leader of the canine kingdom. . . . The master dog has been so ably trained that he approaches histrionic perfection. . . . In nine years Rin Tin Tin has seen the shifting sands of time flow toward him with nothing but gold and brightness. . . . Rinty is the richest dog in the world . . . he has filet mignon for his breakfast. . . . Cerbereus, the three-headed dog that guards the door to Hell, cannot be compared to Rin

Tin Tin the master dog of the movies. Cerbereus pushes people into perdition but Rin Tin Tin saves them.

The tour began at the Albee Theater in Cincinnati. Lee and Rin Tin Tin were the fifth act on a bill that also included Mr. Wu and his Chinese Show Boat ("featuring Miss Jue-Sue-Tai and a dancing chorus of almond-eyed girls with a Chinese girl band"); a cowboy singer; two brothers, Ward and Van, who played violin and harp; a comedy and musical team called Off Key; and a song-and-dance act called Frabell's Frolics. In other cities, the bill included the Murphy Brothers in Rhythm and Taps, a pianist, the Tillers Sixteen Sunshine Girls ("fresh from England"), and, as Lee recalled, "Harry Holmes with a lot of merry nonsense and a very clever bantam rooster that was supposed to lay an egg every performance although I think personally, Harry must have been somewhat of a magician." Duke Ellington and his Cotton Club Orchestra appeared with them in New York City.

Lee and Rin Tin Tin's act was similar to the show they put on at movie theaters. After taking the stage, Lee told the audience how he had trained Rinty using the squeaky rubber doll, the toy he had first given Rinty in France, when he was just a puppy. He explained how Rinty had a "strange love" for the doll, and that to his mind this kind of attachment made Rinty seem like a human being; he was caught in the "magical and inescapable grip" of the doll the way some people were obsessed with baseball or orchids or stamp collecting. Then Lee demonstrated Rinty's training, running him through a repertoire of tricks, many of which he had performed in his films.

Dog training during this period was often limited to the swift kick and the slap, so Lee's approach was not typical. Lee liked to emphasize that he had never "trained" Rin Tin Tin, perhaps because of the association between obedience and fear. Instead, he preferred to say he had "educated" him. In fact, he had trained the dog intensively, relying on the attachment he and Rinty had developed from the time the puppy was just a few days old. This bond, combined with Lee's tenacity as a trainer and Rinty's intelligence and eagerness to please Lee, made their performance both surprising and moving to their audiences. According to James English, who wrote a biography of Lee in 1946 based on Lee's notes, Rin Tin Tin was not "a trained dog but an enthusiastic one," guided by affection rather than tyranny. For Rin Tin Tin, English continued, "work was play and companionship with his master and friend was ample reward."

Lee and Rinty took their vaudeville act to dozens of cities, and they were a success at each stop. The audience seemed to include everyone, of every age and gender. After a show in Portland, Oregon, Lee and Rinty were scheduled to appear at a party at a local high school. But the ads for the appearance in the newspaper were addressed just to boys, which set off a citywide protest. The newspaper ran several stories to correct the mistake, quoting Lee saying, "Rin Tin Tin was much displeased and showed his displeasure by barking energetically when he learned the invitation extended by him to the boys of the city failed to mention the girls. Now Rin has many admirers among the girls and he wouldn't hurt their feelings in the world."

Reviewers of the vaudeville show called Rinty "the Barrymore of dogdom" and said that what made the act exceptional was that it avoided the broad strokes of slapstick. Several other dog acts were on the vaudeville circuit at the time, but most of them consisted of the animal clowning around, teetering around on its hind legs, walking on a tightrope, or jumping through hoops wearing a funny hat. Instead, Rinty's vaudeville performance demonstrated his talent as an actor. It was another triumph. After a show in Kansas City, the Greyhound Bus Company, out of respect and admiration, provided a new deluxe coach bus for Lee and Rinty, to carry them privately and in the finest style to their next show in St. Louis.

They were earning $1,000 a week, a great deal of money, but it was hard work. In one typical month, Lee's schedule included Houston, Galveston, San Antonio, Austin, Waco, Dallas, Fort Worth, Wichita Falls, Abilene, and Amarillo. Before he'd begun the tour, Lee's mother had asked him if she could tag along. Lee apparently declined but reminded her in a telegram: SORRY I COULD NOT LET YOU COME. IMPORTANT WE ALL WORK TOGETHER WHILE BIG MONEY IS TO BE MADE.

After nine months on the road, Lee and Rinty returned to California, filmed another Mascot serial called *The Lightning Warrior,* and then embarked on a vaudeville tour in March 1931. This tour was also a hit, with ads trumpeting "its feature attraction, Rin

Tin Tin, unquestionably the best known dog in the world and the most remarkable canine actor that has ever been brought to the stage or screen!"

At the end of the tour, Lee took Rinty for a rest at his house in Malibu. One afternoon, a rogue wave hit the beach and surged over it, swinging through Lee's house like a wrecking ball. The house was a total loss. A story in the *Los Angeles Times* was head-lined "Storm Wrecks Actor's Beach House." The caption under the photograph of Lee and Rinty standing beside rubble read, "Duncan and Rin Tin Tin, noted motion-picture dog which he owns, looking over the smashed abode. Both were in the house when it was crushed, but escaped injury." Considering how badly the house was dam-aged, it seems miraculous that they survived.

Lee's 1931 tax return shows a total in-come of $17,000, from Mascot Pictures and personal appearances. Item 15 lists the loss of the Malibu house and furniture, for which he had no insurance. Although the value of Lee's 1931 income would be close to $200,000 in today's dollars, the loss of the Malibu property and the mortgages on his two Beverly Hills houses meant he was squeezed. He and Rin Tin Tin had had a triumphant vaudeville tour, but things were tougher than they appeared.

The series of recent calamities — getting dumped by Warner Bros., being swindled, the collapse of his bank, the loss of his beach house — didn't lead Lee to think about what would be, for him, the greatest calamity of all: that someday Rin Tin Tin would die. According to Lee, Rin Tin Tin was still "bubbling over with life and vitality." His work schedule remained busy: he was beginning a new Mascot serial, *Pride of the Legion,* and three others were already lined up. The veterinarian who had just performed his annual exam proclaimed the dog to be in perfect health.

One newspaper report claimed that Rin Tin Tin blacked out occasionally on film sets, but I never found anything to corroborate that, and Lee's notes include no mention of anything being wrong with the dog, although he might have found it too upsetting to think about or too disturbing to admit. Indeed, he resisted imagining Rinty's death so completely that he ignored the plainest fact of their intertwined lives: the man will outlive the dog. In the case of a famous dog like Rin Tin Tin, it would have been useful to prepare a successor. Rin Tin Tin and Nanette had had at least forty-eight puppies, but Lee hadn't trained any of them for a career in the movies. He sold or gave away all but two youngsters. He believed his life began the day he found Rinty. It was impossible for him to imagine his life without him.

3.

He died on a warm summer day in 1932. A United Press bulletin broke into radio programs that afternoon with the announcement: "Rin Tin Tin, greatest of animal motion-picture actors, pursued a ghostly villain in a canine happy-hunting ground today." In his memoir, Lee's description of the event is simple. He had heard Rinty bark in a peculiar way, so he went to see what the matter was and found the dog lying on the ground; within a moment he was gone. The story was soon floated on the great raft of legend. It was rumored that Rin Tin Tin had died at night; that he had died on the set of *Pride of the Legion* during a rehearsal; that he had died while leaping into the arms of Jean Harlow, who lived near Lee on Club View Drive; that he had collapsed on Lee's front lawn and Harlow had raced over to comfort him, where she "cradled the great furry head in her lap, and there he died."

183

The news was met with widespread communal grief. The day after his death, an hour-long tribute to Rinty was broadcast on radio networks across the country. "Last night a whole radio network and thousands of radio fans paid homage to a great dog," one radio announcer explained, "a gentleman, a scholar, a hero, a cinema star — in fact, a dog which was virtually everything we could wish to be."

Theaters posted death notices in their windows, as if they had lost a member of the family. Every newspaper ran an obituary and, in many cases, a long feature detailing the dog's career, as if his life had defined a time period that was now at an end. The *Chicago Tribune* summed up its story by saying that with Rin Tin Tin's death "the greatest of all dog actors became a memory and a tradition."

Fox Movietone's newsreel featured a long piece about the dog's death, titled "Rin Tin Tin Plays His Final Role," which was the main newsreel feature, following a short clip of Herbert Hoover droning on woodenly about his reelection campaign. The footage was taken from one of Rinty's last public appearances, at an orphanage in Buffalo, New York. The orphans are smudge-faced, pale, and dressed in tattered hand-medowns, but they light up with excitement when they see the dog. Lee tells them he will have Rin Tin Tin do some of his tricks, and he needs a volunteer. The kids shriek and bounce as Lee selects one of them, a small boy with a jagged row of dark bangs. Lee, pointing at the boy, tells Rinty to "get the bad guy." Rinty pretends to attack him, and the boy's face flashes back and forth from terror to exhilaration to bashfulness. After a moment, Lee says, "Okay, Rinty, kiss and make up." The dog stands up on his hind legs and licks the boy's face, as the kids in the audience holler in delight. Lee, watching the dog, is beaming, radiant.

Then Lee calls the dog to come to him. Rinty pauses for a split second and then springs into his arms. Dark-coated, bright-eyed, he is just as slim and strong-looking as he ever was, just as light on his feet and explosive in his leaps, and in Lee's embrace, he looks surprisingly small, not at all like a grown dog. Holding him, Lee wears a look of joy so tender and uncomplicated that, for an instant, he is transformed again into a hopeful, lonely boy. The camera lingers for a moment, and then the Fox Movietone announcer says, "Rin Tin Tin: only a dog. But millions who he delighted will mourn his passing."

It is hard to imagine this kind of reaction today to the death of any actor, let alone an animal actor. Did movies simply mean more in 1932? Or was this response particular to Rin Tin Tin? And was this outpouring of grief really for Rin Tin Tin, one individual dog, or was it more for what was being lost with Rin Tin Tin — the innocent belief in a hero, the hope that one silent, strong, and loyal being might have the capacity to be great?

The condolences came from all over the world. "Allow me to say I love you," one man wrote to Lee, "because I loved, and still shall love, your Dog . . . by you and by his many friends like myself, in the world, he shall still live. Rin Tin Tin can never die. . . . He was one of God's spiritual ideas, especially endowed." Another wrote, "Be assured that all who knew Rinty, and there were millions, share in your sorrow for his loss." Another: "I have had the gratification of shaking hands with more than one President of the United States, but all of this I would gladly forgo if I could have said that I had stroked the head of Rin Tin Tin."

Circus sideshow operators begged Lee for

186

the right to display Rin Tin Tin's body, the way they had once competed to display the body of Jesse James. That may sound macabre and degrading, but Hollywood in 1932 wasn't far removed from the world of carnivals and freak shows; in fact, among the other *Variety* obituaries from the month Rin Tin Tin died were notices for Charles Gantz ("a midget, survived by three brothers and two sisters, all normal size"); a gymnast named Irene Berger, who had died in a "thrill plunge"; and medicine show operator Mozell Lamb, a murder victim ("I love him and he was going to leave me, so I shot him," Mrs. Lamb told police).

Cities and towns campaigned to be chosen as Rin Tin Tin's final resting place, knowing that tourism was sure to follow. Lee declined all of these offers. He buried Rinty with the squeaky doll the dog had adored in a bronze casket in the backyard of his house on Club View Drive, with only a handmade wooden cross marking the grave.

In his memoir, Lee talked about the world's response to losing Rin Tin Tin and the way the dog was memorialized in the media. The one thing he didn't do was express what this loss felt like to him. He had begun writing his memoir in 1933, partly for his own sake but also with the expectation that it would be published or used as the basis of a biography. In the section he devoted to Rinty's death, he did something he did nowhere else in tire manuscript: he put a placeholder in — a parenthetical, underlined note saying "Mr. Duncan will give full details of his death" — as if he just couldn't bring himself to talk about it yet.

In public, Lee made few statements about Rin Tin Tin's death, and gave only a few interviews about it. But some time later he published a poem called "Rin Tin Tin, Dedicated by his 'Love Master,' Lieutenant Lee Duncan." In simple phrases, the poem described his life with the dog, ending with these lines:

A real selfish love like yours old pal
Is something I shall never know again
And I must always be a better man
Because you loved me greatly, Rin Tin
   Tin.

4.

If you take the Paris métro to the Mairie de Clichy station and walk north along the Rue Martre, past the long blocks of shabby tire shops and falafel stands, you will eventually come to a small bridge that arches over the Seine. The bank on the far side is steep, slick with moss, and sags toward the river like an old man's shoulders, as if it were just too weary to hold itself up anymore. Le Cimetière des Chiens — the Cemetery of Dogs — is a few steps west of the bridge, sagging on that saggy bank, under a heavy canopy of huge, drooping trees.

I had come to Le Cimetière des Chiens to find Rin Tin Tin on a hot day in August. It was the kind of day when Paris feels becalmed, stewing in the thick air, and the few people outside at midday move at a sleepwalker's pace down the quiet streets. Just a few cars puttered by in the dull sunlight as I walked alone down Rue Martre, and I was alone in the cemetery as I roamed among the tombstones of Titi and Hippy and Poucy and Rhum, looking for the grave of Rin Tin Tin.

When Lee buried Rinty, he probably thought he would spend his life in his Beverly Hills house, and that he would therefore always be near Rinty's grave. But in 1933, just months after the dog's death, Lee's money ran out and the mortgage on the house slid out of reach. When the bank foreclosed he moved to the small house in North Hollywood that he had originally bought for his sister, Marjorie.

There is no mention anywhere of when Lee moved Rinty's casket, but this would have been the logical time to do so, while he still had access to the backyard in Beverly Hills. He could have moved the casket to Marjorie's backyard, but Lee's living there might have felt temporary and he certainly would have wanted to bury Rin Tin Tin somewhere he could always visit. He could have buried him in a pet cemetery. There were a number of them in the United States — the oldest one in the country, Hartsdale Pet Cemetery, in New York, had opened in 1896, and the oldest in California, Cal Pet, in 1918. It is surprising that Lee wouldn't have preferred being closer to the grave and puzzling that he would have gone to the trouble and expense of moving the body to France when he could have buried him nearby more easily. Of course, Rin Tin Tin had been born in France, so burying him there did have a satisfying symmetry. Maybe a fan paid for the expenses, or a friend. Le Cimetière des Chiens has no record of when Rin Tin Tin arrived and was reburied there, and will say only that "someone" paid the annual fee for the grave, at least for a while.

Lee's memoir, unfortunately, doesn't cover this period of time. In fact, the memoir ends abruptly, at the end of page 124, in midsentence, in the middle of one of the condolence letters from which Lee was quoting. The letter is from a fan who sounds fumbling, apologetic, mournful. It begins, "Rin Tin Tin was the unusual, exceptional, even marvelous. . . . Pardon my saying for a livelihood I go from door to door selling articles for household use, and in many many places they own German Police Dogs, some beautiful, some very vicious, but each place I am protected, and I often think this is" — and then there is no more. That is the last page. The rest of Lee's notes were lost, and there is no other trail leading from Beverly Hills to Rinty's Parisian grave.

Le Cimetière des Chiens was founded in 1899 by a group of intellectual pet lovers that included Emile Zola, Marguerite Durand, and Camille Saint-Saëns, after Paris passed a law prohibiting animal graves within one hundred yards of human habitation. Except for the companion dogs of royalty, pets were a relatively new notion at that time. Dogs, the very first domesticated animals, had lived with people for thousands of years, but until the nineteenth century, they usually had jobs — hunting or herding or guarding. Keeping an animal in the house is so familiar now that it's easy to forget how fundamentally odd it is, and what a leap it must have been to share living quarters with a nonhuman life form just to have its company. Dogs worked hard for the privilege, developing as a species the capacity to empathize, or appear to empathize, with human beings better than any other animal; it's this talent, rather than their intelligence, that accounts for their being the preeminent animals in our lives.

Once dogs became valued as companions, they were elevated to a quasi-human status and were often treated like small, mute people. In the 1800s, a wave of bestselling dog autobiographies were published — life stories purported to be written by the dogs themselves — including *Memoirs of Bob, The Spotted Terrier: Supposed to Be Written by Himself* and *The Life of Carlo the Famous Dog of Drury Lane Theatre,* which began, "My mother was so gentle, she would not have hurt a worm . . . my father I never saw as he lived in a distant part of town and visited my mother but seldom." A proper Parisian dog of that era had a wardrobe of shirts, gowns, bathing suits, and underwear, as well as personalized calling cards and stationery, and of course wedding clothes, since dog weddings were common.

At the time, it was believed that dogs had deeper feelings and a greater capacity for expressing them than people did, and that their faithfulness was unimpeachable. This was the period when fascination with the incredible journey first began — that is, the story of a dog separated from its owners by accident that somehow overcomes circumstance to make its way home. This canine Odyssey has been repeated countless times. The stories might or might not have been true, but they were supported by the belief that a dog really could be that loyal. Even Victor Hugo had an incredible-journey story, claiming that his poodle, which he accidentally left behind on a trip to Moscow, made its way home, on its own, to Paris.

Dogs, it was believed, remained loyal even after we were gone. In the nineteenth-century imagination, dogs were the most indefatigable mourners. They were said to visit their masters' graves on their own, lying on the freshly turned dirt for days, inconsolable. If their grief was too much to bear, dogs sometimes committed suicide; newspapers of the period carried frequent reports of these canine deaths. One of the great attractions of having a pet, then, was believing it would miss us and mourn us and always remember us, even if friends and family let us down. The grieving dog was such a fixture in the Victorian mind that it crowded out an unalterable fact: a dog's life is a short one, so most of the time it is we who are mourning them.

Le Cimetière des Chiens is an elegant space, set off from the street by a baroque stone entryway and a curlicued iron gate; it is very Parisian, shady and somber, filled with spindly rose bushes and gnarled topiary. Inside, near the guardhouse, gravel paths radiate outward from an enormous stone sculpture of a Saint Bernard named Barry. More than three thousand animals are buried in the cemetery — mostly dogs and cats but also birds, a horse, several monkeys, and at least one pig.

I read Barry's gravestone ("He Saved Forty Lives") and then started down one of the gravel paths. A few wild-looking cats were loafing on a tombstone, watching me with narrowed eyes and then vanishing as soon as I got close, as if they were some sort of optical illusion. The graves were arranged in haphazard rows, a jumble of shapes and sizes, like a mouthful of very bad teeth: big marble mausoleums beside tiny tombstones beside small granite markers that bore laminated photographs of the deceased. I passed the graves of Funny and Dou Dou and Dick and Ching Ling Foo ("My Best and Most Devoted Friend. He Loved Only Me"); Waddle and Cowboy and Rita and Tushy; Riki-Tiki and Mizouky and Chiquito and Meryl. The headstone for Harry, a stout black Labrador, had a glass globe on top that was filled with three half-gnawed tennis balls. A basset hound named Piggy was memorialized with a photograph of him in better days chewing on a lumpy knucklebone. The oldest graves — for Belgrano, who left this world in 1906, and Mireille, gone in 1903 — were as smooth as pats of butter, the carvings of their names almost melted away.

The cemetery guard was a short man with a rosy face and the body of a bowler, a tight fit in his little guardhouse near the entrance. He had given me a map to the cemetery, and I noticed Rin Tin Tin's grave marked on it along with some other famous animals, but as soon as I saw the name, I folded up the map and stuck it in my backpack. I wanted to find the grave on my own.

While I walked along, I felt suddenly and unaccountably reluctant to find it at all. Maybe I was a little superstitious about something that seemed so significant to me, and I was braced for the letdown that I know occurs when an event you have anticipated for a long time finally takes place. Under the full, fat branches of the chestnut trees, the air in the cemetery was cool and soothing. It struck me that Le Cimetière des Chiens would be a very pleasant place for a picnic if you didn't mind being surrounded by a few thousand dead dogs.

I sat down on a double gravestone for poodles named Oona and Uttawah to bide my time. My mind wandered. Were Oona and Uttawah just friends or were they mates? Could they have been siblings? Why were they buried together? I looked around, leaning a bit heavily on Oona. Someone had left a plastic figurine of Doc, the most senior of the Seven Dwarfs, across from Oona and Uttawah, on Toby the schnauzer's grave. Insects clicked and buzzed in the grass. One of the stray cats reappeared and rubbed its back on the headstone of Iris the collie, using raised letters that said "My Love Is Stronger Than Death" to scratch his itch. Bijoux the spaniel was lucky; I could see he had recently received fresh flowers. Someone had left plastic flowers for Twigsy and also a rubber duckie that looked like a ghost duck, bleached of color by the sun and rain. I wished I had a brought a picnic with me. I decided to walk around a little more. Look at all these graves. A fat husky named Ferris. Next to him, Tessa. Then another Tessa. Many, many Ulysses. Who names a dog Ulysses? So French. I bet there aren't two dogs in the United States named Ulysses.

And then there it was, just across from me: a small rectangle of dark marble, stacked on a slightly larger rectangle, with a tarnished bronze marker that said:

RIN TIN TIN
LA GRANDE VEDETTE DU
CINEMA

Rin Tin Tin, the great film star. On top of the marble was a broken metal fitting that might have once held a statue or urn. Someone had placed purple and white lilacs, fake but nice-looking, in a planter beside the gravestone. Next to that, a red-and-white pinwheel, the kind a child might carry, spun in the breeze, whirring into pink. The ground on one side of the gravestone, damp and velvety with bright green moss, had heaved up and shifted, tilting the grave as if it were being tossed on a wave in the sea.

It was a hunk of stone and a moldering bit of ground, and of course nothing, nothing at all, of the idea of what he had been.

For all I knew Rin Tin Tin wasn't even buried here, which almost stands to reason, since no one had convincingly explained how he might have gotten here from Beverly Hills. But it was enough to know that this was a marker for him, a sign that he had lived. If only feelings and ideas and stories and history really could be contained in a block of marble — if only there could be a gathering up of permanence — how reassuring it would be, how comforting to think that something you loved could be held in place, moored and everlasting, rather than bobbing along on the slippery sea of reminiscence, where it could always drift out of reach.

The modesty of the grave made me sad, but I knew Lee believed that there would always be a Rin Tin Tin, so this was only a click in a turning wheel. The first Rin Tin Tin died but he still lived — and lives still — an idea more than an entity, always different but essentially the same. Remembering was what made him permanent. I brushed away the leaves that had fallen on the gravestone, straightened the plastic lilacs. I shoved the bottom rectangle of marble with my foot to see if I could kick it back into alignment with the other piece. It moved not a bit. The heave must have occurred years ago, and now, as crooked as it was, the stone was firmly settled into place and would stay that way.

The guard was playing solitaire in his booth, twiddling his moustache as he stared at his cards, and it took him a moment to notice me standing at the door. I asked him if he could tell me anything about Rin Tin Tin's grave. My bad French made him grin. He said that many, many people have come looking for it. "A few years ago, an American came," he said. "He wanted to make a big monument for him, a big statue instead of his small grave, but . . ." He shrugged. "No news!" he said, and shrugged again. "No news!"

I asked him who had left the flowers and the pinwheel.

He sighed. "An old lady. She used to come regularly and put the flowers on his grave. At first she put fresh flowers, and then she put plastic flowers." He started to shuffle his cards again and then stopped, tapping the deck on his desk, the sharp knocking sounding like a woodpecker drilling into a tree. I thanked him and started to leave, and as he cut the deck he called to me. "I haven't seen that old lady in some time. No. I think perhaps she is dead. That's what I think."

5.

And then there was Junior. Soon after Rin Tin Tin died, Mascot Pictures announced that Rin Tin Tin Jr., the mature and impeccably trained three-year-old son of Rin Tin Tin, would be stepping in as the successor to his late father. None of these facts were true. When Rinty died, Junior was only eleven months old and mostly untrained, a big clumsy puppy with a black-and-tan coat and a long black tail. Privately, the studio knew the dog wasn't ready. The filming of *Pride of the Legion* was postponed for a year so that Lee could train Junior and introduce him to the public over the course of a national publicity tour. The highlight was a visit to the 1933 Chicago World's Fair, where Junior was featured at the Hollywood concession and rode in a pony-drawn Tom Thumb hansom cab.

Lee never liked the dog. For one thing, he thought he was too big. Rinty never weighed more than eighty-five pounds, but Junior was already close to a hundred and he wasn't yet full-grown. His face was pretty but blank, a bit needle-nosed and pinched. He wasn't smart. His legs were too long. Most of all, he wasn't his father.

Nevertheless, Lee made a go of it; he

didn't have much choice. He needed to make a living, and working with a dog was the only job, except for selling guns, that he had ever had. Even though his training was minimal, Junior did well enough on the tour, making the standard visits to hospitals and orphanages, receiving keys to cities, and meeting reporters at daily papers, although what brought him the most coverage was the fact that on his trip with Lee from Burbank to Chicago he became the first dog to ever fly on a commercial plane. Upon their arrival, according to the studio press release, they disembarked and "were met by a special automobile and escorted to the Palmer House, where they had their own suite." Everywhere they went, in fact, Lee and Junior were treated as celebrities, which must have been at odds with Lee's actual circumstances of being broke, at loose ends, and mourning old Rin. And yet the sleight of hand — presenting Junior as a finished product — seemed to work. Junior was described in the press as "the famous motion picture dog," as if Rinty had not departed this world but simply changed bodies. It must have left Lee with mixed feelings, but Junior was proof that the legacy was established: there would always be a Rin Tin Tin.

Mascot Pictures was quietly hedging its bets. In its 1934 contract with Lee, it specified that the term "artist" referred to Lee and "the son of that certain famous dog named Rin Tin Tin and which is known as Rin Tin Tin Jr.," but added that the studio had the right to use the name Rin Tin Tin Jr. for any other dogs needed to play the movie roles, a provision that had never been in any contract for old Rin. A subsequent contract was even more equivocal. "You warrant that Rin Tin Tin Jr. is an experienced dog accustomed to working in motion pictures . . . and that he will readily respond to instructions given by you . . . You further warrant that Rin Tin Tin Jr. is sufficiently trained and can comply with the requirements of his role. We shall have the right to 'double' or 'dub' the acts, poses, plays, and appearances of the dog and as well, the barks, grunts, groans, and all other sound effects to be produced by the dog to such extent as we may desire."

Pride of the Legion was the first Mascot film that supposedly starred Junior, but the dog in the movie was more likely a stand-in, because it has a much lighter coat and broader face than Junior. Critics noted that the movie, which was released in 1934, had a tired plot, but praised Junior (or whichever dog it really was), saying he was "not the least of the actors by any means." Reviews of Junior's subsequent movies varied. In *Tough Guy,* which starred a young, chunky Jackie Cooper, the *New York Times* reviewer wrote that Junior appeared to be "well fitted to pad along the first-run trail in the footprints of his illustrious ancestor." By contrast, a *Variety* review of *Caryl of the Mountains,* released in 1936, pointed out that the film starred two Hollywood legacies — Francis X. Bushman Jr., whose father had appeared with the first Rin Tin Tin, and Junior — and added that neither Bushman nor Junior had his father's talent. Even the best reviews of Junior's films were brief and flat compared to the kind of reviews the first Rin Tin Tin had always received. Certainly, the world in 1934 was different than it had been in 1924. Maybe everything was a little flat by then.

In 1934 Lee and Junior were earning $330 a week from Mascot, one third what they had been paid a few years earlier working at Warner Bros. To make more money, Lee started to focus on selling puppies; he also put his champion saddle horse up for stud.

He placed a full-page ad that featured pictures of Junior and the horse, Deputy-Master, with the simple headline "A Few Colts and Pups for Sale" in a local magazine. He listed his address as Club View Drive in Beverly Hills, although it is almost certain that he had moved out by then.

In 1936, burglars broke into Marjorie's house in North Hollywood, where Lee was living, and stole several hundred dollars' worth of jewelry and clothing. The *New York Times,* which had always been reverential when it came to the first Rin Tin Tin, used the robbery to make fun of Junior. In a story headlined "Home Robbed, Film Dog Sleeps," the reporter noted tartly that Junior managed to sleep through this real home invasion, even though in his last film he had been shown capturing "a whole robber band" single-handedly.

The story was just a few paragraphs long and tucked away on an inside page, but it spoke volumes. In the 1920s, there was no disparity between Rin Tin Tin's role as a hero in the movies and the public belief that he truly was a hero. The studio publicity that exaggerated his feats and referred to him as a Red Cross dog was partly responsible for this perception, but it was more than that. When old Rin was in his prime, film was still so novel, so amazing, that it had a sort of transformative quality — what a film presented to the audience seemed to be its own reality, without any ironic shade dropped over it.

In the 1920s, the invincibility that Rinty embodied was still possible to imagine, something you could aspire to, even if it remained out of reach. But by 1936, very little seemed invincible. Europe was churning as Spain descended into civil war, Italy invaded Ethiopia, and Germany reoccupied the Rhineland. The Depression was entering its eighth harsh year. The "black blizzards" of dust in the Great Plains destroyed crops for the third season in a row. Hopelessness snapped people in half. The hairline crack between appearance and possibility spread wide and became a chasm of defeat and cynicism. A movie was no longer something more fabulous than anything on earth; it was just a muffling, air-conditioned, momentary escape, and when the lights came back on, there was the hard world again — a place where nothing was more than it seemed, some things were less than they were supposed to be, and hero dogs slept through robberies.

6.

When Rin Tin Tin first became famous, most dogs in the world would not sit down when asked. Dogs performed duties: they herded sheep, they barked at strangers, they did what dogs do naturally, and people learned to interpret and make use of how they behaved. The idea of a dog's being obedient for the sake of good manners was unheard of. When dogs lived outside, as they usually did on farms and ranches, the etiquette required of them was minimal. But by the 1930s, Americans were leaving farms and moving into urban and suburban areas, bringing dogs along as pets and sharing living quarters with them. At the time, the principles of behavior were still mostly a mystery — Ivan Pavlov's explication of conditional reflexes, on which much training is based, wasn't even published in an English translation until 1927. If dogs needed to be taught how to behave, people had to be trained to train their dogs. The idea that an ordinary person — not a dog professional — could train his own pet was a new idea, which is partly why Rin Tin Tin's performances in movies and onstage were looked upon as extraordinary.

Dog training got its start in Europe, and

by the late 1920s, in England, obedience competition was a growing sport. Helene Whitehouse Walker had read in an English dog magazine about these competitions and was intrigued. Walker was the tall, square-jawed, high-waisted American-born daughter of titled English nobility; she was also an enterprising and curious woman who chafed at the endless round of teas and luncheons that was the calling of her class and position. Her wedding to Charles Cobb Walker, a patrician Bostonian with a list of club memberships as long as his arm, had been a celebrated social event, but the marriage had foundered over what she called "differences," and extracting herself from it had cost her the equivalent of more than $300,000. By 1929, she was looking for distraction.

After her divorce, Walker had left Boston with her dogs and her two-year-old son and moved to Westchester County, New York, where she opened a poodle kennel she called Carillon. She was devoted to the breed, and was also eager to rebut the friends who thought poodles were sissies. At the time, purebred dogs were admired for their style but many people assumed that their breeding made them neurotic, genetically compromised, and stupid. Poodles, with their clownish mops of curly hair, were the easiest targets for ridicule, even though they were smart and sturdy dogs that had actually been bred as hunters.

Walker went to England and stayed for more than a month to watch the obedience competitions and also to learn how to train her own dogs. It was an adventurous choice for the time: most dogs that required training, such as hunting or patrol dogs, were sent to professional handlers for weeks or months of schooling and then sent back to their owners with a set of instructions and a bill. Owners simply didn't train their own dogs.

Inspired by what she called the "thrilling sport" of obedience competition, Walker returned to the United States and urged the American Kennel Club to add obedience trials to its dog shows. The suggestion was politely declined. Walker approached smaller dog clubs, asking them to sponsor obedience competitions, but they declined as well. She decided to take matters into her own hands: in 1933, with 150 spectators and eight competitors — two Labradors, three poodles, two springer spaniels, and a German shepherd — she held the first obedience trial in the United States at her father's estate in Mount Kisco, New York.

She was delighted by how the event turned out, and she was stubborn. In spite of her initial rejection by the AKC, she went back to the board of directors; in the meantime she hosted more obedience trials at her father's estate. She also offered small training classes at her home and began promoting her blunt and commanding slogan, "Train Your Dog," everywhere she could. She thought that dog training would have a salutary effect on the world of purebred dogs because it would provide "an incentive to all breeders to breed for brains and for the original purpose of each breed, as well as for show points."

If obedience trials were added to the bill at dog shows, Walker reasoned, it might draw new audiences, especially "people who love dogs but have no understanding of the fine points of conformation." She also believed that obedience had a value in itself — or, as she explained in an interview, she believed a well-trained dog was a benefit to everyone because it demonstrated how well dogs fit "our modern scheme of living." Like Lee, who avoided having Rin Tin Tin do silly routines in his stage show and believed in training dogs to make them better companions rather than amusements, Walker felt it was important "to demonstrate the usefulness of the purebred dog as the companion and guardian of man, and not the ability of the dog to acquire facility in the performance of mere tricks."

Walker's notions disturbed many members of the purebred-dog community. In a *New Yorker* piece called "A Trend in Dogs," a Scottie breeder at the Westminster Kennel Club show is quoted saying, "The mere thought of obedience trials becoming fashionable, with nothing but a tractable nature counting in a dog's favor and with nobody giving a damn about body points, positively makes me ill." The Scottie breeder adds that she considers these so-called obedience people a plague. "The country is full of them, darling," she explains. "Westchester alone is teeming with people who don't give a whoop about lines and proportions any more. All they care about is" — she sniffs — "intelligence." But outside the rarefied world of dog-show people, Walker's timing happened to be perfect. The country was changing, and now that hundreds of thousands of dogs were living in suburban houses and city apartments, people wanted to learn how to manage their pets.

In 1932, shortly before she held her first obedience trial, Walker advertised for a new manager to run her kennel. She ended up hiring a young woman named Blanche Saunders, who was a farmhand at Green Chimneys, a property that was owned by circus people who practiced trick riding and elephant training on the grounds. Saunders had worked on farms since graduating college with a degree in animal husbandry, but she had begun to be bored with farm animals and decided to answer Walker's ad.

Saunders was angular and blond, with a wide forehead, a decisive-looking jaw, and a pursed mouth. The daughter of a Baptist minister, she was the only girl among six siblings and very comfortable on large machinery. She had a penchant for clunky shoes and oxford cloth shirts and refused to admit that she was a very good cook because she thought it made her sound too girlish. In her introduction to Saunders' 1974 memoir, *The Story of Dog Obedience,* Walker recalled coming to Green Chimneys along with her poodle, Tango of Piperscroft, to interview Saunders for the job. "She came running to meet me, all energy and enthusiasm," Walker wrote. "She was in blue jeans with a red bandana around her head and had just finished a day's work driving a tractor on the farm."

Saunders and Walker came from very different worlds but they found immediate kinship, and Saunders left Green Chimneys for Carillon. Her job there was to manage the daily workings of the kennel, but she became interested in the obedience training Walker was so enthusiastic about, so she asked if she could try her hand with one of the poodles, Carillon Epreuve, who was known around the house as Glee. Right away, Saunders saw that she had a knack for dog training; soon it became a calling, and Walker found the companion who was as devoted to the idea of obedience work as she was.

In 1935, Walker submitted yet another proposal to the AKC concerning obedience trials. After three months of deliberations, the board of directors at last agreed to include obedience at its shows. Instead of bringing the two women on to run it, the AKC took charge of the new obedience program. Walker and Saunders were disappointed, but they now had time to attend to another mission: taking the idea of training to the general public, not just to the dog-show world. As Saunders later wrote, "Mrs. Walker and I were at last free to give full effort to the arousing of public interest in training dogs." According to Saunders, as soon as they began urging people to train their dogs, "questions and pleas for guidance" had poured into Carillon Kennel from all over the country. They then decided to take their passion about training dogs on the road.

First, they converted Walker's Buick sedan to suit their unusual needs. They pulled out the backseat and replaced it with a wooden platform for the three poodles — Glee, Joyeaux, and Bon Coeur — who were coming along with them to perform in the training demonstrations. Then Walker bought a twenty-one-foot-long house trailer, which would serve as "the home of the human uprights," as Saunders put it, that they would pull behind the car. They packed the trailer with maps, food for the dogs and themselves, and a list of the dog shows scheduled for the next several months.

They left New York in the fall of 1937, around the time Lee and Junior were working on the last of their serials for Mascot films. Walker and Saunders drove until Harrisburg, Pennsylvania, which was holding a large all-breed dog show; Walker persuaded the show's organizers to let them give a demonstration during a break in the proceedings. They had divided their responsibilities: Saunders put the poodles through their obedience routine while Walker narrated and handed out *Train Your Dog* pamphlets to the spectators. From the very start, they drew huge crowds. In her memoir Saunders recalled that at most of their stops, "the ringside was crowded because everyone was anxious to see the 'two crazy women from New York with their three trick Poodles.' "

They were a spectacle for many reasons. Poodles were rare at the time — in 1930, the AKC listed only thirty-four poodles in its registry; trained poodles were a curiosity twice over. In addition, house trailers were rare. To encounter two women traveling together, unaccompanied by men, was also unusual; to find these women in a house trailer with trained poodles was downright extraordinary. ("The courtly sheriff in Louisiana . . . looked at us in amazement when he heard that we had no men folk with us," Saunders wrote.) Saunders carried a gun in case anyone found their unusualness too intriguing. "When we parked for the night," she wrote, "the poodles became experts at finding hobos asleep under a bush and would chase them with fierce determination."

They traveled the way Lee had done so many times with Rin Tin Tin, stopping in all the small towns and midsized cities. They performed in Cincinnati, Louisville (where they needed a mule team to pull the trailer out of a sinkhole), Dallas, Fort Worth, Galveston, Hollywood, and even Juárez, Mexico. They passed homeless families camping on the side of the road — not a rare sight in 1937 — and lines at soup kitchens in most of the towns.

Although they suffered through sand squalls and a plague of stinging red ants, and had to minister to the dogs when they were injured by cactus spurs, Walker and Saunders also got the notice they were looking for, and the idea of dog obedience began to gain acceptance. Magazines, including *Reader's Digest, Town & Country,* and *Pageant,* began reporting on their travels. Some magazines took what Saunders called "a different slant." *Parents Magazine,* for instance, ran an article about them called "We Sent Our Child to a Dog School."

They were gone for three months and headed home at last in November 1937. By the time they got back to New York they had traveled ten thousand miles. They had performed before thousands of people and brought their passion for dog obedience to the public for the very first time. Within a few months of their trip, the number of obedience trials at American dog shows doubled and forty-two new obedience-training clubs had sprung up around the country. One unplanned result of their celebrity was that the number of poodles in the country grew even faster than the craze for obedience. The breed rose from a position of near-obscurity to one of the most popular in the country, exploding just the way German shepherds had a decade before.

Walker and Saunders' friendship must have been extraordinary. I have seen a picture of the trailer they used on the trek, hitched to the rear of the white, bulbous Buick (the caption reads "21-foot House Trailer in which the Writer, With Mrs. Walker and Three Poodles, traveled Coast to Coast on Behalf of Obedience"). What I wish I had is a picture of them together. Their relationship had the contours of a romance, or certainly an intense closeness, not just because they shared this interest and spent so much time in each other's company but because they had set out to achieve something difficult and managed to do it together — and the satisfaction of that would have been impossible for anyone else to understand.

Walker remained active in the obedience world and in poodle clubs for the rest of her life, but in 1943, she decided to close her kennel and gave Saunders the rights to the Carillon name and a few of her best dogs. Saunders was no longer her kennel manager at that time — she had left in 1941 to study with the German dog trainer Josef Weber, who along with several other prominent trainers had immigrated to the United States after World War I. After Carillon closed and Saunders moved away from Brewster, I do not know if the two women ever spent time together again.

7.

During this period, Lee was in limbo. He was growing tired of Hollywood and felt uninspired by Junior. He felt depleted if he wasn't excited about a dog. At least his personal life was advancing: after a seven-year engagement, he and Eva Linden were getting married. Her parents had long disapproved of the match — Lee was eighteen years older than Eva — but in 1936, they finally gave in.

The wedding was held in Yosemite National Park. It was an unconventional place for a wedding. The choice reflected Lee's tastes much more than those of Eva, who was a city girl with a taste for art and music. So did the wedding's canine theme. "The bridal supper table will be very effective with its centerpiece representing a miniature log house," reported the *San Fernando Valley Times.* "Standing at a window [of the log house] looking out at his master will be a silver likeness of the departed Rin Tin Tin, the world-famous movie dog, which was made in France. Other silver dogs and horses will stress the appointments, to emphasize the great love for animals which is so dear to the heart of the bridegroom."

When they returned to Los Angeles after their honeymoon — which was also in Yosemite — Lee told Eva that he wanted to move. He wasn't thinking about finding a different house in Los Angeles; he wanted to move to Riverside, a town on the banks of the Santa Ana River, a long sixty-mile ride from Los Angeles on a washboard road that wound around sage scrub and chaparral and rocky breaks. Riverside was California's orange capitol. In 1870, a Riverside resident had planted three Brazilian navel orange seedlings in the front yard of her house. One of the trees was trampled to death by a cow and another died of unknown causes, but the third tree survived and flourished, and in time it became the parent tree of the entire California navel orange industry. Within a decade, the orange industry was thriving and Riverside was said to be the richest city per capita in the United States. Some twenty thousand acres of citrus were cultivated within the city limits, and Riverside's oranges were shipped all over the country under dozens of different labels, such as Desert Dream Oranges, Riverside's Best, Riverside Gold, Sunny Mountain, and Cal-Crest.

Lee had visited Riverside in 1928, when Rin Tin Tin was filming *The Race for Life* at the local fairgrounds, and he liked the look of it. Although he was not thinking about leaving Beverly Hills at that time, he took an interest in a forty-acre spread on low, sloping land near the river, but the place wasn't for sale. In 1937, though, when Lee was eager to move out of the city, the ranch came on the market at an attractive price — land in Riverside was going for 25 cents an acre — and he was able to put together enough money to buy it. Later that year, he and Eva, who had been living at his sister Marjorie's, moved to Riverside.

It was a modest place, and the house was a little ramshackle, considerably less grand than the name they gave it, El Rancho Rin Tin Tin. In spite of its wealth and a few fancy buildings like the Mission Inn and Benedict Castle, Riverside was still just a market town, without any of Los Angeles's sophistication or polish. Movie people came to the Mission Inn now and then for a weekend in the desert, but otherwise Hollywood could have been a million miles away. Perhaps that is why Riverside suited Lee at that moment, when he seemed like he had had his fill of Hollywood, and he adapted immediately. In Los Angeles, he'd always worn the most stylish clothes, sweater vests and pleated knickers and starched, snow-white shirts, but now he refused to wear anything other than Western shirts with pearl snaps and a straw cowboy hat with a four-inch brim. It was almost as if that other version of him had never existed. Once he was in Riverside, he picked up where he'd left off in 1916, when he was a ranch kid in a checkered shirt and torn dungarees. Even when he traveled to New York City to appear on *The Ed Sullivan Show* in the 1960s, he wore — to the everlasting embarrassment of his daughter — his cowboy clothes and his big straw hat.

It's hard to know for sure why Lee fixed on his childhood, which had never seemed very happy, as his point of reference. It's human nature to set a point in our minds when we feel triumphant and to measure everything that comes after it by how far we fall or rise from that point. For Lee, I would have expected that point would have been the glorious years when Rinty was making movies like *Clash of the Wolves,* when he and Lee were mobbed in theater lobbies, had endless money, and saw no end to their possibilities. Instead he retreated to his childhood — both actually, by moving to the ranchlands of California, just like the ranch where he lived as a boy, and also symbolically, by completely abandoning the trappings of his successful Hollywood years. He certainly wasn't trying to forget those early years with Rinty: as soon as he moved to Riverside, he converted a tack room in the barn into what he called the Memory Room, where he kept all the newspaper clippings and memorabilia from Rin Tin Tin's early years.

It seemed like a paradox, but the distinction eventually dawned on me: the Memory Room was set up to preserve the great successes of Rinty's life, while Lee's return to living on a ranch was a chance for him to reconnect with the great success of his *own* life. For Lee, that great success wasn't the moment when he and Rinty had so much acclaim. It was when his mother had come to retrieve him from Fred Finch, pulling him back from "the dark well or canyon" into which he felt himself falling. Elizabeth had rescued him from being forever orphaned and alone, just as he, in the dark well of war, in the rubble of that ruined kennel, had rescued the puppy Rin Tin Tin. "Then came the ride back to the country, the life I love best of all," he had written. And now came the ride back to Riverside, to the life he loved best of all.

8.

Eva was less enthusiastic about ranch life. By her daughter Carolyn's description, Eva thought she was marrying a rich older man with a famous movie dog, and the retreat from Hollywood was a stinging disappointment. "It wasn't at all what she thought she was getting," Carolyn said. "My mother didn't expect to be on a dirty, horrible ranch." Eva got a job with one of the orange shippers after they moved to Riverside, then gave birth to Carolyn, and tried to adjust to what her life had turned out to be.

Carolyn is now in her sixties, divorced, with three grown children. She lives alone in a small house in Michigan on a road as long and straight as a gunshot. Her neighborhood is neither city nor country: old farm gates open onto raw-looking subdivisions, gas stations border green cow pastures, and the few cars that whip by are a random mix of freshly washed sedans, muddy pickups, and panel trucks. Carolyn works part-time caring for an elderly neighbor, and helps take care of the toddler son of one of her daughters, who is a veterinarian.

My visit was on a chilly fall day, the weight of the sky pressing down on a landscape stripped bare and drained of color. Carolyn's kitchen was warm and cluttered, and we sat drinking tea near an oil painting of Rin Tin Tin that hung above a StairMaster. Next to the painting was a photograph of Lee and Eva before they moved to Riverside: Lee is dressed in white flannel trousers and a crewneck sweater, Eva is in a fox stole, and they look chic and sharp, almost glittering. On another kitchen wall was a picture of Carolyn at three or four years old — a round-faced girl with bright brown eyes and silky hair, sitting cross-legged on the ground, surrounded by German shepherds. I asked Carolyn what else her father had left her, and she waved her hand toward the pictures and then shrugged. "My father was a dreamer," she said, after a moment. "There was an empire, but the only thing that was real in the empire was my father, and when he was gone there was nothing."

When Eva met Lee, in the 1920s on a film location, her expectation that he would provide her with a comfortable life was reasonable, but things changed; by the late 1930s their money was always coming and going, and Lee's career was rocky. Eva's secretarial job paid their bills. Lee promised Eva that he would build her a nicer house as soon as he could, and he did apply for a permit to tear down the old house shortly after they arrived in Riverside. But twenty years passed before they did any construction, and then the first thing Lee built was a new dog kennel. Everything else might have changed, but his attention to the dogs was, as always, absolute. Eva, and then Carolyn, too, orbited around that but never came close. I asked Carolyn if she felt sibling rivalry toward the dogs. She laughed and said, "No, there was never any rivalry. The dogs always came first."

Eva was disappointed by the life she ended up with, while Lee exulted in what Carolyn calls "his dreamland." He was in his mid-forties when they moved to the ranch. He wasn't old, but by then he had been marked by the heavy tread of big reversals: he had made a fortune and lost it; he had found his life's great companion but outlived him; he had rocketed into celebrity and out of it. He seemed happiest settling in with his memories; he became, as Carolyn put it, "an old man with all this history and all these pictures." Lee would have several more spins through luck in his life, but the move to Riverside marked a turning point and he turned with it; it was as if he were now viewing his life in a different way, compressed and distanced, through a long lens aiming back toward the field in Flirey.

Junior made four more movies after the move to Riverside, but he didn't star in any of them, and the reviews mentioned him only in passing or not at all. It wasn't really Junior's fault. Movies in the late 1930s still featured dogs, but mostly as supporting players — family pets or cute companions to the leading man. The gravity and nobility of the German shepherd almost seemed like an anachronism. According to Lee's biographer James English, Lee had his own ideas about why Junior never enjoyed more celebrity — he thought the problem was that Junior wasn't known to have a family life. Anytime Rin Tin Tin appeared in a film with Nanette or had a story written about his life as a father and "husband," so to speak, his popularity soared. His movies often featured a scene, near the end of the film, with Nanette and their puppies. Junior was never publicly linked with a mate and none of his movies featured him as a father. Lee believed that "his popularity suffered accordingly."

But Junior was the dog he had to work with, and he tried. In postcards to Eva from movie locations, he wrote, "Junior has been doing some fine work in this picture" and "Rin worked fine all day, I am so proud of him, he improves every day." It's not clear if he believed this or perhaps was just trying to reassure Eva, who was home working at the orange plant and taking care of whatever new litter of puppies they had — and, later, Carolyn — while Lee was on the road.

Junior's last film was the 1939 pastiche *Hollywood Cavalcade,* produced by Darryl Zanuck and directed by Malcolm St. Clair, who had worked with old Rin more than a decade earlier on *Find Your Man* and *Lighthouse by the Sea,* among other films. It's a corny tale about old Hollywood, with walk-on parts by nearly everyone under contract to 20th Century Fox at the time, including the Keystone Kops, bathing beauties, and the sly, snappy Don Ameche. Junior was cast in the role of his father, Rin Tin Tin, and Lee appeared in a small part as an inexperienced, naïvely optimistic young man, going door-to-door in Holly-wood, begging to have someone put his dog in a movie.

9.

Here you can pick your narrative. Rin Tin Tin III, the next Rin Tin Tin in line, who was born in 1941, might have been one of Junior's puppies, a chosen one who stood out from among all the other puppies, the embodiment not of his father but of his il-lustrious grandfather, old Rin, and who, like his grandfather, was marked for destiny. This is the narrative many people, including Daphne Hereford, choose to believe. Or you can believe that Rin Tin Tin III was a beautiful puppy purchased by Lee, quietly and without mention, from another breeder, and that he was a puppy as clever and responsive as old Rin, with that same com-pact build, but with a lighter sable and cream coat that was easier to light for film.

The version of the Rin Tin Tin III story that Lee put forward is laid out in James English's book. English had first met Lee in 1947, when he wrote a story about Lee for *Boys' Life* magazine, called "Dogdom's Royal Family." They later worked together, using Lee's memoir for background, on English's book *The Rin Tin Tin Story,* which was published by Dodd, Mead in 1949. In the chapter called "Training a New Rinty," English described Rin Tin Tin III as "a clumsy-footed puppy who stood out in one of Junior's litters as had none before him. . . . It was like finding the original Rinty again. . . . Duncan knew he had found Rin Tin Tin III and once again he commenced thinking about the movies. This pup had it."

According to Carolyn, however, Rin Tin Tin III was unrelated to old Rin and Junior. She told me that Lee loved the idea of the continuing bloodline, but he was more interested in finding a perfect dog. Since he wasn't impressed with Junior, it makes sense that he might look outside his own kennel. He just preferred that it be kept secret. Lee believed he had a knack for knowing a good dog. He trusted his instinct more than he trusted DNA.

The question of pedigree is, in a sense, rhetorical. By definition, all German shepherds are related, all descended from von Stephanitz's dog Horand. Pedigrees do mean a lot to dog people, of course, but in the continuing story of Rin Tin Tin, pedigree doesn't seem as important as the idea of a character continuing, and lasting, across time. In that regard, the issue of bloodline seems like a will-o'-the-wisp, a distraction, a technical issue. The unbroken strand is not one of genetics but one of belief. Once upon a time, a hapless puppy was found, became a star, inspired people, stood for something, and endured. I am not concerned with chemistry or the specifics of genetics or with literal relations. The stuff that stays with us and manages to outlive its limits is what drew me to this story and what I wonder about — and what I hope might explain something about life to me.

Lee could have made the whole issue of lineage irrelevant if he had shifted the narrative and made himself the central character of the legend. He could have chosen for the narrative to revolve around the great dog trainer Lee Duncan and his kennel of great movie dogs, instead of revolving around the great dog Rin Tin Tin and his descendants. Other dog trainers in Hollywood were doing exactly that, marketing their talent rather than some unique quality of their animals. Carl Spitz, who trained the dog that played Toto in *The Wizard of Oz,* opened the Hollywood Dog Training School in 1927 to showcase his technique. It was Spitz whom directors hired for their movies; the dogs were almost incidental. The Weatherwax brothers, Rudd and Frank, were preparing their collie, Pal, to star in the upcoming Lassie movie, and to them, too, the dog was fungible — they were also preparing a kennel of other collies that would be interchangeable with Pal.

Some trainers, like Blanche Saunders, *were* celebrities; no one remembers the names of Saunders' dogs, but during her lifetime, she became synonymous with dog obedience. After working with Josef Weber, Saunders seemed to detour from the obedience world and opened a poodle grooming shop in a town house on the Upper East Side of Manhattan. Her client list included du Ponts and New York governor Tom Dewey. She also published a booklet called *The Poodle Chart* with schematics for trimming the breed's mass of hair. But dog obedience remained her passion. In 1944, she began offering ten-week dog-training sessions for the public, which she conducted at gyms and armories around the city. "Etiquette Course for Dogs Open — Mongrels May Attend," announced an article in the *New York Times.* The course completely sold out each time it was offered, but hundreds and sometimes thousands of people who hadn't been able to reserve a place in the class itself came just to watch, looking on in astonishment as Saunders demonstrated that it was possible, for instance, to quiet a barking dog by holding its mouth firmly shut. At least twenty thousand people graduated from Saunders' training courses. "Miss Saunders' talents are now so much in demand that getting your dog into one of her classes is roughly comparable to getting your son into Harvard," one magazine noted.

There seemed to be no end to the interest in Saunders' training techniques. She frequently appeared on radio and television. In 1948, she conducted an obedience demonstration with twenty-two of her students before an audience of seventy thousand who had gathered in Yankee Stadium to watch an Indians-Yankees game. "Even baseball players ran from their dressing rooms buttoning their uniforms as they came, in order to miss none of the fun," reported the *AKC Gazette.* A Cleveland sportswriter noted that "the dogs got more applause than DiMaggio." Saunders performed in Yankee Stadium seven more times. She also held a demonstration before an audience of thousands at the Rockefeller Center skating rink.

She wrote several books about obedience, including *The Complete Book of Dog Obedi-*

ence, the first guide that helped amateur owners train their pets, and *Training You to Train Your Dog,* which was made into a three-part documentary narrated by actor Helen Hayes and broadcaster Lowell Thomas. In 1947, to her great satisfaction, the Girl Scouts of America added dog training to its scouting merit badges.

One of the last photographs of Saunders before she died, at age fifty-four, of a heart attack, was taken right after one of her classes in 1964; it shows her demonstrating to a Girl Scout the proper method for putting a training collar on a dog. Saunders no longer looks like the tomboy who drove a tractor and sprinted beside her dogs wearing saddle shoes and men's khakis. Her hair is cropped, frosted, and teased into a bouffant, and she is wearing an A-line skirt and a white blouse with a round collar, the sort of prim outfit you might expect on a boarding school headmistress. At that point in her life she drove a black Lincoln Continental rather than a tractor and had taken on the style of a Manhattanite. She never married, and after leaving Helene Walker, she lived alone except for her dogs. In the foreword to *The Story of Dog Obedience,* Walker wrote, "Blanche Saunders died the way she lived — quietly, and just after doing what she loved best, teaching people how to train dogs."

If there was a moment when Lee might have put himself forward instead of his dogs, and made a name for himself as a training expert, this was it. After all, he had proved himself by training Rin Tin Tin, and he could have parlayed it into personal fame at a moment when people all over the country were gobbling up any information they could about training their dogs. But he didn't. While Saunders was performing in Yankee Stadium, Lee was at home in Riverside, preparing Rin Tin Tin III and looking for another chance at the movies.

Rin Tin Tin III, who might or might not have been a direct descendant of his namesake, looked very little like the thin-lipped, narrow-hipped, dark-haired Junior. Rin III had a sable coat, heavy shoulders, a boxy chest, a blunt nose, and a dark shadow around his muzzle that always made him look like he needed a shave. According to Lee, he was a quick learner. By the time he was a year old, he supposedly knew five hundred different commands, and Lee thought he was as expressive as old Rin. He was also a more agreeable dog. Lee had insisted that he be the only person to handle old Rin and Junior, so both dogs were unaccustomed to strangers, and old Rin, especially, was unfriendly. By the time he was training Rin Tin Tin III, Lee had changed his philosophy. He wanted the dog to be more sociable, so he allowed his daughter, Carolyn, to play with him, and then he began encouraging visitors to the ranch to spend time with the dog.

Lee had another bite at the movies in 1939, when he got a part for Rinty in *Law of the Wolf,* a cut-rate western produced by Metropolitan Pictures and written by Bernard B. Ray, a one-man movie factory who wrote under a dozen different creative rearrangements of his name, including Ray Bernard, Bernard DeRoux, Raymond Samuels, and Franklin Shamray. Publicity for the film announced that the role of the dog, called "Rinty" in the movie, was going to be played by "a grand son" of the original Rin Tin Tin. It's hard to know with certainty which dog appears on screen, or even what the term "grand son" really meant — the peculiar phrase, sounding like but not quite being "grandson," almost seems like a clever way of dodging the question of whether the dog was in fact a grandson of the original Rin Tin Tin. Some sources, including the Internet Movie Database, maintain that the dog in the film was Rin Tin Tin III. Dan Condon, a collector of silent-film memorabilia and a student of German shepherds, disagrees; he believes the dog in *Law of the Wolf* was neither Junior nor Rin Tin Tin III, but some other dog Lee used, perhaps because Junior wasn't performing well and Rin III was still too young. In its praise for the film, *Moviegoers Daily* said it would attract "patrons of western films who remember the uncanny feats of the screen's original and most famous canine hero" — both a fond reference to old Rin and a pointed failure to mention Junior.

Even though Lee deflected attention away from himself and instead to his dogs, he did have one persistent wish for notice that seemed to contradict his constant modesty: he had his mind set on getting the story of how he found Rin Tin Tin memorialized on film. Lee was thrilled when two writers, Everett George Opie and Ruth Weisberg, began work in 1940 on a screenplay for Warner Bros. that was described as the "true life story of Rin Tin Tin and Lee Duncan." Opie and Weisberg's project was only the first attempt of many to make a movie about Lee's experience. Over the next seventy years, the project was taken on again and again, without success, but Lee never lost hope. "He was always talking about doing a movie about it," Carolyn told me. "Always, always, always."

In 1941, Junior, who was only eight years old, died of pneumonia. This time, however, there were no national broadcasts or major obituaries. Junior's death went unremarked and apparently unnoticed by the public, and I have never been able to find any mention of what happened to his remains. I am certain that Lee mourned the dog. Even if Junior had been, ultimately, a disappointment, he had been old Rinty's son.

Junior's death might have simply been eclipsed by world events: it occurred just a few weeks after the Japanese had attacked Pearl Harbor. Lee had learned of the attack from the radio as he was driving home from Palm Springs, where Rin Tin Tin III and Junior had appeared in a dog show. As soon as he heard the news, he decided that he would try to reenlist in the air corps if they would take him. He would find out soon that he was too old to reenlist; instead, it would be Rin Tin Tin who played a significant role in the war.

10.

Right after Pearl Harbor, the U.S. military called for the public to donate their dogs for use in the war. Thanks to Blanche Saunders and Helene Whitehouse Walker, the dogs of America were now willing to sit and stay on command, and it was hoped that they were that much more ready to work on the battlefield. "It is an uncontestable fact that the eight years of preparatory work in conditioning the people and dogs of this country to obedience training is what enabled Dogs for Defense to get underway in record time," Saunders wrote, with obvious pride.

At the end of World War I, most of the military dogs in Europe had been returned to their owners or, more often, destroyed — except in Germany, where the training had continued apace. Germany had used more than 30,000 dogs in the war, and the German military knew their value, so they had kept an active corps. Another 25,000 trained German dogs had been sent to Japan during that time, where they joined a small cohort of Rin Tin Tin offspring, bred from the puppies acquired by the Japanese consul in the 1920s. (Rin Tin Tin had enduring popularity in Japan. In 1941, years after his silent films had vanished from theaters in the United States, Lee received an annual royalty check worth about $11,000 from Japanese distributors for the same movies, which continued to be shown in theaters there.)

Even though the Treaty of Versailles, signed in 1919, limited the size and activity of the German army, it was being rebuilt — first in secret and then more openly. In 1932, the German government made the defiant announcement that it would no longer abide by the Versailles restrictions. Soon after, compulsory military conscription in Germany resumed. A new dog army was mustered as well. Most of the dogs were donated by German citizens, who for years had been advised to train their pets for a possible military use. In the mid-1930s, the German military asked families to hand those dogs over to the service. According to a Berlin newspaper, one recruiting rally brought the army almost 16,000 privately owned dogs.

As von Stephanitz had hoped, the German shepherd had become the most prized dog in Germany. There were 60,000 members of the breed club, and it was still growing. As the Weimar Republic imploded, von Stephanitz focused on his dogs; his only politics were canine. When many of the club's members joined the Nazi Party, he put it out of mind and busied himself with the club's stud registry, a breed survey, and his own book project, *The German Shepherd Dog in Word and Picture,* the definitive text on the breed. The Nazis were more interested in von Stephanitz than he was in them. Of particular interest: von Stephanitz had created a universe parallel to the Nazi ideal — he had created a pure "race" of dogs, weeding out inferior animals to accomplish it. He had established a singular German breed that had proven its value and superiority to the rest of the world.

Von Stephanitz's resistance to politics was finally tested in the early 1930s, when the Nazis declared that they wanted control of Verein für Deutsche Schäferhunde, the German Shepherd Dog Club. They wanted the dogs for their military value, but they wanted the club for its great symbolic value as the governing body for these uniquely German and specifically engineered animals.

At first, von Stephanitz refused to step aside. He was then told that if he didn't comply he would be sent to a concentration camp, so he finally resigned. It had been his life's work. In 1936, right after the Breed

Book and Stud Registry were handed over to the club's new Nazi leaders, von Stephanitz died. By 1939, when the Blitzkrieg began, Germany had a canine corps of 200,000 dogs.

Nazis admired wolves because of their success as predators — they were the dominant creatures in the Nazis' view of nature as a violent, hierarchical battleground — and German shepherds were admired for their *germanischer Urhund,* their similarity in appearance to wolves. Hitler loved the breed. In the 1930s, he owned two German shepherds, a mother and daughter, both named Blonda. In 1941, after both Blondas had died, his secretary, Martin Bormann, gave him a black-and-silver female named Blondi. Hitler became so attached to the dog that he allowed her to sleep in his bed. He did not offer the same privilege to his lover, Eva Braun.

Around that same time, Anne Frank celebrated her thirteenth birthday. She loved Rin Tin Tin and wanted to take her friends to see a Rin Tin Tin movie for her party, but Jews had been forbidden from attending movie theaters. Her parents managed to get a copy of *Lighthouse by the Sea,* one of old Rin's earliest films, and showed it to Anne and her friends at home. In her diary, Anne wrote that the Rin Tin Tin movie had been "a big hit" with her classmates. She often thought about the dog. A few days before her party, she had written, "This morning in my bath I was thinking how wonderful it would be if I had a dog like Rin-tin-tin. I would call him Rin-tin-tin too and I'd take him to school with me, where he could stay in the janitor's room or by the bicycle racks when the weather was good."

Hitler cared deeply about animals and animal welfare. "In the Third Reich," he once announced, "cruelty to animals should no longer exist." Some of the earliest laws enacted by the Nazi Party pertained to animal protection, and violators could be sent to concentration camps. Vivisection, tail docking, and neutering were banned. Hunting and horseshoeing were regulated and restricted. Cooking lobsters and crabs by boiling them while they were still alive was outlawed. Veterinarians were elevated to the highest level of Nazi Party membership. Even though there were no wild wolves in Germany, the species was placed under strict protection. Schoolchildren — who were rewarded for reporting suspected non-

Aryans in their neighborhoods — were offered courses on animal welfare from primary school through college. In 1933, the extensive Reich Animal Protection Act included a ban on the use of animals in film.

Hitler's concern for animals seems perverse, considering the ease with which he sent millions of human beings to their deaths. But of course, everything he did was perverse: he loved Blondi so much that he tested his suicide pills on her, and then apparently was horrified to see her die. So what accounted for this concern for animals? Some of these laws, such as a ban on kosher butchering and on Jews having pets, were probably enacted because they furthered the goal of religious persecution; the restriction on vivisection might have been an effort to inhibit Jewish scientists. But the Nazi reverence for nature and natural order was more far-reaching and fundamental than a simple anti-Semitic attack. The pagan-like worship of nature as an immutable force was at the core of the Nazi belief system. Nature, with its inviolable schematic and pitiless ranking of strong over weak, was held up as a model and a justification for the Nazis' worldview, and therefore nature, and animals, had to be honored and protected. Within this scenario, Aryans viewed themselves as dominant predators, and the rest of the world as prey; therefore, they reasoned that their behavior followed the order of the natural world. They believed they were not disrupting civilization but actually restoring it to a more organic arrangement, with Aryan supremacy providing a universal and correct alignment.

Nazis also used their attention to animal well-being as a way to further humiliate their victims. By elevating animals in the natural order and legislating their comfort and safety, they were, by implication, degrading Jews and Gypsies and non-Aryans to a status even below barely sensate creatures like lobsters: a Jew could be put in a gas chamber, but a lobster could not be cooked in a pot of boiling water.

This grotesque contradiction was illustrated by the Angora Project, a rabbit-breeding program operated by the SS at the Auschwitz, Dachau, and Buchenwald concentration camps. Raised by inmates at the camps, the rabbits lived in gorgeous hutches and were fed lavish meals; their fur was trimmed and used as insulation in Luftwaffe pilots' winter jackets. But Heinrich Himmler, the chief of the SS, who ran the project and kept a notebook documenting it, also wanted the rabbits for another purpose; he liked the starving prisoners to be reminded, as they prepared meals for the animals and cleaned their cages, that they had less value in the Nazi world order, deserved less dignity and fewer rights than the animals they cared for.

Anyone who loves animals seems to be essentially a good person — or at least, conversely, anyone who would deliberately hurt an animal does not. Unfortunately, the Nazis' relationship to animals explodes this assumption. I had only recently lifted the veil on some of my own family history — examining unanswered questions and odd gaps, questioning our mysterious lack of relatives and the refusal of my grandparents to visit their hometown in Hungary. My grandparents were both from affluent, assimilated Jewish families and had left Hungary at their leisure, in the 1920s, with their good china and their silver and their favorite oil paintings, settling first in Mexico and then in the United States. They often told me stories about their early years, and these stories were crowded with brothers and sisters and cousins I had never met. Whenever I asked where this relative or that one lived now, the stories ended abruptly and I was hustled away to have a snack or play in the yard. Eventually, I forgot about these phantoms, the ones who were mentioned but then whisked out of the story, like actors jerked off a stage by a director's hook. I was never told they died. They simply disappeared from the narrative, as if they had never really existed.

Much too late to have asked my grandparents more about it, I learned that these siblings and parents and cousins, these weightless placeholders in the old stories, had died in the concentration camps, the director's hook catching them and yanking them away just before the end of the war, when they probably thought they had managed to outwit it. I realized that if my grandparents had ever gone back to Hungary to visit, there would have been no hometown left that they would have recognized, no one there who had been family or friend.

11.

The dog heroes of World War I — Satan of Verdun and Rags of Gallipoli and Michael the Messenger Dog and Stubby the Hero Dog — had demonstrated how useful dogs could be in battle, but the U.S. military didn't realize it in time to develop a canine corps. It was no better off when World War II began. There were between 13 and 15 million dogs in the United States at the time, but the entire force of American military dogs consisted of fifty huskies stationed in Alaska. Shortly after entering the war, though, the military announced that it wanted 300,000 dogs trained and deployed to Europe and the Pacific as soon as possible. The majority of the dogs would have to be donated by civilians; there was no other way to obtain so many adult dogs. If all went well, the dogs would be sent home at the end of the war.

The idea for Dogs for Defense, the group that organized to help collect the dogs, came from a group of professional breeders and dog handlers in New York, led by Arlene Erlanger, who owned Pillicoc, a poodle kennel. Once the group had secured the support of the American Kennel Club and made arrangements with the Quartermaster Corps — the army division that managed animals and equipment — it began the process of separating American families from their dogs.

Like Helene Walker, Erlanger was a proper New York matron who trailed ladies' maids and chauffeurs in her wake. But she was also pragmatic and strong-willed. She had lobbied the Army without success to develop a canine corps during World War I, and she was determined not to let another war go by without the United States using dogs in it. After Pearl Harbor, she told a *New York Sun* reporter, "The dog must play a part in this thing. Other countries have used dogs in their Armies for years and ours has not. Just think what dogs can do."

In a photograph I saw of Erlanger, she is seated beside Quartermaster Major General Edmund Gregory. He is in a medal-encrusted uniform; Erlanger is wearing a navy blue overcoat, white gloves, and a pillbox hat, and has a chinchilla stole draped over one shoulder. She looks as though she might be on her way to a country club luncheon, but in fact she was meeting with Gregory to hand over custody of hundreds of guard dogs she had just managed to get donated to Dogs for Defense. After organizing the drive to collect dogs, Erlanger did not return to a life of suburban repose. As the war went on, she wrote the technical manual for the U.S. Army, *TM 10–396 War Dogs,* with a standard training protocol, and later was hired as a special consultant to the Quartermaster General, producing training bulletins and films.

In the early days of the war, German submarines began to surface along the eastern seaboard and the Gulf Coast and there was concern that spies and saboteurs had infiltrated the United States, so the first mission of Dogs for Defense was to guard domestic airports, military installations, and public utilities. The public was asked to donate animals between one and five years old, taller than eighteen inches, and not "storm shy or noise shy." They could be either purebred or mixed breed, as long as they met the other requirements.

Ads for Dogs for Defense appeared during newsreels at movie theaters and in newspapers and magazines. One of those ads, sponsored by Purina Dog Chow, featured a drawing of a soldier with a German shepherd by his side. In the background, six soldiers march in formation, their rifles shouldered. The headline reads, "Joe and Shep Take Over — and Release Six Men for Other Duties!" The ad explained the importance of dogs in the war effort: "It has been proven here and abroad that one well-trained dog is equal in keenness of perception at night to at least six human guards. That's one big reason the United States Army is now recruiting dogs for war duty — why Major General Edmund B. Gregory, Quartermaster General of the U.S. Army, estimates that thousands of trained dogs will be needed! Dog volunteers are needed now!"

Within a few months, Americans had given nineteen thousand of their pets to Dogs for Defense, packing the kennels at the War Dog Reception and Training Centers in Virginia, Nebraska, Mississippi, Montana, and California: there was Jack, a three-year-old Belgian shepherd, who was offered for service by Joseph Verhaeghe of Floral Park, New York; Butch, a Doberman pinscher, owned by Mr. Walter Dipping of Chicago, headed to the Marine Corps; Chips, a German shepherd who eventually earned a Distinguished Service Cross for clearing out an enemy pillbox in Sicily "with utter disregard for his own safety," enlisted by Mrs. Edward Wren of Pleasantville, New York; and Peppy, a Doberman, the house pet of Mr. J. F. Bryan of Long Island, who would go missing in action for three days in Guam after being shot. Other dogs included actress Greer Garson's poodle, Mary Pickford's German shepherd, Rudy Vallee's Doberman, and violinist Jascha Heifetz's Great Dane. Even Lee donated a dog — Truline von Pondview, the mother of Rin Tin Tin III, who was eventually killed in action in the South Pacific.

So many dogs were being given to Dogs for Defense that the number of field trials and dog shows around the country immediately fell off. A typical 1942 headline from the dog column of the *New York Times* announced, "Dogs for Defense Out for Recruits — Demand for K-9 Additions Is Unceasing Because of Their Value on All Fronts — Suffolk County Kennel Club Votes to Abandon Annual Show at Huntington." Many of the shows that were held, including the Westminster Kennel Club show, donated their proceeds to Dogs for Defense.

If you donated your pet to Dogs for Defense, you received a card in the mail that read:

We are happy to advise you that your dog, with name, brand number and breed as follows, has arrived at this Depot in good condition. At this time we are not able to predict your dog's adaptability to the rigors of Army training. You will, of course, understand why the interests of military secrecy will best be served if further information is withheld from this point forward. Thanking you for your generous donation at the time of this national emergency, I am, [Signature of Commanding Officer].

Half of the dogs that were donated were sent back to their owners within weeks because they failed the physical or were too small or too nervous. The remaining dogs started an eight-week obedience program, practicing their attacks on stuffed dummies of Hitler and Emperor Hirohito. At first the dogs' progress was disappointing. The handlers and obedience teachers leading the program had experience in a show ring but not in teaching dogs how to attack an infiltrator or sniff out a land mine. The approach was scattershot and the program was still only semi-official; Dogs for Defense was a civilian group, and the U.S. military hadn't yet formalized the canine corps. The following year, however, the secretary of war officially established the War Dog Program within the jurisdiction of the Quartermaster General, and — with Arlene Erlanger's training manual on hand — the canine corps was under way.

The families who donated their dogs soon overwhelmed the Quartermaster Corps with letters, Christmas cards, and birthday cards for their dogs. There were also thousands of notes sent to the quartermaster himself, asking how this or that dog was doing, whether Skipper had passed basic training, if Thor had mastered airplane spotting and messenger work yet, if Ginger or Lucky or Tippy or Cappy was thriving on army rations. At first the staff tried to answer each letter, but as the number of dogs grew, the mail became unmanageable and all inquiries were answered with certificates of appreciation on War Department letterhead.

The soldiers at the front who were actually using the dogs occasionally wrote to the owners, especially if the news was bad. The first dog to die in action was Rollo, a Doberman pinscher, killed by machine-gun fire in the Solomon Islands. Many more fatalities followed. "Now I have to tell you the worst," a Marine named Guy Wachtsletter wrote to Mr. and Mrs. Leo Raymond of Ridgefield, Washington, about their dog Tubby. "Tubby was shot and killed the night of August 31. He has to his credit eight Japs. . . . he behaved like a true Marine at all times and didn't even whimper when he died. He was shot through the heart and died instantly. We have buried him in the Marine cemetery along with the other real heroes of this campaign and if it is at all possible I'll send you a picture of his grave. He has a cross with his name and rank. He was a corporal."

There had been no call for citizens to

donate dogs during World War I. If there had been, it wouldn't have been quite as emotional a gesture as it was during World War II. In 1917, dogs were still seen as an elevated type of livestock. They were commonly used as hunters and shepherds, so training them as soldiers would not have seemed dramatically different. In all of Rinty's early films, for instance, he is portrayed as a companion but not really a pet — he is rarely even shown inside houses, and his intimacy with his masters comes from being a coworker rather than a member of the family.

But by the time World War II began, dogs were a familiar fixture on the stage set of modern domesticity. Americans had continued their steady move from countryside to city, and dogs were accompanying them. They had been promoted from farm workers to companions, from outside animals to hearth-warmers. As soon as dogs became our escorts — our friends — putting them to work, and especially work that could kill them, required a great commitment to the cause. The war in 1942 was that sort of cause, when doing something hard probably seemed easy compared with the prospect of a world controlled by Adolf Hitler.

The army acknowledged the emotional

difficulty of giving a dog away. "Appreciative of the sentimental and monetary value of these dogs being lent to them by their owners for the duration of the war, the Army provides the utmost care and attention for them at all times," according to *Fighting War Dogs of World War II,* a brochure published in 1944 by the U.S. military. The brochure, promoting Dogs for Defense, included articles such as "Dog Catches a Jap," "Skippy Has 200 Flying Hours with AAF," "Queenie Dies in Action," and "Terrier Goes from California to Africa."

One story, "Boy Offers Dog as Sacrifice to War Effort," quotes a Boy Scout named Eugene Knispel. In a letter to the Quartermaster General, Knispel wrote, "Being a Boy Scout and having the privilege to own a very fine, intelligent, young Belgian Police Dog, I deem it my duty towards my country to offer him to be trained for Defense. How proud I would be if my dog could belong to your K-9 Corps. Would you be kind enough to let me know how to go about enrolling him?"

Eugene Knispel is now a veterinarian in New Orleans. When I reached him by phone at his clinic, Dr. Knispel was completely startled by my call; he is now eighty-one years old, and it had been close to seventy years since he'd thought about giving away his dog. He told me that the dog had been named Ferdinand, after the bull in the children's book *The Story of Ferdinand,* a gentle pacifist who refuses to perform in a bullfight. When the war began, Eugene was living with his mother, who was divorced, in an apartment on 97th Street in Manhattan. It was a tough neighborhood in those days, and because his mother worked, Eugene was often alone. He was very attached to the dog, whom he described as "not only my friend, but my protector." Ferdinand must have seemed like quite a prize, because Knispel said only a few other kids in the neighborhood had a dog, and, what's more, Ferdie looked like he could have been a cousin of the famous Rin Tin Tin. It was a hard knock when Knispel's mother decided to take a job working on an estate on Long Island, where the dog would not be welcome. Knispel was thirteen when they moved, a difficult age to lose anything, especially a dog. He hadn't known what to do with Ferdie until he heard about Dogs for Defense — he thinks it was probably in a newsreel at a movie theater. "I felt proud offering Ferdie," he says. "I hoped he'd do well. After Pearl Harbor, for us kids, our motto was 'Hitler stinks.' "

He didn't really remember whether Ferdinand was accepted by Dogs for Defense or not, or what had become of him. What he did remember is that he and his mother soon left Manhattan without the dog and he never saw Ferdie again.

12.

Although Lee wanted to reenlist, he was fifty years old and no longer eligible for active duty. His reputation as a dog trainer, however, made him valuable, and army officials invited him to Camp Haan, in Riverside, to help evaluate and train the donated dogs. Other Hollywood dog trainers, including Earl Johnson and Carl Spitz, were also working with the army, but Lee had a unique asset: Rin Tin Tin III. The famous dog could inspire people to donate their dogs for the war. Lee brought Rinty to Camp Haan, where he was tattooed with his army serial number and rank (sergeant), and put through the same six-week training as the other dogs.

As in World War I, the dogs were trained as sentries, messengers, scouts, mine detectors, airplane spotters, and cadaver dogs. The U.S. Army Air Corps also began experimenting with dropping the dogs by parachute behind enemy lines. (One accounting of the program states that a purebred boxer named Jeff "made thirteen jumps, twelve successfully.") General Douglas MacArthur wanted to use dogs in more than just a support role, so he sent a tactical unit of eight dog handlers and their Doberman pinschers — the official breed of the Marines, where they were affectionately known as Devil Dogs — to the Solomon Islands. The Marines and their dogs worked as an integrated team; the dogs made the amphibious landing and lived alongside them in foxholes. The dogs excelled at rooting out enemy troops and relaying messages when radios failed, which was common in the sodden South Pacific. The experiment was considered a great success for the war effort but less so for the dogs. Five were killed in combat and the remaining dogs were destroyed because they became infected with typhus.

There was never a chance that Rin Tin Tin III would be sent overseas. He was assigned a public relations job as the celebrity spokesmodel for what was now known officially as the K-9 Corps. A 1943 press release from Camp Haan explained, "One of the hardest working and most 'all out' of the civilian volunteers in this war is a dog.

A beautiful, intelligent, fearless animal, untiring in his effort to aid his country to the best of his very great ability. He is none other than Rin Tin Tin III, the grandson of the famous moving picture actor for whom he is named. . . . At first it was his owner's intention that Rin enlist as a regular army war dog but it developed that Rin Tin Tin III could be of greater service by remaining in the capacity of a volunteer, free of the many restrictions necessitated by army life." The German shepherd was soon named the "official dog breed" of the U.S. Army, and Rin Tin Tin III was held up as a singular example of what an American dog should be during wartime.

Rin Tin Tin III and Lee made appearances throughout California to promote Dogs for Defense. Back at Camp Haan, Rinty was also used in various tests, many of which were dangerous. In one, he wore a canine gas mask in a functioning gas chamber, and in another, he carried wire across a course mined with live ammunition to assess a dog's ability to weave among land mines. In his off hours, he greeted the movie stars and entertainers who visited Camp Haan, including Bob Hope, Jack Benny, and singer Kate Smith. The Camp Haan newsletter reported that after she visited the dogs' kitchen, "Miss Smith was thrilled at the cleanliness and order prevailing throughout."

Hollywood was going to war, and the war was also coming to Hollywood. One of its unlikely fictional heroines was a British bitch named Lassie. The character had been introduced to the public in 1940 in the bestselling young adult novel *Lassie Come-Home,* which told of a beautiful collie owned by the Carracloughs, a poor Yorkshire family. When Sam Carraclough loses his job, the family is forced to sell Lassie to a rich, brutal neighbor. The story describes Lassie's "suffering aristocratic majesty" and her determination to be reunited with the Carracloughs' young son, Joe.

Eric Knight, who wrote *Lassie Come-Home,* was born in England but raised in the United States. As a child, he never had his own dog, but he loved collies, which were the most adored dogs in Yorkshire. Knight worked in New York as a playwright and a reporter, and on an assignment for the *Saturday Evening Post* he went back to his childhood home in Yorkshire to investigate the region's poverty. He was told that some families were so strapped that they had had to sell their collies just to make ends meet. His magazine piece, a fictional-ized account of one such family, drew great praise, and a publisher urged him to expand the piece into a novel. A few months later he completed *Lassie Come-Home.*

As far as we know, Lee never met Eric Knight, but they led uncommonly parallel lives. They were born just a few years apart in the 1890s. Both lost their fathers before they were old enough to know they had fathers, and both spent part of their child-hoods away from their mothers. For Knight, it was when his mother took a job in Russia and he was sent to Massachusetts to live with relatives. Both men served in World War I and were involved in World War II. (Knight was a major with the U.S. Army Special Services.) Both saw characters they created come to life for the public. Unlike Lee, however, Knight never saw the full impact Lassie would have on popular cul-ture. Three years after he published *Lassie Come-Home,* he was killed in the crash of a Special Services flight to Surinam.

In 1943, the year Knight died, his book was made into the film *Lassie Come Home.* (The expression "come-home dogs" from the book title was British slang for dogs that find their way back to their masters, so the producers dropped the hyphen to make the title more universally understandable.) The film starred Roddy McDowall as the wistful Joe Carraclough. Sam Carraclough, the boy's father, was played by actor Donald Crisp, who was particularly familiar with animal actors: his wife, Jane Murfin, had owned Strongheart along with her first husband, Lawrence Trimble.

More than a thousand dogs auditioned for the lead. The character of Lassie was female, but in the film, and later on television, male dogs were cast in the role. This was because males have more luxuriant coats than females and, unlike females, they don't go through an annual shedding period, during which they look mangy and threadbare. Males are also larger than females, so child actors look more endearingly childlike next to them (and because of this optical illusion, older, more experienced children could be used to play younger roles).

The dog that won the part was a tricolor male named Pal, who was owned by animal trainer Rudd Weatherwax. Weatherwax had trained some star dogs, including Asta, the wire-haired terrier in the *Thin Man* movies, but his greatest hope had been to find a star-quality German shepherd, because they were the only breed regularly cast in leading film roles. When Weatherwax's Hollywood business was slow, he trained problem pets for private clients. Pal had come to Weatherwax's kennel as one of those problems; he was a dedicated car-chaser and barker, and he was driving his owner crazy. Weatherwax managed to cure Pal of barking but couldn't break him of chasing cars, so his owner simply abandoned him at the kennel. Weatherwax liked Pal, but there was little call for collies in the movies, and he didn't need a pet, so he gave the dog away to a friend.

A few months later Weatherwax heard that MGM was casting *Lassie Come Home,* and he decided to get Pal back and take him to the audition. Other than his car-chasing, Pal was well trained, and he performed well enough to win the part. He was a beautiful and expressive animal with a special talent for looking miserable. This was an important star turn throughout the movie, and the result is extravagantly poignant; it was reported that Louis B. Mayer, the head of MGM, burst into tears when he first screened the film. When he dried his eyes, Mayer realized the appeal the film's star could have. Dozens of different portraits of Lassie — that is, Pal — were released, and a press barrage ensued. After the film premiered, Weatherwax toured the country with the dog, performing in theaters and arenas throughout the country, just as Lee and Rinty once had. Within three years of the film's release, collies became the third most popular breed in the United States.

13.

It was a novelty in 1943 for a collie to be a movie star: German shepherds had dominated Hollywood for decades. Other breeds and the occasional mongrel got movie roles, but ever since Strongheart appeared on screen, no dog other than a German shepherd had ever starred in a film or become a celebrity. What's more, collies were such a contrast to German shepherds. Both were herding breeds, and they were about the same size, but in every other way, they were opposites. German shepherds were muscular, with thick, short coats and a tight outline. Their faces were keen and bright, with dark eyes and an intense, impatient expression, as if they were waiting for you to finish your sentence and get on with the urgencies of the day. Their posture, in a permanent quarter crouch, was unrelaxed, ready for action. They were well known as soldier dogs and police dogs; they were tough and rugged and businesslike. Collies, on the other hand, seemed contemplative and shy, with their hooded eyes and tipped-over ears and long, slim, fragile-looking muzzles. Even when they wagged their tails, they looked like they might break down and cry any second. They were bred to work in rough weather, but their coats, which had as much loft as a down comforter, made them look fancy, and their legs and feet looked too delicate to support their billowy bodies.

In addition to being the first collie to star in a film, Lassie was the first female dog character to be the lead in a feature. Lassie's character was not just coincidentally female — it was distinctly female, by traditional definitions: she was valued because she was beautiful, she was gentle and soulful, and she was willing to suffer for love. Before Lassie, canine characters in popular culture had always been male: they were action stars in action movies. Females, if they appeared at all, were always given minor roles. Many generations of Nanettes appeared on film alongside Rin Tin Tin, but only in cameos, as Rinty's loving wife. One female German shepherd, Sandow, starred in three silent movies, including *Avenging Fangs,* but she was always disguised as a male dog.

But the way we viewed dogs had changed significantly by this time. In the United States, pet ownership was exploding. Between 1947 and 1953, the number of dogs in the United States grew from 17 million to 22 million, and the dog population was growing four times as fast as the human one. It was more than just numbers, though; the way dogs lived with us had changed. They were not living in a shed in the backyard; they were living inside the house as part of the family. Before this, dogs had been ideal heroes because we knew them but we couldn't really know them: they were familiar but they weren't us. They were mysterious and enigmatic strangers. But as more people owned dogs, shared quarters with them, and let them lick up dinner leftovers, dogs lost some of that mythic otherness. People began to know dogs more and idealize them less; they became interested in stories about loving dogs rather than stories about marveling at them as superheroes. Lassie inspired love rather than awe. She was not larger than life. She was noble but not meant to be extraordinary. She was never described the way Rin Tin Tin had been — Lassie was the perfect devoted pet, a maternal sort of friend, not the Dog Wonder or the Wonder Dog of All

Creation; not the Mastermind Dog or the Marvelous Dog or the Miracle Dog or the Dog Hero of Young America. She was elegant, melancholy, long-suffering, nurturing — an emotional vessel rather than a warrior, an athlete, or a super intellect, as German shepherd stars had been.

Besides popularizing collies, *Lassie Come Home* was also the first time a dog movie was made expressly with children in mind. Rin Tin Tin's films, as well as nearly all other movies starring dogs, were action films. They were full of crime and danger and adventure. The actors in Rin Tin Tin movies were all adults, and if children were featured at all, they were mostly incidental and usually just babies.

Lassie Come Home was a departure. The story of Lassie's journey is the narrative spine of the movie, but the thematic center is not the clever way Lassie overcomes hardship, as it might have been in a Rin Tin Tin movie; it's the power of the relationship between a boy and his dog. The grown-ups in the movie are secondary, and they are either evil or ineffectual. The film presents the idea that children and dogs have interesting and compelling inner lives — and, more important, that children and dogs have a unique connection.

Lassie Come Home and Lassie's ascendance came at a time when Rin Tin Tin was most absent from Hollywood. In 1943, Lee and Rinty were still enlisted at Camp Haan, working with Dogs for Defense. Rinty hadn't been in a film since *Law of the Wolf,* which was released in 1939. Lassie and Rin Tin Tin didn't really overlap in Hollywood at this point, but the rivalry between the two dogs was set in motion. Press agents always delighted in rivalry between stars: if no real ones were available to exploit, they would often fabricate them. Friction between celebrities was exaggerated to tantalize moviegoers and keep them interested in stars even when they didn't have a film in theaters. Famous Hollywood rivalries really did exist — sisters Joan Fontaine and Olivia de Havilland, for instance, wouldn't speak to each other — but many others were mostly faked, such as the one between Fred Allen and Jack Benny. Dog actors had been pitted against each other in the press as well, but it had been decades since Rin Tin Tin had topped Strongheart in popularity and prominence, and no other canine actor had come close to Rinty's appeal for years, so he hadn't even had a reasonable rival. Lassie offered a new sort of competition. MGM played up the difference between Lassie and

Rin Tin Tin, contrasting Lassie's gentle nature to Rinty's tendency to be involved in at least four or five fights in every film. Lassie, according to MGM, could do "everything but snarl."

Lassie Come Home was regarded as one of the best films of 1943, and MGM rushed to capitalize on its popularity by producing four sequels. These films had little to do with Knight's book and were panned. By the time MGM released the last of the films, *The Painted Hills,* in 1951, the studio had fallen behind in paying Weatherwax for his work. MGM offered him the rights to the Lassie character in lieu of cash. Weatherwax accepted and toured the country for the next several years with Pal, who was billed as "famous movie dog Lassie." In the meantime, Rin Tin Tin, who had never costarred with a kid, caught on to the trend for targeting a younger audience and made his first boy-and-dog movie, *The Return of Rin Tin Tin,* in 1947, a few years after *Lassie Come Home.*

14.

According to James English, MGM approached Lee in 1942 with a request for Rinty to appear in a war dog movie. Lee declined the "fat movie contract" because he was too busy with work at Camp Haan, but it seems more likely that the project just stalled. MGM did dispatch two writers to Camp Haan to begin taking notes on the war dogs, but, according to English, the writers were drafted into the army soon after arriving at Camp Haan and "that was the end of the war dog picture."

Nevertheless, Lee felt hopeful about his new dog's prospects. He liked the symmetry with the past. The first Rin Tin Tin had been a war dog, and so was Rin Tin Tin III. Lee took it as a sign. Maybe the charm had skipped a generation — Junior's generation — and been strengthened through the trials of war. Lee began telling everyone that grandfather and grandson were "remarkably similar" — the way they behaved, their response to training. Even their misfortunes seemed alike: Rinty III was injured by a Jeep during field maneuvers, which reminded Lee of old Rin's broken leg. It was an omen, he believed, that this was another extraordinary dog.

In the meantime, Lee and Rinty were busy, and life felt purposeful. They visited army hospitals and orphanages, just as Lee and old Rin had done, and Lee helped process the dogs that were being trained at

Camp Haan. He and Rinty would remain there until the war was over and the army told them they were no longer needed.

The dogs of war came home with a certificate from the Quartermaster Corps:

> HONORABLE DISCHARGE. The War Dog _____ Tattoo No. _____ having served with the Armed Forces of the United States of America is hereby awarded this Certificate of Faithful Service and Honorable Discharge.

Owners were assured that the dogs hadn't been altered by their service in the war, but many were still uneasy. The 1946 hit film *The Courage of Lassie* was about a gentle collie whose war experience makes her into a killer (until Elizabeth Taylor helps her reclaim her previous pleasant temperament). According to Lee's biography, rumors had begun to spread that "there was no way to rehabilitate a war dog. They had been taught to be vicious, they had a killer's instinct." The Quartermaster Corps announced that before the dogs were returned to their owners, they would be "reprocessed" to a "pre-war state of docility" by means of ample petting and lots of play-time.

The army, looking to reassure families, published pictures of demobilized dogs relaxing at home, over captions like "This is Caesar on the front lawn" and "Here is Spike in Civilian Life." They also published excerpts from letters that described success-ful reunions. "DOLF arrived yesterday in excellent condition. . . . He knew each and all of us immediately." "Thank you for your good care and training of our dog MIKE . . . he still remembers the tricks he knew before he entered the service." "I want to thank you for the wonderful dog you returned to us. SMARTY is a perfect example of health and alertness. It was a genuine sacrifice for Herbie to donate his dog to the armed forces, but now he is receiving his reward by receiving a dog more beautiful and bet-ter trained than he ever thought possible."

Newspapers also reported on successful reentries. According to one 1944 story, "Goofy, The Warrior Dog, Comes Home," service in the army had actually improved the dog's behavior. After seventeen months at the front, Goofy was happy to be home with his family in Pennsylvania and even had a joyful get-together with his best friend, a Belgian shepherd named Wacky.

Then the mailman arrived. "The mailman was nervous about Goofy," the story reported. "He remembered that Goofy had bitten him before joining the army." Goofy sniffed the mailman's shoes but didn't bite him. The mailman, sighing with relief, remarked that they must have taught him manners in the army.

Dogs for Defense was disbanded at the end of World War II, but dogs remained part of the military, and most of them still came from private donations, although the terms of the donations changed. In the future there would be no progress reports and no trip home at the end of service. Donated dogs became permanent property of the U.S. military, as had always been the case with other animals that the military procured — horses, camels, mules, donkeys. Dogs were used in Korea and Vietnam, in Desert Storm and Desert Shield, and in Iraq and Afghanistan.

A few years ago, I watched an army unit audition some potential recruits. The testing took place on a carpet-green soccer field in a suburb of Boston on a bright morning in May. When I arrived, half a dozen people were gathered at the field, resting against their cars, their arms crossed, watching each dog go through its paces before three army officers, who were wearing fatigues and clutching clipboards to their chests. Most of the dogs were Doberman pinschers and German shepherds, and each of the owners said they'd brought the dog because it was too aggressive to be a pet, or too dominant, or too mean. They viewed the army as a sort of last-chance resort for bad dogs. This was entirely different from what was taking place in 1942, when sending your dog to the K-9 Corps was like offering a piece of yourself in the hope of being able to serve.

Everyone I tell about Dogs for Defense is astonished by it. Some are horrified. People who didn't grow up during World War II, who have only known wars that seemed optional or ill considered or entrepreneurial, have trouble imagining the intimate sacrifice of sending a pet to war. Never mind that many of their fathers and grandfathers fought in the war: giving a pet away for that purpose seems somehow more shocking. Most of us realize that bad people do bad things and good people have to fight them. A dog has no such knowledge, and the thought of sending it off to war seems like a betrayal of the human-dog relationship, which is founded in trust and in the dog's unspoken promise not to eat us when it probably could.

15.

By 1947, after all the dogs that survived the war were petted into docility and sent home, Lee and Rin Tin Tin III headed back to El Rancho Rin Tin Tin. Lee was once again at loose ends. His tax returns show scant earnings — $1,150 from selling a few colts; $210 from the sale of puppies; and $3,225 for boarding horses. Eva's secretarial salary was paying their bills.

As always, Lee's thoughts turned to the movies. After spending four years at Camp Haan, Rinty was mature and well trained. Lee didn't have much footing in Hollywood anymore, but he was determined to try again with this new Rin Tin Tin.

The movie industry was nothing like the Poverty Row he had walked down with Rin Tin Tin in 1920, but it was still a surprisingly small town. People bumped into people and made deals. At a horse show, Lee met a retired movie executive named George Schaefer, who happened to be toying with the idea of starting a new production company. Lee described Rin Tin Tin III to him. Schaefer was a fan of old Rin,

and after the horse show he came to Riverside to see Rinty III. According to Lee,
Schaefer was so impressed that he "tele-
phoned for his attorneys and associates to
join him at the ranch," and that evening,
at Lee's dining room table, Schaefer incorporated a new production company, Romay Pictures, to produce a film starring the
dog.

Once again, Lee also had an idea for a
screenplay. At the time, hundreds of European war orphans were being placed in
American foster homes. Lee thought a
movie could focus on an orphan boy who
overcomes his war trauma by developing an
attachment to a dog. Perhaps the dog could
in some way be orphaned, too, and the dog
could also be saved from loneliness by the
boy's devotion. It was the story Lee never
tired of, no matter how many years he was
away from Fred Finch. Even now, so long
after he had lost his first dog, he never
stopped believing that a dog could make
you whole. Now he was circling back, hoping it would start his life up again.

But did anyone still remember Rin Tin
Tin as a movie star? It had been years since
Junior's bumbling efforts in *Law of the Wolf*
and *Hollywood Cavalcade,* and even longer
since old Rin had been in his prime.

Schaefer, clearly, was willing to take the chance.

Schaefer's partner, William Stephens, wrote a script based on the story Lee suggested, and *The Return of Rin Tin Tin* was shot that year. The young actor Robert Blake (then known as Bobby Blake) stars as Paul, an emotionally damaged orphan from an unnamed war-torn country. Paul's American foster mother is unable to form a bond with the troubled boy, so she places him at a California mission in the care of a wise priest — a version of Lee's experience at Fred Finch. Rin Tin Tin III plays a dog that has escaped a cruel owner and finds refuge at the mission just as Paul arrives. (As gossip columnist Louella Parsons noted, the film was "based on the old reliable formula of a boy, a dog and a priest.") In the end, Paul and Rin Tin Tin heal each other. "I can't love nobody!" Paul sobs in a pivotal scene, hugging the dog. "But I love you, Rin! I love you!"

Rinty performs the requisite leaps and jumps, and once again he plays a character who is wronged, who suffers, and whose goodness ultimately saves him. But his role in the film was quite different from roles old Rin had played. In his movies, the first Rin Tin Tin was the star, but he was also much more. His thrilling stunts were pivotal to the plot. His perspective was the omniscient one in the story. His intelligence and resolve provided the plot's deus ex machina. His performance was the film's power. Less was asked of Rin Tin Tin III in *The Return of Rin Tin Tin.* He was a beautiful animal and he was billed as the star of the movie, but in fact he is just one character in an ensemble, less central to the story than the mop-topped, wincing Robert Blake. The dog's stunts are impressive, but they embellish the story rather than propel it. The relationship he and Blake develop is the axis of the film, but the character that struggles and changes is the boy, not the dog.

Unlike old Rin, this new Rin Tin Tin has none of that internal clash between his wildness and his civility, between his wolfishness and his capacity to become attached to humans. He does not symbolize any friction between superego and id. Rinty's struggle here is just circumstantial: he needs to stay away from his cruel owner. The first Rin Tin Tin always managed to seem a little better, a little smarter, a little more spiritual than the other characters in his films. In *The Return of Rin Tin Tin,* for the first time, he is just a dog.

Before releasing the film, Schaefer hired

Buchanan and Company to research whether audiences were still interested in Rin Tin Tin. In November 1946, the *Brooklyn Eagle* carried news of the Buchanan study:

A nationwide survey, covering cities of all sizes from rural communities to the largest cities in the country . . . has revealed that the best-known motion picture "personality" ever to appear on a screen is Rin Tin Tin, the animal star. . . . The survey revealed that 70.3 percent of those people queried — ranging in age groups from six to fifteen years and sixteen to forty-five — knew the name of Rin Tin Tin. This is a larger percentage than has ever known of any film star's name. Of the people who had heard of Rin Tin Tin's name, 94.6 percent identified him correctly as the animal star of motion pictures.

The numbers astonished everyone, even Lee. The filmmakers were elated. To ensure that this huge number of people who recognized Rin Tin Tin would see the film, Romay launched an aggressive publicity campaign, almost contemporary in its reach. One contest offered a "genuine RIN TIN

TIN pup" to the person who came up with the best name for the puppy. *True Comics, Parents Magazine,* and *Calling All Boys* agreed to feature the movie on their covers. Gaines Dog Food, which had supplanted Lee's long relationship with Ken-L-Ration, placed full-page ads featuring Rinty in *Life* and the *Saturday Evening Post* ("A Wise Dog feels it in his bones — the marvelous difference when EVERY INCH of him is nourished by GAINES!"). Theater owners were given advice on how to draw patrons to the film: they might offer huge barrels full of animal crackers in the lobby as an enticement; encourage war veterans to march in formation to the theater on opening night; ask schools to encourage students to make Rin Tin Tin drawings in art class and write "Why I want to see Rin Tin Tin on the screen" essays in English class. The school's orchestra members and their dogs could parade through town.

He had died fourteen years before *The Return of Rin Tin Tin* was released, but the first Rin Tin Tin seemed more present than ever. It was as if he had never gone away. Lee was "constantly amazed" that children who were far too young to have seen a Rin Tin Tin film, who couldn't possibly be nostalgic for the old dog, responded to the new one as if he were an old friend; they "called Rinty by name, knew him, loved him, asked for autographed pictures." Lee supposed they had learned about the dog from their parents. One contest to promote the film was called Memories of Rin Tin Tin. It was an essay competition; the topic was "Why I Liked the Old Rin Tin Tin and Am Looking Forward to 'THE RETURN OF RIN TIN TIN.' " According to the publicity material, "Millions of people remember the greatness of Rin Tin Tin and you can take advantage of this to resell the adults in your town on him by promoting this contest."

Popular culture is a period of time captured in a look and a gesture. Popular performers are made by time and then undone by it, as they age out of relevance. Rin Tin Tin, and the idea of heroic devotion that he represented, was proving to be something more. Parents were passing him along to their children. He had beaten time. He had become a classic.

The reviews were enthusiastic:

"Every bit the performer and as camera-wise as his celebrated grandfather, Rin Tin Tin III carries on a distinguished heritage."

"The current dog star is Rin Tin Tin

III . . . He carries on the tradition nobly and measures up to his predecessor in talent and screen personality."

"The dog definitely justifies his star billing."

The only sour note came from the American Humane Association, which complained to the Motion Picture Association of America about several scenes in the movie. In one, Rinty's former owner tracks him down and beats him. The scene was "objectionably suggestive of cruelty to animals." (In a side note, the AHA also disapproved of a scene in which the priest, Father Matthew, is shown telling a lie, "a specious line of reasoning unbecoming a Priest and is certain to give widespread offense.")

Lee took good care of his dogs. But in early Hollywood, animals that were not recognizable stars often had a rotten time. Horses got the roughest treatment: they were tripped, shocked, raced into open trenches, run ragged. To make a horse fall on cue, wires were strung around its ankles or threaded through holes that were drilled in its hooves; the rider simply yanked the wires to pull the horse up short. In 1935, 125 horses were wire-tripped in *The Charge of the Light Brigade,* and 25 of them were killed outright by the fall or euthanized as a result.

Four years later, the director of the Tyrone Power movie *Jesse James* wanted a shot of a cowboy on horseback jumping into water. A stunt-man rode a blindfolded horse into a greased chute on a cliff above a lake. When the horse hit the water, it broke its back and had to be destroyed. This was a defining moment in the film industry. Only the first frames of that shot were used in *Jesse James,* but the entire sequence of the animal plunging toward the water — hunched, helpless, stiff-legged — was circulated by people concerned with animal welfare. The American Humane Association, which had been founded in the late nineteenth century to protect animals and children, issued a report reproaching the movie industry, citing *Jesse James* as a particularly egregious example of how animals were treated. (In England, the animal protection group Dumb Friends League called for similar reform the same year.) The Motion Picture Association of America, responding to the complaints, added a section to its production code in 1940 prohibiting the use of tilt chutes and trip wires, as well as other abusive practices, and the AHA opened a Hollywood office to enforce the new standards.

The scenes in *The Return of Rin Tin Tin* that were "suggestive of cruelty to animals" remained in the film despite the AHA's misgivings. There was never a charge that Rinty was actually being hurt, just that the scene depicted cruelty. *The Return of Rin Tin Tin* was released in the same year as *Gentleman's Agreement, Duel in the Sun,* and *The Bachelor and the Bobby-Soxer* — formidable competition. It still managed to be a success, drawing audiences that were as devoted to the dog as those that had gathered to see old Rin a decade earlier.

16.

"HEY KIDS! Big Special Stage and Screen Show with a Dual Appearance of the Most Famous Dog in All the World. On our stage In Person Lee Duncan and Rin Tin Tin III. See this Marvel of Canine Intelligence in an Amazing Array of Uncanny Stunts and Feats. His Understanding of his Trainer's Commands Astonishes Everyone . . . And on our Screen See this same 'Dog With a Brain' in *The Return of Rin Tin Tin*!"

In November, Lee left Riverside with Rinty and set out on an eight-week tour of the country to support the film. The studio publicist had been swamped by requests. "Rin Tin Tin is certainly popular," she wrote to Lee, forwarding notes from veterans' groups, hospitals, Boy Scout troops ("The scouts wish Rinty to autograph special slips of paper"), kennel clubs, and orphanages. Mayors and governors asked Lee and Rinty to stop by when they were in town.

Eva and Carolyn accompanied Lee on a few of the visits. The press paid them little attention. One article mentioned that Eva was a "weary but well-dressed looking woman"; Carolyn was "their plump eight-year-old daughter." Otherwise, they receded into the background or stayed at home in Riverside.

"Famous Dog Will Be Here Wednesday!"

"Orthopedic Kids Hated to See Rin Go!"

"Rin Tin Tin Welcomed by Mayor."

"Dog Star Signs City's Guest Register."

"Movie Star from Famous Family Comes to Town with a Fur Coat."

Lee wouldn't stop working. He went on yet another tour, another round of personal appearances. A visit to the local Goodwill, the hospital, the orphanage; a stop at a dog show, a county fair, a parade; a demonstration at a kennel club, a town hall, on the tarmac of the local airport. He wanted the story to keep winding off its spool, trailing the silvery filament of memory.

Dear friend,
Thank you for writing.
We have lots of action and
adventure planned...so keep
watching our program.
Best regards,

Rip, Rusty, and

THE PHENOMENON

1.

By the time I managed to locate Bert Leonard, all that was left of him fit into a small unit in a self-storage facility in Los Angeles that was hemmed in by concertina wire and a row of spindly palm trees. Coincidentally, the facility was right down the road from the house Bert owned when he was producing *The Adventures of Rin Tin Tin* in the 1950s. Because it was one of the most popular television shows in the world, Bert had been able to afford a Tudor mansion with a tennis court in a fine neighborhood near Griffith Park. Years later, when his money ran out, he was forced to sell. Now the only real estate he still had was a plot in Forest Lawn Cemetery in the Hollywood Hills, where he was buried in 2006, and this storage unit, which enjoyed few of the particulars of the neighborhood. It was on a bleak and creepy back lot, as blank as a tomb, and the chain-link fence running along the sidewalk was clogged with flyers and newspaper pages that the wheezy California wind had slapped up against it.

Bert's unit was in one of the buildings farthest from the entrance. A short man with fading Iron Maiden tattoos and a patchwork denim vest was tinkering with a car engine nearby, but otherwise the place was still, except for the distant gurgle of traffic. As I climbed a short flight of stairs, a light above the landing snapped on, and I was so startled that I blurted out something like "Hey!" and then had to take a moment to calm myself down. In the stuffy quiet, I heard a soft flutter. A little bird had made her nest on a rafter in the hall. She hopped to attention as I stood there, and then she watched with a shiny eye as I reached for the lock on Bert's door. Why would a bird choose to live here, in a storage building, on a pad of hot concrete, instead of in, say, the Santa Monica wilderness? Nature is so mysterious. I fumbled for the key.

I had been looking for Bert Leonard for years. In his day he had been the quintessential Hollywood character, but there was no longer any evidence of him there — no relationship with any movie studio, no projects in development, no deals about to be made. He had no address or phone number that I could find. I called all the friends of his I could locate, and after telling me how fond they were of Bert, and also how much money he owed them, they each admitted they hadn't talked to him in ages and didn't know where he might be. It was incredibly frustrating; I was desperate to ask him about working with Lee and how he came under the spell of Rin Tin Tin and a million other questions that felt crucial to me.

And then I found him, but in the worst sort of way: I ran across his obituary. That led me to his daughter Gina. A few months later, we met at her house in Los Angeles and talked; it was edifying, of course, but I wasn't satisfied. I was getting ready to leave Gina's house when she mentioned, almost off-handedly, a storage unit. She might have the key. She went upstairs, and I sat in her living room, wound up and eager, the way you feel right after you pull the lever on a slot machine. A minute passed, and then Gina came downstairs and handed me a key, warning me that she had no idea what was in the unit. She said there had been a problem with it when Bert was still alive —

unpaid rent, that sort of problem. For the moment, Gina's mother, Jenny — one of Bert's four ex-wives — was taking care of it, but no one in the family had had a chance to look through the stuff to see whether it was even worth keeping.

The key fit into the lock but the shackle was stuck. I thumped the lock against the sheet-metal door, and it rang like a bell, the sound skipping down the empty hallway. Another thump and it opened.

Storage units have a deep, mute privacy about them. I once followed around an auctioneer who was selling off the contents of units whose renters had fallen behind on their payments. No one was allowed to examine the contents in advance of bidding, and whenever one of the units was opened, it was as riveting and uncomfortable as watching someone's clothes being torn off. We couldn't begin to guess what we would see once the lock was clipped off and the steel door of the unit was rolled away; it might be a bunch of broken dinette chairs; a pile of dirty laundry; a tumble of books, lamps, and knickknacks; or a mountain of gold.

The last few years of Bert's life had been difficult. He was deeply in debt and had no permanent home, so he had to get rid of anything that was not essential to him or was hard to carry around. What he'd held on to was now in front of me, stacked to the ceiling of unit 3482. The room was about the size of a New York City parking space, and it was so crowded that it was difficult to wedge myself in, but I went at it, shoulder first, until I was inside, jammed against a file cabinet. I dug a flashlight out of my pocket and pointed it at the tallest stack of boxes, which had bulged and spread like pancakes under their own weight. I could hear the little bird in the hall whistling a reedy tune as I swept the light over the squashed boxes and their labels, which said "Rin Tin Tin," "Rin Tin Tin," "Rin Tin Tin."

2.

There was a lull in Lee's life between when he and Rinty III made *The Return of Rin Tin Tin* in 1947 and when he met Bert in 1953. In the past, Lee had always lined up the next film or the next publicity tour before he finished the current one. But this time, after they toured, he and Rinty came back to Riverside and stayed.

He spent hours in the Memory Room, where he received visitors and told them stories about the early days with Rin Tin Tin. He also became preoccupied with training his horses. If he was working with one of them and it was time to pick Carolyn up at school, he sometimes went to collect her in a horse-drawn carriage, which she found mortifying.

At that point the Duncans were comfortable but by no means rich. Eva continued to work as a secretary, and they still hadn't been able to afford a new house; it was always on hold, always the thing they would do when Rin Tin Tin had his next big success. So where was that success? *The Return of Rin Tin Tin* had been reasonably profitable and popular, not a blockbuster but not a flop, either; but somehow, nothing happened after it. Lee had a contract with Romay Pictures for a new Rin Tin Tin series, but before the next film was made, the company had shut down after going bankrupt. On film, German shepherds were actually enjoying a resurgence: Harvey, Rex III, Zorro, and Mr. Lucky starred in films in the late 1940s, and a charismatic shepherd named Flame, trained by a young man from North Carolina named Frank Barnes, was playing the lead in three different series.

The movie Lee most wanted to get made was his story — the story of how he had come out of the orphanage, gone to war, found a puppy, and made the puppy a star. It was not really vanity as much as it was a kind of validation, and it was always on his mind. There had been that first false start at Camp Haan; now Lee proposed the story to Everett Freeman, a Hollywood writer who had just completed the screenplays for *The Secret Life of Walter Mitty* and *Jim Thorpe — All-American.* Freeman, intrigued, began working on a film treatment. It looked like the film would go forward, but then Freeman wrote with disappointing news, saying that "the material, thus far, has not developed into a successful dramatization" and he was abandoning the project. (He added that Lee's story had inspired him to write a man-and-his-dog musical with "the makings of a wonderful movie" that could use Rinty in the starring role, but Lee wasn't interested.)

Lee was in his fifties. He wasn't old, but without offering any explanation he told James English that he didn't think he would do any more extended road trips. He might have simply gotten weary of life on the road, but the statement seems to imply something more than that.

At least Lee was giving some thought to the future. Rin Tin Tin III was also no longer young. The dog was seven when *The Return of Rin Tin Tin* was made, and even though he was still active and only slightly past his prime, he was beginning to slow down. Lee designated one of Rin Tin Tin III's pups as the next official Rin Tin Tin. He also seemed to designate his own successor: he began telling people that Carolyn, then just eight years old, would eventually be in charge of the dogs, as if he were also preparing for his own departure from the stage.

3.

The real excitement in the entertainment business at that moment was focused on the new medium of television. The technology had been developed in the late 1920s, but American companies didn't begin mass-producing television sets until after World War II. In the mid-1940s, there were only 17,000 sets in the country, most of them in the Northeast. Then, very suddenly, television got its footing. By 1949, 250,000 new sets were being sold in the United States every month, and more programs were being developed all the time. The first children's show, Bob Emery's *Small Fry Club,* debuted in 1947, and in 1949, *Hopalong*

Cassidy became the first children's show with a western theme. Actor William Boyd, who had started his career as a romantic lead in silent films, played the white-haired Hopalong, a sincere, fatherly cowboy who urged fans to swear to an eight-point creed that included being kind to animals and taking care when crossing streets.

Hopalong Cassidy sprang out of the television in a way movie characters never had: he became merchandise. One million Hop-along Cassidy jackknives were sold in the first ten days they were available. He wore a black shirt, so children's clothing manufacturers, which had always considered black too grim for kids, began producing the shirt in small sizes and sold out of them almost immediately. Along with Hopalong hats, lunchboxes, watches, plates, towels, soap, and dozens of other products, merchandise from the show quickly added up to a $200 million industry.

In Hopalong's wake followed a host of other westerns, including *Sky King; Steve Donovan, Western Marshal; The Gene Autry Show;* and *The Lone Ranger.* At the center of all these shows was a strong but somewhat remote male who handed out perfect justice — an idealized father, in other words, which probably appealed to the generation of youngsters who might have lost a father for a short time, or forever, in the war. Westerns suited a postwar world perfectly: they portrayed a universe in which armed authority solved problems, and in which even good people were capable of violence if violence was called for.

In westerns, the emptiness of the landscape had the unformed, open feel of early America. People were inscrutable strangers or went by nicknames; they had no past and no connections, whether they were orphans or not. The distinction between good and bad was sharply drawn. Westerns put things right with the world. During the war, men were, by necessity, often absent from home and women had new authority. But in a western, the way things had always been was restored, the familiar order reinstated. Men towered over the landscape and women shrank in it, reduced to being tiny decorations. For Americans, a western was a fisheye mirror of a national character; for people in other countries, who consumed these entertainments as quickly as they could be made, a western was the fantasy of rebirth, the past cast away — an inspiring sort of newness, raw and elemental. By the end of the decade, nearly thirty prime-time westerns were in production and westerns accounted for seven of the ten top-ranked shows.

No one had forgotten Rin Tin Tin, but people in the entertainment business wanted to put him on television, not on a movie screen. To counteract the growing influence of television, movies were getting bigger and more spectacular — and less suited to the solemn dog stories that were Rin Tin Tin's specialty. Lee was skeptical; he didn't think much of the new medium. Nevertheless, producers and directors began visiting El Rancho Rin Tin Tin, trying to convince him that television would be an ideal home for Rinty. Michael Curtiz, who had directed *Casablanca* and *Mildred Pierce,* came to call, and wrote a treatment for a Rin Tin Tin television series, which he considered financing himself; nothing came of the project, and it's hard to know whether Lee rejected it or Curtiz decided not to risk his own money. Lee had other suitors: producer Richard Talmadge; director William Collier Jr.; Apex Film Corporation (which ended up producing the Lone Ranger show); Harry Webb, who had produced and directed films at Mascot Pictures; and Chester Franklin, who had directed many of old Rin's films, including *Tough Guy, The Silent*

Accuser, and his first star vehicle, *Where the North Begins.* Another producer, Alfred Seale, wanted to develop a documentary-style show starring Rin Tin Tin — almost like a canine talk show — with Rin Tin Tin as the host and guest spots for, as Seale suggested, "seeing-eye dogs, hero dogs (i.e., a dog who has wakened a family in a burning house), field winners, dogs who have contributed to medical science, etc."

Lee turned them all away. He had always been so committed to keeping Rin Tin Tin in the public eye that his resistance is puzzling. But maybe he was being contrary simply because he felt the right thing hadn't yet come along.

4.

Bert never expected to work in television; he was a film guy. He dismissed television as a fad that would pass or at least never challenge the film business. Bert had come to Hollywood in the late 1940s after graduating from high school, spending a little time at New York University, and serving as a navy fighter pilot in World War II. After the war, he lived for a while in Mexico with his brother, Roger, and once said that he began each day "screwing the six broads" who were living in Roger's house. He loved women; he had a tendency to fall for those who were inappropriate or unavailable. By the time he was in his twenties, he had already been married and divorced.

He was curious about the movie business. His uncle, Nathan Spingold, was on the board of directors at Columbia Pictures, but Bert wanted to make his own way, and he refused to ask Spingold for a job. He moved to Los Angeles and got an entry-level position with Sam Katzman, a producer who went by the nickname Jungle Sam. Katzman was proud to be known as the biggest, crankiest cheapskate in Hollywood. His movies were terrible. One of his affectations was to walk with a cane that had a middle finger carved at one end. Whenever anyone dared to ask him for money, he raised the cane as his answer. Katzman liked Bert and began teaching him the business. No one had ever treated Bert like a son before that. His own father, a traveling salesman, was mostly absent during Bert's childhood. He showed up only when Bert became successful and there was money around to be borrowed.

Where Lee Duncan was a cipher — opaque in his manner and veiled in dreams — Bert was his opposite — bold and brash, carnal, concrete. He was small and broad, with peachy cheeks, a tangle of pitch-black hair, and an impish smile. He was not exactly handsome, but he had a shine in his eyes that captured people. He didn't mind confrontations, and he took pride in firing off argumentative letters to people he disagreed with. In New York's Hell's Kitchen, where he grew up, there were plenty of kids with fast fists, but Bert had the fastest. He boxed with the Catholic Youth Association and never lost a match. Even as a grown man he was always ready for a fight. He once fought an actor, George Maharis, during an audition for Bert's show *Route 66.* Maharis, who was younger and fitter than Bert, lost the bout, but he got the part.

Once Bert began working at Jungle Sam's he was so intrigued by the process of film-making that his preoccupation with women, at least for the moment, receded. Whenever the other young employees at Jungle Sam's invited him to parties, promising Bert that he would end up with a girl or two, he declined. He preferred spending his free time learning how to load the camera or adjust lights. "These other guys hated me because I didn't want to get laid," Bert told a friend. "So that was my introduction to the film business."

In 1949, Bert was promoted unexpectedly while on a film shoot when the production manager dropped dead. Katzman, anxious to keep up with the shooting schedule, asked Bert if he thought he could finish the film — that is, manage it through its completion — and Bert said he could. Over the next four years, he managed the production of eighty more Katzman movies, most of them sensational quickies such as *Killer Ape, Jack McCall Desperado,* and *Sky Commando.* He made himself indispensable to Katzman, who wanted him to stay at the studio forever. To keep Bert from wandering, Katzman gave him an unlimited betting account with the two biggest bookies in Hollywood and an assistant to place and manage his bets. There wasn't a horse race in the country that didn't interest Bert, so he made ample use of Katzman's credit line. But he was not fooled. He knew that Katzman expected him to end up so deeply in debt that he could never quit the job.

5.

A few years ago, during a deposition for one of the many lawsuits that eventually arose concerning the rights to the Rin Tin Tin character, Bert was asked how he first got involved with Rin Tin Tin. The deposition was videotaped, and I came across a copy of it in Bert's storage room. Bert was in his late seventies at the time of the deposition, but his face was still as smooth and round as a kid's, and he was wearing a fashionable collarless shirt. When the lawyer asked him to describe how he got his start with Rin Tin Tin, Bert became impatient. "That's like . . . like saying, how did they build this building," he said, his voice starting to rise.

Bert's relationship with Rin Tin Tin was assembled from so many small bits and pieces and grew to be so essential to him that it was difficult to single out one simple moment when it all began. But at least one such point was the Sunday afternoon in 1953 when Bert drove out to Riverside with a stuntman, Hugh Hooker, who thought Bert and Lee should meet. Bert knew who Rin Tin Tin was; as he later told a reporter, "I was only ten when the original Rin Tin Tin died, but I, like millions of others, never forgot him." Still, he was reluctant. Bert wasn't interested in television, but he was thirty-one years old, he'd already been working in Hollywood for five years, and he wanted more autonomy, regardless of the betting account covered by Jungle Sam.

After thinking it over, he agreed to ride out to Riverside to see what he might see.

Their first few minutes together must have been awkward: Lee, who was certainly wearing his usual cowboy clothes, with maybe a dog or two by his side, maybe holding court in the Memory Room; and Bert, jangling and hurried, young, maybe chewing on one of his favorite cigars, wondering what exactly had brought him out this way. In his later recollections of the meeting, Bert implied that a few of the directors wooing Lee were at the ranch when he and Hooker arrived, so his youth and lack of Hollywood status would have been that much more uncomfortably apparent. Working in Bert's favor was the fact that Lee liked young people and also liked to think he had a talent for recognizing the spark of specialness in an individual. Lee was sure he had discovered that talent with his dogs, and he thought he had the same aptitude with human beings. In Bert he saw something that he liked.

Bert also saw something he liked, and he left the meeting resolved to win Lee's approval. The idea for the show came quickly. "I was shooting something at the Corrigan Movie Ranch for Katzman, and I was thinking about all those directors, all trying to please Lee Duncan so they could get the rights to Rin Tin Tin," Bert told his friend Rob Stone, in a long conversation Stone taped with him before he died. "I took a walk and went up to . . . Fort Apache, and I sat down and had a box lunch, and in about three and a half minutes I had the whole format."

It had dawned on Bert that a military western might be a perfect vehicle for Rin Tin Tin and the story could be a classic setup — a boy, a dog, a man, and a fool, thrown together by circumstance, facing life and its vicissitudes together. Later, he would say that even though his idea was good, "the only genius connected with the show was the dog himself." Bert's genius, though, was in finding the perfect story for Lee.

As Bert envisioned it, the show would be set in Arizona around 1870 — more than forty years before Arizona became a state, when it was still wide-open territory. The boy and his dog would be lone survivors of an Indian raid. A U.S. Cavalry troop, led by a serious and principled lieutenant and a warm but bumbling sergeant, takes the boy and his dog under its wing. The solemn, gallant dog would serve as a canine double for the solemn, gallant lieutenant, and the childish man a foil for the mannish boy who is trying his best to appear grown-up.

Bert scribbled down his idea and convinced Douglas Heyes, a screenwriter, to work on it with him. "We put together a whole presentation the following weekend and went out to see Lee," Bert told Rob Stone. "And Lee being a flyer, an army man, he loved my idea of the cavalry, and he said, I'm going to do this with you. He was a flyer and I was a flyer, so we had that in common. He said, I'll do it, and I said, how much do you want? He told me ten percent and I said it sounded okay. I made the deal right there. We shook hands. He never wanted to sign another contract. He said, Bert, you've got my handshake." Bert gave him ten dollars to make their agreement official.

The show was called *The Adventures of Rin-Tin-Tin.* (Bert hyphenated the name, just as Lee had, although Lee usually didn't capitalize each part of the name.) The title focused attention on the dog, even though the show was, in fact, an ensemble piece, and Rinty was actually less central to the story than the boy, who was called Johnny in the proposal. Bert said the range of subjects that could be explored in the show was "limitless," and he included a dozen suggestions for episodes involving long-lost gold mines, Apache coyote gods, land-grabbers, kidnappings, battles with Comanches, and outlaw gangs. For some reason, the stories came naturally to him, even though he was neither a Westerner nor a dog person. He just liked thinking up narratives. "God must have given me this thing for stories," he liked to say. "I always thought a story had to have a point, and it had to have great feeling, and it had to grab you in the first minutes with some kind of feeling and excitement. And I could do that." Lee liked the military theme and western setting, but what must have appealed to him the most was the story of an orphan boy and his dog.

The official Rin Tin Tin was no longer Rin Tin Tin III. Instead, it was Rin Tin Tin IV, the "bundle of fur" that James English mentioned toward the end of his book. Rinty IV had been a very young puppy when his father, Rinty III, came home from Camp Haan. The anointing of the puppy as the primary dog at El Rancho Rin Tin Tin took place without any fanfare or notice. Rinty III was born in 1941, so by 1953 he would have been an elderly dog, perhaps retired, or he might have already died.

There was no mention of the changing of the guard, which seems to indicate that Lee finally appreciated the power of Rinty's legacy. With the fourth generation of Rin Tin Tins coming to the public's attention, Lee knew that he had created something that meant more than any individual dog or moment — something with a kind of elastic reality. The intensity of his connection with old Rin was so special that all the dogs that followed merged in Lee's mind into one dog — one vessel for containing and carrying forward what old Rin had begun. When old Rin was alive, Lee never talked about a succession, almost as if he didn't dare mention the possibility that Rin Tin Tin would die. Now he prepared for it; he let it be known that while Rin Tin Tin IV was the current standard-bearer, three more Rin Tin Tins were being readied and there would not be disruption. He would make sure that there would always be a Rin Tin Tin.

Lee realized that drawing attention to each new incarnation of Rin Tin Tin made the continuity less seamless. Instead, one dog now just gave way to the next, quietly and completely, as if they lived in a universe that had managed to exist outside the boundaries of time.

6.

Bert drafted a formal description for the show and flew to New York to meet with television executives. After explaining that the half-hour series would feature "the famous motion picture dog, Rin-Tin-Tin," the proposal continued: "In contemplating any television series (or any project in the business world) one must first ask himself: WHY? Why, then, a TV series on the adventures of a *dog* — even one with so celebrated and memorable a moniker as Rin-Tin-Tin?" The show was aimed at children. They would love it, Bert explained, because they all go through a phase during which they devote all their affection to "some dog — the only creature with whom [they] can share unselfish loyalty and complete, wordless understanding."

The next section of the proposal was a surprise. It began, "A child's grief over the loss of his dog is the most monumental sorrow he will ever experience." Could Bert have written that? Could he even have thought such a thing? He grew up in New York City, without a dog. The paragraph continued: "After that [loss], he is prepared for anything that growing-up may do to him. A child and his dog together, enjoy the most rewarding of companionships — one which is never topped for pure rapport again in this life." My guess is that Lee wrote this, or maybe he had told Bert about losing his pet lamb and his first dog.

The next section seems to be in Bert's voice again: "Today, many kids aren't privileged to know this great and intimate experience. City-living, apartment-dwelling, the pace of a mechanized era, all make it increasingly tough on the old child-and-dog relationship. . . . Rin Tin Tin is the most famous name in the dog world. In this proposed TV series, he represents the ultimate of those noble characteristics which every kid attributes to his OWN dog — or which every luckless, dog-less kid cherishes for the pooch he hopes to have some day. As the ideal dog, therefore, he is the natural idol of every kid, with or without a dog — and as such is a powerful magnet for TV viewers of ALL AGES." Along with Rin Tin Tin, the show would feature "a rugged kid of the proper age: nine or ten years old" and, as the lieutenant, someone "clean-cut, virile, and dynamically right in his estimate and handling of any situation. Second, he must be attractive to women but *not* unduly attracted *to* any women he may meet in his adventures." There would be action: "We'll supply it in large quantities." Bert, who would produce the show, described himself with some hyperbole. "There is no film-maker in Hollywood who has been so importantly identified with the production of such a vast number of motion pictures during the last seven years — or indeed, in *any* similar period in Hollywood history." He included Lee in the proposal as well; Lee was "the real star of the series, the man *behind* the dog . . . his remarkable owner and trainer . . . a pioneer of the motion-picture industry . . . His reputation as Rin Tin Tin's trainer and manager has made his a name of distinction in the Hollywood scene."

The executives at Screen Gems, the tele-vision arm of Columbia Pictures, loved the proposal and told Bert they wanted twenty-six episodes as soon as possible. They expected to syndicate the show — that is, to sell it to individual stations rather than to a national network. A network show had more impact and more prestige than a syndicated one, but in 1953 there were only four major television networks — CBS, NBC, ABC, and the DuMont Television Network, which was one of the very first but would be out of business by 1956. Screen Gems didn't expect to attract a major advertiser — the prerequisite for a network show. The best such hope had been Quaker Oats, the parent company of Lee's old supporter, Ken-L-Ration, but it passed because it was already committed to another animal show called *Zoo Parade*.

Bert and screenwriter Douglas Heyes wrote four scripts and sent them to Screen Gems. The executives were not pleased. "They said, we've read your scripts and we, collectively, think they stink," Bert recalled. "And I said, Yeah? Obviously I don't agree. And they said, What are these, morality plays? And I said, I don't know what you're planning on making, but that's what I'm making. They said I was wrong, and I said, I don't think I'm wrong — it's got action, it's got people, it's got the dog, and that's what it should be. And they said, You're going to go against our seven combined years of experience? And I said, Yeah, if I listen to you and I fail I've learned nothing. If I go my way, I learn something. I'm the best fucking production manager in the business — you think I need you guys? Forget the contract — I'm out the door."

The executives called his uncle, Nate Spingold, the head of Columbia Pictures, to tell him they thought Bert was crazy and that Spingold needed to straighten him out. "Nate said, Send me the scripts, let me have a look," Bert recalled. "Nate reads them and says, These are brilliant, you Screen Gems guys are crazy. And that was the end of the discussion. That was the last bullshit I ever heard, but from that point on those Screen Gems guys hated me."

Despite their doubts about attracting a major sponsor, Screen Gems showed the scripts to the head of Kenyon & Eckhart, a large advertising agency in New York, before selling the show in syndication. To Screen Gems' surprise, the agency liked the show and suggested that Nabisco, which manufactured Shredded Wheat cereal as well as Milk-Bone dog biscuits, might be interested in sponsoring it. After looking over the proposal and scripts, Nabisco agreed. The only stipulation was that Bert guarantee the show would contain no crime, violence, sex, or tasteless material; nothing "critical, contemptuous or scornful of the United States of America"; and no scenes showing cast members eating competitors' products — especially zweiback crackers and "edible ice cream holders." In addition, Rin Tin Tin could never be shown eating ordinary pieces of meat, since that would compete with the prepared dog foods Nabisco manufactured.

Bert agreed, and with Nabisco on board, ABC decided to buy the show. It would air on Friday nights at 7:30 p.m. on every station in the ABC network.

In 1954, a new television show was something special, an event, announced with flourish. A show starring Rin Tin Tin was even bigger news because of the dog's heritage. He was, in the words of many press releases and news stories, "the first fourth-generation Hollywood star in history." As the Associated Press story put it, "The fabulous Rin Tin Tin is ready to romp to what may be his greatest fame — as a television star. When [the show begins] a new generation will be watching the heroics of a star that thrilled their parents a couple of decades ago." The television columnist for the *Los Angeles Mirror* wrote, "Rin Tin Tin IV is carrying on the family tradition, set to bark on television in a series all his own."

Except for DuMont, ABC was the smallest of the networks, with only 40 affiliates, compared to NBC's 164 and CBS's 113. But ABC was on the way up. In the spring of 1954 the network was in the spotlight, thanks to the Army-McCarthy hearings, the Senate's investigation into whether Communist-hunting Senator Joseph Mc-

Carthy had meddled improperly in the army's treatment of one of his staff members. CBS and NBC, expecting the Senate hearings to be tedious, ran only evening recaps, while ABC, which had little other daytime programming, decided to broadcast the full proceedings live. As it turned out, the Army-McCarthy hearings were fiery and theatrical and drew millions of new viewers to the network.

In addition to *The Adventures of Rin-Tin-Tin,* that fall ABC was introducing a number of new shows: the first telecast of the *Miss America Pageant,* with Bess Myerson and John Daly hosting; bandleader Lawrence Welk's musical variety show; and a program called *Disneyland,* produced by Disney Studios to coincide with the opening of its first amusement park, in Anaheim, California.

Bert came back from New York thrilled by the reception the show had received, but dreading one remaining bit of business — quitting his job. Katzman did not take the news well; after Bert told him, he chased him out of his office. "He was pissed at me until about two weeks before he died," Bert later recalled. "I was at the race track and I ran into him. He looked shitty. I said, Sam, you can't die until you make up with me. He was my mentor, my father. I couldn't let him die still being mad."

In a sense, leaving Katzman and taking on the Rin Tin Tin legacy from Lee, Bert was trading one father for another. Katzman was more of a mentor, but Lee became the person Bert respected and felt indebted to, and with whom he shared a new devotion. His presence in Lee's life was just as profound for Lee, who never had a son, never had a brother, and never knew his father. Lee was entrusting Bert with his life's work; Bert was the heir he had hoped he would find. Somehow he forgot that he'd promised his daughter that role. Carolyn remembers her father announcing to her that Bert was "coming in" — his precise phrasing. I thought it an odd way of describing what was happening, although on second thought, it seemed fitting; it was as if Lee was trying to say that Bert was "coming in" to the family, which is what it felt like to him — much more than an ordinary business arrangement. Carolyn also remembers how keen Lee was about Bert. "He said, Bert is a really nice young man, he has a young family, and he's going to do wonders throughout his career, and he's going to make a lot of movies and promote Rin Tin

Tin from here on out."

When Bert entered the Duncans' lives, Carolyn was fourteen, edging toward adulthood; she had always been half in the shadow of the dogs and now she was in the shadow of this newcomer from Hollywood, who in an instant had stepped into a role she had strived for ever since she could remember. Even now, a grown woman with children and grandchildren, her face crumples when she talks about her father and Bert, how "their visions joined into what it would be, what it could be." She talks about it with a quiet weariness, an emotion rubbed smooth, the sort of feeling that comes from having worked very hard to forget that something once hurt very much. "I saw my role with Rin Tin Tin really fading," she said. "I knew that I — that I wouldn't be part of it." She never really felt close to her father again.

7.

The cast of *The Adventures of Rin-Tin-Tin* was assembled in early 1954. Ten-year-old Lee Aaker filled the important role of the boy, who was still known as "Johnny" in early drafts of the scripts, although Bert was considering "Dusty" and "Rusty" as alternative names. Aaker, whose mother owned a dancing school in Los Angeles, was a small, sturdy kid with floppy hair, a snub nose, and a wide face that looked as soft as putty. He had been acting professionally since he was eight years old. He costarred in several major films, including *High Noon, Greatest Show on Earth,* and *Hondo,* and at the time of the audition had just finished shooting an episode of *Ford Television Theater,* "And Suddenly, You Knew," starring Ronald Reagan.

For the role of Lieutenant Rip Masters, Bert wanted Richard Denning, a veteran actor who had starred in *The Creature from the Black Lagoon.* Denning was unavailable. Instead, the role went to a former professional tennis player from Texas named James Brown — classically handsome, tall and deep-voiced and dark-haired, with a flash of white teeth and a strong chin. Joe Sawyer, a character actor with a mashed, meaty face, was cast as softhearted Sergeant Biff O'Hara. Rand Brooks — Scarlett O'Hara's weakling husband Charles Hamilton in *Gone with the Wind* — was cast as Corporal Boone.

Lee was asked to train and direct the dog, but he decided against it. The long hours in Los Angeles didn't suit him anymore. He seemed content mentoring Frank Barnes, the trainer who was then hired for the job. What he cared about more was having his dog in the show. This Rinty was big and blond with a saddle of dark fur, an aquiline nose, and a bright, beckoning look in his eyes. He was only two years old, but Lee had spent long afternoons at the ranch training him and thought he was camera-ready. Lee also had prepared a cousin of Rinty's, Rin Tin Tin II (the nonsequential numbering was done by the AKC), and another named Hey You, to use as Rinty's stand-in. When Hey You was a puppy, he had been pecked in the eye by a chicken and was left with a noticeable scar. But he was good at snapping and snarling on command, and Lee thought he'd be perfect for fight scenes.

One afternoon, as the show was in pre-production, Lee brought Rinty to the set for Bert to see. He ran Rinty through a series of commands and did a scene. Bert watched him and was dismayed. He wasn't a dog person, but he knew what he wanted, and it wasn't Rinty IV.

Sam Manners, the production manager for *The Adventures of Rin-Tin-Tin,* had been present when Lee brought Rinty IV to audition. Manners is one of the few people who worked on the show who is still alive. When I talked to him at his home in Los Angeles recently, I asked him what exactly was the problem with Rinty IV. He looked at me for a long moment and then started laughing.

"Why didn't we use him?" he repeated, cupping an ear toward me. "Why? I'll tell you why." He settled back in his chair. Then he said, "We could never use Duncan's dog because it was stupid. It couldn't do anything! Bert almost died when he saw that Lee's dog just couldn't do a thing."

Rinty IV stupid? I knew that old Rin was short-tempered and Junior was inept, but I was astonished to hear Rinty described as stupid; it was hard to believe that Lee would have presented a dog that wasn't up to the job, especially because he could have chosen another one of his dogs if the one he had anointed as Rin Tin Tin wasn't working out. I decided to ask Manners to elaborate, thinking he might have confused a dog or two — after all, the audition took place fifty years ago. But he insisted that he remembered like it was yesterday. A few weeks later, I was talking to one of the show's stuntmen, Max Kleven, and he repeated what Manners had said — Rinty IV just wasn't good enough to star on the show.

Bert decided to use one of Frank Barnes's dogs: a cream-and-black German shepherd whose father, Flame, had been a movie standout in the 1940s and early 1950s. Bert thought that Flame Jr., whom everyone called by the initials JR, was "absolutely brilliant." Bert told Rob Stone that, on command, Flame could open a specific drawer in a file cabinet, take out whatever object he had been told to retrieve, and deliver that object to whomever he was told to give it to.

Sometime after that excruciating audition, Bert informed Lee that he was going to use JR as the main actor in the show, and that another one of Barnes's dogs, Blaze, would be his double most of the time. Hey You would be used in the fight scenes. As for Rinty IV, Bert said he would be used occasionally, although there was no specific role for him. Most of all, Rin Tin Tin would receive fans of the show who wanted to visit El Rancho Rin Tin Tin. It was as if he were being made the king in a constitutional monarchy — the embodiment of the character, but with nothing much to do. "This Rin is a ranch dog," Eva Duncan told a reporter for *The New Yorker* in an interview that year, which sounded as if she was acknowledging that living on the ranch was in fact his main job.

Throughout the run of the show, the matter of not using Lee's dog was handled gingerly. In 1958, Rin Tin Tin was nominated for a PATSY Award, the animal equivalent of an Oscar. The awards ceremony and gala at the Ambassador Hotel was going to be hosted by Roy Rogers's horse, Trigger. (The previous year's hosts were actors Piper Laurie and Ronald Reagan, and the PATSY went to Francis the Mule.) Before the event, Bert's secretary sent him a note saying that Lee Aaker and his mother planned to attend, as did Lee and Eva Duncan, and Frank Barnes and his wife, Pauline. For the ceremony itself, a dog — a Rin Tin Tin, whether factual or fictional — had to be present. "As it stands now," the secretary wrote, "JR will be the dog — but you can understand the abyss over which we tread on this question."

Lee never discussed Bert's decision not to use Rinty IV, and he never wrote about it. It might have been so disappointing for him that he chose to push it out of his mind. Maybe he hadn't trained Rinty as well as he thought he had. He had certainly begun to accept the idea that Rin Tin Tin had become something different from a single dog. In fact, the exact definition of who Rin Tin Tin actually was had gotten a little muddled. There was the character on the television show, who was named Rin Tin Tin; there was the dog, Rin Tin Tin, who was living at the ranch in Riverside; and there were Frank Barnes's dogs, who played Rin Tin Tin on the show. In truth, they were all part of the legacy now. They were a repertory company of animals filling an identity that the public knew as Rin Tin Tin. Whichever dog showed up to put his paw print on headshots, to meet kids at a county fair — that dog was Rin Tin Tin for that moment. No public acknowledgment of the array of dogs that appeared as Rin Tin Tin was ever made.

Lee's connection to Rinty IV was nothing like the one he had had with old Rin, which would have made this disappointment easier to bear. His feelings about Rin Tin Tin IV are actually hard to gauge. I never found anything in his papers about the dog at all — nothing extolling his particular talent or abilities and nothing referring to Lee's work with him. What I did find was an interview Lee gave to a small California newspaper in 1954. Under the headline, "Rin Tin Tin Discoverer Still Hopes for Dog as Great as Ancestor," the reporter quoted Lee saying,

"I have spent a fortune breeding Rinty's progeny with dogs I thought might duplicate all of Rinty's great characteristics . . . but there is always something missing." The story continued,

> With his memories and his hopes, his scrap books and mementos, Duncan resides amid a living memorial to the famed canine star, who could leap almost like an antelope and mug for the cameras almost like a human being. . . . One small building at his ranch is a Rinty I museum. There's an assortment of framed citations and photos on the walls and on tables are the mementos. There is a story in back of each one and Duncan takes great delight in relating them.

Lee never wavered in his belief that there would always be a Rin Tin Tin. But at this point he accepted that there would never be another single, singular Rin Tin Tin — there would never be another battlefield puppy found by luck and chance, who by luck and chance had his life transformed into a wonderful odyssey. There would never be another dog he traveled with through the Sierras as a young man, alone. And Lee would never be that young man again. The idea of the dog had now fanned out to include all these other dogs. Lee must have agreed with Bert's opinion about Rinty IV, or at least he made his peace with it. Soon after the dog's disastrous audition, Lee signed an amendment to his contract with Bert that included the phrase "Flame, the dog which does all the work for Rin Tin Tin . . ."

8.

As soon as the cast was assembled, Bert shot the pilot episode of *The Adventures of Rin-Tin-Tin* and shipped the film to New York, where Screen Gems could preview it for potential advertisers. The sales brochure promised "clean action entertainment and outstanding merchandising plusses for juvenile audiences." It continued:

A screenful of human interest in every show: a heartwarming series about Rin Tin Tin . . . the most famous canine of all time!

A heroic boy, Rusty (Lee Aaker), the companion and partner of Rin Tin Tin

Dramatic conflict of Man vs. Nature, with raging rivers, forest fires, mine explosions, wild animals and Indian warfare . . .

Rin Tin Tin's personality, not unlike the Fairbankses and Barrymores, has *outlived time and medium* . . .

Rin Tin Tin is cast in an environment in which the fullest advantage is taken of this dog's almost human intelligence. . . . There is none of the artificiality of the environment of an FBI-dog or an atomic spy dog, stalking the city streets or flying jet planes. There is no sex element, nor any influence which will in any way detract from the wholesomeness of the action.

MERCHANDISING OPPORTUNITIES BETTER THAN EVER WITH RIN TIN TIN. Manufacturers put in their bids for a license in anticipation of what is considered one of the hottest merchandising propositions in the field today. . . . Their enthusiasm is based upon one premise: that Rin Tin Tin is a pre-sold character! There is no question of biding their time to see if Rin Tin Tin catches on — Rin Tin Tin caught on a long time ago!

The final page of the brochure featured a haiku-like description of the show:

The *majesty* of the rugged frontier . . .

The *magic* of the most famous name in dogdom . . .

The *mystery* of an almost human animal intelligence . . .

The *magnetism* of a small boy's engaging personality . . .

The *merriment* of the good old days in an Army Cavalry fort . . .

The *magnificence* of Nature's tests and trials for men . . . all . . . in the greatest selling medium of our time

The head of sales reported back to Bert with good news:

Friskies, the dog food product — anxious to purchase the show. Henri, Hurst, and McDonald, representing Armour Meats: agency EXTREMELY excited about show. Several brand-advertising managers have seen show and are highly enthusiastic regarding it. Dancer, Fitzgerald: On basis of reaction have second screening for Peter Paul Mounds executive. Very good possibility that Chunkies will purchase about 8 markets. BBD&O: Had excellent screening for top broadcasting executives. Nestle: Had meeting with VP in charge of advertising. Enthusiastic but account just renewed *Space Patrol.*

Bert wanted to shoot *The Adventures of Rin-Tin-Tin* in color. In the proposal, he wrote, "Color TV is no longer a distant dream, but will generally be available in the *immediate* future." He was a little ahead of history. In 1954, color television was still quite unusual. The technology had existed for decades but was being adopted slowly. The very first color show in the United States — the Tournament of Roses parade — had only just been broadcast, on New Year's Day of 1954. Almost all the 30 million televisions in the country were black-and-white. Even ten years later, in 1964, less than 5 percent of Americans who owned televisions had color sets.

Screen Gems wanted to make *The Adventures of Rin-Tin-Tin* on the cheap; color was out of the question. Bert had learned to keep a tight budget from his years working for Sam Katzman, but Screen Gems wanted an even tighter budget, hoping to spend no more than $50,000 per episode, which was $5,000 less than Bert proposed. The studio suggested that the number of extras and background players could be reduced if the actors were thought of as interchangeable. Instead of having one actor play a cavalry officer, another play a Comanche brave, and another play a townsperson, why not have one actor play all three? According to Screen Gems, children wouldn't notice if a familiar-looking face started to pop up in different and even contradictory roles. That's what makeup was for. If different characters who were played by the same actor needed to interact with each other, it could be solved with camera angles. Shoot one side of the fight or conversation, and then change costumes, change camera angles, and shoot the other one.

Bert had to try to make it work. Each extra was issued a complete set of costumes — a cavalry uniform, a Native American deer hide suit, and a pair of britches and a muslin shirt for playing a local citizen — and was told to bring all three costumes to the set every day. The cast was constantly changing costumes. At one point, they ran out of dressing rooms and someone draped a couple of tarps over a rope stretched between two trees to accommodate the frequent changes. The cast of twelve worked constantly. "They'd be playing an Indian one minute and a trooper the next," Sam Manners recalled, chuckling as he described it. "We cheated with the camera angles. We sometimes had the same person killing himself."

The fight over whether or not the show would be in color was just a beginning: Bert clashed with the studio about almost everything. At one point I started a file called "Bert's Conflicts with Screen Gems Etc." just to organize the angry letters and telegrams I had come across. It is amazing that Bert did produce the show, considering how often he threatened to quit. I could have started a second file with notes in which he announced to Screen Gems that "this will be our last year together" or "I will be discussing terminating our contract with my lawyer" or variations thereof.

I don't think he was bluffing. He had absolute confidence in himself, and he bristled anytime he was reminded that he was a young man producing his first television series who had to answer to senior executives. In general, the studio's involvement struck him as an insult. "THEY have final script approval? THEY have final production approval?" he scribbled in a note to himself after a phone call with Screen Gems. "In any artistic or production dispute they have final say? Then I might as well be an EMPLOYEE." He complained to his uncle Nate Spingold that the executives at

Screen Gems "talked down" to him and that it was "becoming more and more difficult to live with these people."

In 1954, however, studios were still supreme in Hollywood. Writers and directors and, to some degree, actors, were viewed as fungible goods, easy to move around as needed and ultimately replaceable. That year, François Truffaut published his essay "A Certain Tendency in French Cinema," which counterpunched, arguing that directors were the true authors of their films, the way writers were the authors of their books. In Hollywood, as of 1954, the "auteur" theory hadn't yet changed most minds, but Bert embraced it. He was fearless and determined when it came to his show, entirely possessive of it, which he made clear in memos, letters, phone calls, telegrams, and personal confrontations. Sam Manners bubbled over with stories of Bert's quarrels and altercations, and after he finished telling me several of them, he leaned back in his chair and sighed. Then he brightened and said, "Ah, Bert. I loved him. He antagonized everyone he ever knew."

Bert was especially affronted whenever his judgment was questioned. He sparred regularly with the two Briskin brothers, Irving and Fred, who were among Screen Gems' top executives and were supervising *The Adventures of Rin-Tin-Tin.* Before filming even began, the Briskin brothers questioned Bert's choice of Douglas Heyes as the show's head writer. Bert was furious. He pounded out a note that made quick mention of Heyes's qualifications and then launched into what he considered the real problem: the Briskins' disrespect. "I have spent seven months thinking and creating this show. . . . I am not an amateur in making pictures. I will always take advice — to accept or reject at my own discretion." The note apparently took Irving Briskin aback. He replied, "BERT LEONARD: I don't like the tone of this note and think it is entirely uncalled for — maybe we three had better meet and get things settled quickly. . . . You haven't got a DIME in these pictures & I want to protect my money." In a note, after yet another of Bert's inflammatory memos, Briskin scolded, "Bert, I think we'll all be better off in the future if you stop making federal cases out of ordinary suggestions." One of Bert's grievance letters was sent back to him with no reply, except for a comment from Fred Briskin, scribbled in thick black pencil in the right margin, which said, "BERT: What can you accomplish by writing a letter like this other than make an enemy?"

He tangled most frequently with Ralph Cohn, the founder of Screen Gems and the nephew of Harry Cohn, the head of Columbia Pictures. Cohn was only a few years older than Bert, but he wore his seniority with a flourish. He was involved with *The Adventures of Rin-Tin-Tin* from the beginning and paid scrupulous attention to the show's every detail. Bert sent his first belligerent memo to Cohn just one week after Screen Gems had decided to make the show, following a perceived slight of which there is no record. "I personally feel that my ability to see this series through to a successful conclusion is *not* to be questioned," Bert wrote. "The fact that I have an open mind and am willing to discuss and incorporate certain of your suggestions does not mean that I am willing to subjugate my thinking on this series to anyone's. This is *my* show and I intend to run it."

He was right to feel that Cohn had reservations about him. In February 1954, Bert had gotten hold of a letter Cohn had written to Irving Briskin criticizing two scripts for the show. Cohn complained to Briskin that even though there was nothing "actually wrong" with the scripts, he thought they were "inadequate." For instance, he noted, the show lacked a trademark phrase — "in the sense that 'Hi Yo, Silver!' is a trademark of the Lone Ranger," as Cohn put it — even though he had asked Bert to develop some. He didn't like that the "Apache Chief" episode began with a scene of Apache warriors and "The Education of Corporal Rusty" with a scene of Rip Masters. He wanted the show to always open with Rin Tin Tin.

He urged Briskin to make sure Bert kept the focus on Rin Tin Tin. "The dog is the most interesting element in the series," Cohn wrote. "His actions, smartness, and relationship to the characters should be accentuated throughout." He wanted more scenes "in which the dog is involved purely for entertainment, and which demonstrate its extraordinary intelligence." Cohn went on: "[Rin Tin Tin] should be developed much more fully as a character which the kid audience will come to love for his talents, and will try to emulate with their own dogs. I asked for bits of business between the boy and dog which would make every kid in the audience envy our boy and try to imitate him."

Cohn also wanted to cut several items, which he listed for Briskin:

1. Scenes in which children in the stories are subjected to undue horror or fright. In the Indian script, the children's lives are threatened by the Indians. Large advertisers, intensely aware of PTA, Child Guidance Groups, etc. . . . will not buy a program to which these groups object. 2. Overlong, pointless dialogue scenes. 3. Western-type dialogue. Heyes maintained that it was Southern more than Western, but I asked for avoidance of it. 4. Lines and words in lines that were over the heads of children. Example: 'Disembowel potatoes' in one script.

In closing, Cohn said he thought Bert needed guidance "in almost every detail." He mentioned that Bert was planning to have the boy "ride a cute white mule" in the show. Cohn hated the idea and said he had pointed out to Bert that a white mule — even a cute white mule — "would not represent the wish fulfillment of every boy or girl in the audience." He wanted the boy to ride "a beautifully marked Indian Pinto pony."

The letter, with its prickly tone and fixation on minutiae, could have been topped only by one thing: the sight of Bert Leonard and Ralph Cohn — both New Yorkers, both opinionated, bossy, and blunt — actually facing off on a Hollywood soundstage in early 1954 over the question of whether an orphan on the Great Plains in 1870 would be more likely to ride an Indian pinto pony or a cute white mule.

Bert's injuries were not all narcissistic. He loved the characters he had created for *The Adventures of Rin-Tin-Tin* and felt protective of them. Ralph Cohn was in charge of overseeing the radio version of *The Adventures of Rin-Tin-Tin,* which was meant to complement the television show. The radio show, in Bert's opinion, was a disaster; he thought the scripts were weak and the actor playing Rin Tin Tin was "way off on his barking." He made sure to let Cohn know his opinion. After reviewing one of the scripts, Bert wrote, "I can only tell you, Ralph, that this is one of the most miserable jobs of writing I have ever encountered. . . . The writing is unimaginative and the relationship of the people are foreign to the way they are being handled on the TV show. If action on these points is not forthcoming immediately, I will have to turn this matter over to [my lawyer] to protect my interest."

Just a few weeks later, Cohn told Bert that he thought Rusty should mention "Ivanhoe" during a radio episode. Bert was as aghast at this suggestion as Cohn had been at his plans for the cute white mule. His note to Cohn pointed out that "Rusty . . . living at Fort Apache and having no schooling or education, would know nothing about Ivanhoe or the Crusades." Then, for good measure, he added, "Ralph, you told me you were closely supervising creation and adaption of the radio show. Yet character relationships and treatment of the dog do not follow in line with established and proven thinking. For example, Rin Tin Tin would not sleep under the barracks but [would be] quartered in Rusty's room, as every kid knows. And Rin Tin Tin does not growl or menace Rusty under any circumstances. Rip Masters does not consider taking a razor strop to the boy. In all situations the boy and dog are treated with the dignity they deserve for the heroes they are." Satisfied that he had made his points to Cohn, he signed off, "Anxiously awaiting your answer."

In early spring Bert was scrambling to settle all the details of the show so they could begin shooting; he and his wife, Willetta, also had their first baby, a boy they named Steven. Names were an issue elsewhere in his life. Even though Bert had decided to call the boy in the show Rusty, Irving Briskin infuriatingly persisted in referring to the character as Dusty and then, suddenly, told Bert that he wanted the boy to be called Dakota Bill. Briskin also was concerned about how the dog would be addressed. Would he be Rin Tin Tin? Rinty? Just Rin? Even though this was a decision Bert undoubtedly would have considered his to make, Briskin announced, in a memo to Bert, "I am cautioning you here not to use the name 'Rin Tin Tin' when it is spoken, particularly by Dusty. Never have him call him anything other than 'Rinty,' and please avoid the use of people calling him 'Rin.' By those who do not know him, such as strangers, they can refer to him as 'Rin Tin Tin,' but immediately people around him should call him only 'Rinty.' "

They still hadn't settled on a catchphrase — the "trademark" that Rusty/Dusty/Dakota Bill would always say to the dog, that they hoped would become as popular as "Hi-yo Silver!" In his first draft, writer Douglas Heyes used the phrase "Go get 'em, Rinty!" but Irving Briskin — who seemed to relish criticizing Heyes — found it objectionable. "DON'T LIKE THIS" he scrawled across a copy of the script. "IT'S ORDINARY. MAYBE 'FIGHT, RINTY!', OR 'TROUBLE, RINTY!' " He also attached a longer note, full of sharp remarks. "We have agreed that this would not be the expression we would use. We feel that you should get something better than that, like 'Fight 'em, Rinty' . . . or something other than an ordinary expression like 'go get 'em.' . . . I would also call your attention to what I call sloppy writing. You are going to try in one scene to have the Major walk in and call attention, you are going to have Dusty dive into a footlocker, you are going to have O'Hara rush across the aisle and open up another footlocker, you are going to have Rinty jump into a footlocker, then you are going to have O'Hara jump to attention. All of this in one scene! This is bad script writing and you are only kidding yourself. Again, I would like to warn you this is a story of a dog and a boy. I am not interested in the adults."

Bert told Briskin that he and Heyes had tried out all sorts of catchphrases, including "Charge 'em, Rinty!"; "Attack 'em, Rinty!"; "Fight 'em, Rinty!"; "Trouble, Rinty!"; "Forward, Rinty!"; and "Go, Rinty!" Then he remembered a cavalry expression, "Yo-ho!" which was used as a call to the troops if a bugle wasn't available. He liked the sound of it. "This could be used as 'Yo-ho, Rinty!' " Bert wrote. "I still personally like 'Go get 'em, Rinty!' because I think it has a certain rhythm and drive, and at the same time its literal meaning encompasses all the various actions into which he might be sent. However I am open to suggestions on this matter." Everyone loved "Yo-ho, Rinty!" and Heyes was instructed to delete "Go get 'em, Rinty!" and replace it with "Yo-ho, Rinty!" in every script.

Now they needed only to figure out a short "signature" sequence that would open every episode. After hours of tinkering, Bert finally had a forty-five-second opening that he was sure would "act as a calling card to all the kids to come and watch Rin Tin Tin." The troops would line up for inspection. Then Rusty and Rinty would squeeze their way into the line and salute along with the troops. Bert thought it would be charming to see the dog and the boy — half as tall as the other troops — in formation, trying hard to look grown-up and serious and, in the case of the dog, human. Bert sent Cohn a script for the sequence, which came to be one of the most recognizable openings on television for years:

A. CLOSEUP RIN-TIN-TIN

— in a big head-and-shoulder close-up against a simple sky background. Over this: BUGLE CALL BEGINS

EXT. INSIDE FORT APACHE STOCKADE
— DAY

B. ANGLE TOWARD BARRACKS WITH BUGLE IN FOREGROUND

— as Troopers pile out of the doors, carrying rifles — dashing toward camera the one-shot formation, filling the screen

C. ANGLE ON CATWALK UP TO RIN-TIN-TIN

D. MEDIUM SHOT AT STABLE AREA — RUSTY

— a rugged kid of eight or nine, coming from b.g. to f.g. carrying a much too large army saddle, puts it hastily on a saddle rack, and rushes toward the o.s. formation. He wears a makeshift cavalry uniform and a cavalry hat. Over this: SUPERIMPOSE:

(Title)

WITH RUSTY "B-COMPANY"

E. ANGLE ON RIN-TIN-TIN

As he leaps from the high catwalk to an army wagon below, thence to a rock, and finally hits the ground running.

CAMERA HOLDS on him as he, too, dashes for the formation

F. MEDIUM FULL SHOT
as Rin-Tin-Tin reaches the empty place in line, and sits up at attention next to Rusty.

G. TWO SHOT RIN-TIN-TIN AND RUSTY
At attention. (Bugle call has stopped.)

> VOICE
> Eyes — right!

After introducing Masters and O'Hara, the sequence comes to a close:

Music hits a climax as we SUPERIM-POSE:
(Title Card #1)
AND *STARRING*
(Title Card #2)
RIN-TIN-TIN
FADE OUT.
INSERT FIRST COMMERCIAL

9.

Bert had suggested to Screen Gems that he shoot in Mexico to save money, but it was decided that the show would be filmed at Corriganville Movie Ranch, a two-thousand-acre spread in the valley north of Hollywood, near the Santa Susana Pass. In

1954, the ranch's owner was Ray "Crash" Corrigan, a stuntman and actor with credits in such movies as *Bela Lugosi Meets a Brooklyn Gorilla* (he played the gorilla) and *Captive Wild Woman* (he played an ape). Corrigan bought the land in 1936 after being told that there was Spanish treasure buried on it. He never found treasure, but he soon realized that the ranch — studded with cactus and rock and pocked with caves and pools — was a classic western landscape and close enough to the studios in town to be an ideal movie location.

The studios began using the ranch regularly; Corrigan also opened part of it to the public as a sort of western-themed amusement park (out-of-work actors performed gunfights and brawls for entertainment). John Ford used Corriganville for his classic film *Fort Apache.* Howard Hughes built a Corsican village set on it for filming *Vendetta.* Gentle, vaguely medical pornographic films known as "figure studies" were shot in a section of the ranch known as Silvertown. Sam Katzman shot dozens of films at Corriganville, so Bert knew the ranch well. For *The Adventures of Rin-Tin-Tin,* he took over the Fort Apache section of Corriganville, not far from the spot where he first came up with his idea for the show. At the same time, on other parts of the ranch, *Lassie, The Lone Ranger,* and *Have Gun Will Travel* were being filmed as well.

The business of renting out a location like Corriganville for westerns was profitable for years — each time the genre started to seem out of date, it was retooled to suit the moment. From 1936 until the last set closed in 1966, Corriganville Movie Ranch was used in 3,500 different productions, more than any other location outside a studio. After westerns fell out of favor in the 1960s, Corrigan sold the property to Bob Hope, who subdivided a section and built Hopetown Homes, a neighborhood of suburban split-levels with aggressively irrigated lawns, curiously adrift in the empty, parched acreage. Then Camelback Mountain was dynamited flat to make way for the Ronald Reagan Freeway. That sliced the property in two, and before long the northern edge of Los Angeles inched its way up and over what had been the quiet, wild acres of the ranch. I was curious to see if anything at Corriganville still looked like the scenes from the show, so I went to visit it one morning. I was meeting a man named Greg Anderson, a local amateur historian who knew the area well and had offered to show me around.

When Anderson approached me in the parking lot that morning, I couldn't help but notice that he was dressed in an 1870s army uniform. "I'm in character," he said, in response to the alarm on my face. He smoothed the brass buttons on his coat. "This one is cavalry. I have a Cheyenne look, too, and a few others, but this seemed right for today."

We headed down a path lacy with light filtering through the oaks, Anderson narrating what had been filmed in what spot and which movie star had stood on which hunk of granite and under which gnarled tree. We came to an empty concrete swimming pool veined with cracks, tufts of stiff grass pushing through. There were scrapes and chips along the edge. "Skateboarders," Anderson said with disgust. "And to think that Johnny Weissmuller used to swim in this pool." I grew up watching and hating those Weissmuller Tarzan movies, which played on late-night television in what seemed like an endless, dark loop. I must have seen this pool hundreds of times in those movies, but I would never have recognized it without the fake vines and fake palm trees used to dress the set.

As we walked along, Anderson told me that he had always been a fan of westerns.

When he discovered that so many of them had been filmed here, he became fascinated by the place and the many identities it had been able to assume. He began taping every western on television in order to learn how to recognize as many Corriganville rock formations as possible. "After a while, I wouldn't even really watch the movie," he said. "I would turn the sound off and study each scene really carefully to figure out the location." He assured me that he could watch any western that had been filmed here — no matter how much set dressing had been done — and tell me exactly which rock was which. He had spent a lot of time working on it, hours and hours.

This seemed like an unusual sort of hobby, but no matter how specialized or particular a hobby might be, it always seems that someone has dug into it. Immersing yourself in a single interest so thoroughly sometimes means that the interest stops being something you do; instead you become a servant of that interest. But for many people, that kind of engagement is a comfort. Maybe embracing one thing that is so explicit is like whittling all you know and feel and care about into a single point — one that is so fine it can be threaded through life's eye.

Anderson stooped to pick up a piece of

trash that was tumbling by. "You know, I have all this knowledge of this stuff now," he said, glancing at me. "It makes me feel like I'm important."

We left Johnny Weissmuller's pool and ducked under low branches. I asked Anderson if he could show me Fort Apache, where *The Adventures of Rin-Tin-Tin* was filmed, but he told me that the fort had been dismantled in 1967. He could tell how disappointed I was. As a consolation, he pointed out some other interesting movie rocks and said he could take me to see the crest of the hill where Rin Tin Tin posed at the end of every episode. We walked beyond the trees and the land opened up, the sky a huge sheet of blue, the upsweep of the black mountains in the distance and before us rocks scattered like a toss of giant dice. The hill was there, past the rocks, and the jut of the crest looked exactly as it had when the dog posed on it every week and filled the screen of the TV. It was around midday, and the color was blasted out of the red dirt and the gray rock and the tawny chaparral, the light bleaching everything, blazing against the granite, so that for a moment you could picture it all in black and white.

10.

In the fall of 1954, the American television schedule included puppets and comics, average families and aging celebrities, cowboys, detectives, and Mickey Mouse. Longtime stars Arthur Godfrey and Red Skelton hosted prime-time television shows. *The Jack Benny Program* featured a new comedian named Johnny Carson. On ABC, most nights began with a fifteen-minute segment of *Kukla, Fran and Ollie,* an ad-libbed puppet show featuring Ollie, the one-toothed dragon, and the red-nosed, arch-browed Kukla. Family life was showcased in *The Adventures of Ozzie and Harriet* and *Father Knows Best* and the most popular show on television, *I Love Lucy. The Lone Ranger* held down Thursday night. The first prime-time game show, *The $64,000 Question,* premiered, as did the drama anthology *The Millionaire.*

Another dog with Hollywood history was also debuting on the 1954 fall television schedule. Rudd Weatherwax had made a deal with CBS to develop a show around Lassie, and the Campbell Soup Company had agreed to sponsor it. Like Lee, Weatherwax was more interested in making movies than television, but after the 1951 film

The Painted Hills, no offers for Lassie had come his way. In 1953, an independent producer approached him with the idea of bringing the Lassie character to television. By that time, Pal, the dog that had starred in the movies, was too old to work the long days on a set, but Weatherwax had several of Pal's puppies — Lassie Junior, Baby, Spook, and Hey Hey — trained and ready for the new show. The show was being cast around the same time as *The Adventures of Rin-Tin-Tin;* in fact, Lee Aaker was one of the finalists for the lead in the show.

Like *The Adventures of Rin-Tin-Tin, Lassie* featured a fatherless boy and his dog. The boy on the Rin Tin Tin show is an orphan who has lost both parents in an Indian raid; the boy on *Lassie* was less alone in the world, living with his widowed mother and his grandfather on a farm somewhere in rural America. Lassie's world was gentle and pastoral. The dog provided companionship and lessons to the boy, Jeff, and helped him out of squeezes, which were usually no worse than an unexpected confrontation with a wild animal. (In later seasons of the show, Lassie lived with a different family, whose young son, Timmy, is far more disaster prone, and in time is threatened by a tiger in the woods, trapped in a mine, nearly drowned in quicksand, exposed to radiation, menaced by an escaped circus elephant, poisoned by nightshade berries, chased by a rabid dog, carried off in a balloon, struck by a hit-and-run driver, locked in a shed by an armed robber, and nearly killed by dynamite carried by an escaped lab chimpanzee.)

Overall, the tone of *Lassie* was quieter and more domesticated than *The Adventures of Rin-Tin-Tin,* which often included "shooting, knifing, punching, war, arrow shooting, Indian attacks, scuffles, gun-butting (but no sword play, strangling, torture, or flogging)," according to the Motion Picture Association of America's analysis. In fact, *The Adventures of Rin-Tin-Tin* was considered rough enough that censors in Britain removed certain scenes — especially ones that showed Rinty fighting — and Germany banned the show from playing on religious holidays. Some of the Rin Tin Tin episodes were almost comically violent, a matter that Bert and Screen Gems often squabbled over. In one such squabble, Bert conceded several points to the studio:

The actual kill of the mountain lion will be done off scene, and the savageness of the situation will be held down. . . . We will get enough of it to make it exciting but definitely not gruesome. In Scene 103 we will show chicken feathers as if the wolves had gotten to the chickens, which I don't think is too horrible as long as we don't show any of the dead chickens, and we will eliminate the dead horse.

And finally:

Rusty will not be caught in a bear trap, but will be treed by the wolves, which will not be as bloodcurdling as the other situation.

11.

The Adventures of Rin-Tin-Tin was broadcast for the first time on October 15, 1954. The debut episode, "Meet Rin-Tin-Tin," was the story of how the "Fighting Blue Devils" of the 101st Cavalry came to be stewards of Rusty and Rinty — or, as Sergeant O'Hara puts it, "How we found them two little orphans." Only after I had learned Lee Duncan's personal history did I realize how this story recalled his own time as an orphan, and also the orphaned French boy who had lived with his squadron during

World War I — the "little chum" who had served as the squadron's mascot until French authorities took him away.

Bert and Lee were confident that Rin Tin Tin would be a triumph again, but even so, the reception *The Adventures of Rin-Tin-Tin* received must have been overwhelming. The show was an instant success by every measure. It had one of the fastest ratings climbs in television history and from its start was ABC's second-highest rated show overall, trailing only the Walt Disney show. Nine million of the 30 million televisions in the United States tuned to *The Adventures of Rin-Tin-Tin,* several million more than were tuned to *Lassie,* which had premiered on CBS a month earlier. It was also a critical success. "Crammed with action, gun-play, and chase scenes of pre-musical-cowpoke Westerns," wrote a critic in *TV Guide.* "It makes fine viewing for kids and nostalgic viewing for grown-ups." Even *The New Yorker* paid its respects, running a "Talk of the Town" interview with "the proud, tall, long, four-year-old, hundred-pound, gray-and-white great-grandson of the original Rin Tin Tin." At the end of the piece, which was mostly an interview with Eva Duncan, the writer, Philip Hamburger, noted that after dinner at the Stork Club, where he turned up his nose at the roast beef, Rin Tin Tin "drank milk out of a champagne glass" and "pushed a molting goose called Susie down Broadway in a baby carriage."

Lee and Rin Tin Tin were once again the center of the nation's attention. How many years had passed? Decades, lifetimes, it seemed — and yet here they were, as if Rin Tin Tin was a fresh new discovery. The show was broadcasting in seventy other countries besides the United States, including Canada, France, Lebanon, Kenya, Pakistan, Nicaragua, Cuba, Thailand, Germany, Bermuda, Brazil, Italy, New Zealand, Surinam, and Japan. Just as in earlier decades, Rin Tin Tin was everywhere. He was a single point connecting people all over the world, from all different cultures and circumstances, all of them watching as the camera angled up to the crest of a hill where a big dog stood at alert, a depthless silhouette against a western sky in a placeless place somewhere in the timeless history of America.

Success kept them busy. At Corriganville Movie Ranch, the cast and crew worked six days out of seven, racing to shoot two episodes a week. They shot thirty or forty scenes every day. The schedule was so intense that none of the actors had time to launder their costumes. Directors rotated in at noon on Wednesdays. Robert Walker, a Hollywood veteran, directed the greatest number of episodes until, according to Sam Manners, he got fed up with Hollywood and left to become a Mormon priest. The stunt-men, who were paid $17 to fall off a horse, were black-and-blue from the long days.

There was a flood of requests from schools and civic groups, hospitals, rodeos. Every-one wanted a visit from Rinty or from anyone connected to the show. Screen Gems, delighted and also besieged, hired a Kenyon & Eckhart executive named Wau-hillau LaHay to manage the enthusiasm. LaHay was a political reporter before she joined Kenyon & Eckhart, and some years later, when she decided to leave the ad busi-ness, she became the White House cor-respondent for Scripps Howard newspapers. Her father was a lobbyist for the Cherokee Nation and the leader of the Oklahoma statehood movement, and LaHay liked to describe herself as "an Indian lass from Muskogee, Oklahoma." She had an ener-getic social life, especially by the standards of the time; when she began working on Rin Tin Tin, she was midway through her third marriage. She had worked her entire adult life but liked to shock people by saying that she believed the best thing any woman could do was "find a nice man, marry him, have babies, and shut up."

LaHay took on Rin Tin Tin with her usual zeal. Even her memos seemed to crackle. She began by issuing a thirteen-point list of publicity ideas, including "Make Rin Tin Tin reporter for a day at the *Journal* — have him cover interview of guy like Milton Berle — make it very cute" and "Dog presents pup to winner on 'Queen for a Day' " and "Set up photo shoot of female dogs swooning at Rin photo." She rousted Lee from Riverside and sent him to New York with Rinty for three days of magazine interviews, press conferences, a meeting with Boy Scouts, a performance at a rodeo in Madison Square Garden, and an appearance on the television game show *I've Got a Secret,* where celebrity panelists tried to guess contestants' "secrets" (Lee's being that he had trained Rin Tin Tin).

Lee was accustomed to doing press tours, less accustomed to being managed with such vigor by someone like LaHay, although he seemed to roll along with it. She wrote to him with advice and suggestions all the time. Before one press event, she sent a note telling him to be sure to mention cats as well as dogs in his opening remarks because "many of these people are very fond of cats . . . and we don't want them to think we're forgetting their pets. It might hurt their feelings."

She wanted more publicity for Eva and Carolyn Duncan. In the past, they had avoided almost all attention, but LaHay wouldn't hear of it. "You have to go to work, darling," she wrote to Eva. "First off, [I want] a picture of Carolyn and Rinty in a training pose. Not just the two of them looking at the camera, but an actual working picture. Like making him sit up or beg or what the hell. Exactly how old is Carolyn? (We can lie a little.) The Teens in the News section is very anxious for this, so the sooner, the better, honey."

LaHay crafted a marvelously fictitious biography for Rin Tin Tin that circulated to the press — one more addition to the many versions of his life that had been concocted over the years. In LaHay's account, Rinty's mother was a German police dog from Buffalo, New York, that had been recruited for the army expeditionary forces by Flight Commander William Thaw of the 135th Aero Squadron — the same Thaw who really had been a pilot in the Lafayette Escadrille — and that this Thaw-recruited,

Buffalo-born police dog had given birth to Rinty in the basement of an American Red Cross hospital in France. According to La-Hay's account, Lee somehow found Rinty in the hospital and "kidnapped him"; later the puppy accompanied Lee on his many (fictional) combat flights. Rinty, as LaHay explained, lived in sybaritic luxury. His valet curried him every morning with a butter-soft rubber brush and bathed him every afternoon in a porcelain tub. He lived in a miniature stucco palace with electric lights, plumbing, a sterling silver food trough, a radio that was always tuned to classical music, and a large mailbox, which was bursting with ten thousand fan letters a week.

The part about the fan letters was true.

Dear Rinty, I watch your show every Friday night and I think you are the smartest dog in the world.

Dear Rinty, I like it when you leap through glass at a bad man. Say hello to Rusty for me.

Dear Mr. Duncan, My name is Janice. For a girl, I like dogs and horses very much. Rin Tin Tin is and always will be my favorite dog.

Dear Mr. Duncan, I like Rusty just like a brother and I do mean brother. I have made up a song I will write down here but first I would like to know if you could send me a picture of Rusty and Rin Tin Tin. I have not got the notes and tune to the song but I am working on it.

The fans of *The Adventures of Rin-Tin-Tin* wrote thousands of letters each week requesting photographs and autographs. Other fans wrote with urgent questions. Did Rinty really have a solid gold dog license? Did he really know how to count/read/fly? Were his meals catered by Romanoff's Restaurant in Beverly Hills? Did he wear a hairpiece on his tail to make it look so bushy? (Duncan assured fans that Rinty "grew every single tail-hair himself.")

Some fans wrote just to say hello. In the Riverside archives, in the enormous stack of fan mail sent to El Rancho Rin Tin Tin, I found a batch of letters one little girl had written to various Rin Tin Tin cast members, sent in care of Lee and Eva. I was marveling over the Duncans' patience with the girl — Eva had replied personally to almost all of the girl's many letters — when I came to Eva's final reply, which she had sent after almost a year of regular correspondence. "I must say, Marcy, you are the most 'writingest' fan we have," Eva wrote. "Please let me get this straight with you . . . I would be deeply grateful to you if you would PLEASE stop sending mail to Rancho Rin Tin Tin! Don't you think you are overdoing it a little? There is mail for either Rusty or Boone or Sergeant O'Hara in our mail box every week from you."

Lee got hundreds of letters from dog owners, for whom he had become a sort of paradigm, the perfect dog owner of the perfect dog. By 1954, more than 40 percent of American households included at least one dog. Mixed breeds were the most common, and the most popular purebreds were beagles, boxers, cocker spaniels, and dachshunds. German shepherds and collies, the two breeds now in prime time, were the fifth and sixth most popular breeds. Just as he had in the 1920s and 1930s with old Rin, and then again in the 1940s with Rin Tin Tin III, Lee stood out as the person who could serve as an intermediary between people and this nation of dogs.

This perception was strengthened after he wrote a story in 1956 for a popular general-interest monthly, *The American Magazine,* called "Your Dog Can Be a Rin Tin Tin." The story was prominently featured beside a piece by then Senator Lyndon Johnson called "My Heart Attack Taught Me How to Live." Lee described his training philosophy ("You must be a little smarter than your dog, and you must have the patience to get to know him really well. The rest comes with experience"). His dogs were gifted, he added, but he assured readers that every dog had the potential to be as obedient and responsive as Rinty.

This was an interesting departure from the early days of Rin Tin Tin, when the emphasis was on how peerless he was: he was a "dog among millions," as James English wrote, a dog you could dream about but would never be lucky enough to own. Now, instead of being a miracle, he was a model. He was the dog you could aspire to have, and maybe even manage to have, at home. In the early days of Hollywood, movies were alchemy, and movie stars, including Rin Tin Tin, were unattainable; they lived on huge screens in the dark, with the power to awe and amaze. Television, however, was a small box in your living room, and the stars on it were also scaled down, familiar and friendly and available. This intimacy made all the difference in the world.

After "Your Dog Can Be a Rin Tin Tin" was published, Lee was swamped with requests and questions and confessions. People with dogs they could no longer take care of asked if Lee would take them in.

People with misbehaving dogs hoped he could work a miracle. Could he suggest how to keep a dog from digging holes? Barking at the mailman? Stealing food from the table? "Dear Mr. Duncan, my male dog is a coward," one letter began. "Now my female dog is shy and also a coward. Would you please take a few minutes of your valuable time and help a fellow dog lover?" Another letter, from a dog owner in Baltimore, began, "How do you teach a dog to stay out of incinerators? Because every time my dog is off the leash he is in it."

People often asked Lee how to get their dogs (or, in one case, their cheetah) into show business. Other fans, sure their dogs were more than ready to be stars, wrote to brag: "I am writing to tell you about my beautiful and intelligent Samoyed. He has learned to count by barking. He counts two for the number of parts the Bible is divided into, four for the number of Gospels, ten for the commandments, and four for the number of ribs I broke when I fell last year." Others complained to him of their dogs' lack of genius. "Dear Mr. Duncan, I am writing to you about my two dogs, Pogo and Topper," a man from Kansas City wrote in 1955. "They are not too exceptionally bright but they catch on to most things.

They can do things like jumping through hoops, etc. My problem is that I can't get them to limp. I've tried working with a sling but after I take it off they still won't do it. Would you please tell me what method you use in teaching your dogs to limp?"

German shepherd owners, in particular, turned to Lee. Some wrote with minor questions: How did you cure a German shepherd suffering from dry skin? What food did Lee think was right for the breed? How did he spot a good puppy? Others presented what sounded like serious problems. One note, written on flowery stationery, began, "Dear Lee, My German shepherd dog has one terrible trait and that is viciousness."

Many people said they remembered Rin Tin Tin from the period when the dog had appeared in air-conditioned movie palaces in the downtowns of the big cities — the old, crumbling city centers, which were now being abandoned for the suburbs. Rin Tin Tin marked the turn of time for the world they knew then, which by 1954 had begun to fade. "In this day and age, there are few things absorbing enough to take one's mind off the greedy and streamlined tempo of living, but yesterday I lived in the golden, silent 1920s again," one man from North

361

Dakota wrote to Lee in 1954. He said he had grown up watching Rinty's early movies, and he and his friends believed that everything depicted in Rinty's movies really happened — they thought the movies were more or less documentaries, and that cameramen followed Rin Tin Tin around recording his exploits. Later they concluded that Rinty was too talented to be real — they decided he had to be a mechanical dog. Eventually they came to realize that Rin Tin Tin was in fact a real dog, extraordinarily talented and extraordinarily trained. In closing the man wrote, "This shepherd definitely had a part in my boyhood that will never be forgotten. And now at last Mr. Duncan I have the opportunity to thank you for having a part in such a beautiful story, for having had some part in my happier boyhood days, for finding that wonderful wonder dog, Rin Tin Tin."

In the 1920s and 1930s, Lee and Warner Bros. had been flooded with unsolicited screenplays for old Rinty, and now Lee and Bert received the same gush of television episodes from fans. The proposals ranged from pedestrian to absurd. One suggestion, for an episode the writer called "Rin Tin Tin and the Imposter," included "a half-breed Indian, a Gorilla-type man, an Air Robber, and a Sweet Girl of Fourteen Years." Most solicitations were returned to the sender with a standard gentle refusal, such as "Thank you for submitting 'Rin Tin Tin and the Imposter,' which I am returning herewith," or "I am returning to you the script entitled 'The Pebble That Grew and Grew.' Unfortunately, the story has no value to us."

A few, at least, must have caught Lee's attention. One called for Rusty to be "made painfully aware of the fact that he has no father . . . this all builds to make Rusty suffer the agony of all unwanted children." When Rusty decides to run away, "Rin Tin Tin senses his inner trouble and refuses to be left behind." The episode resolves with an unorthodox but fascinating plot twist: the 101st Cavalry arranges to adopt the boy. The sergeant makes Rusty "the legal son of each and every man in the outfit . . . while most boys only have one father, he has fifty."

Bert received countless suggestions, too. He was developing two new shows to go on the air in 1956 — *Circus Boy,* which would star child actor and future Monkee Micky Dolenz, and *Tales of the 77th Bengal Lancers* — and was eager to work on others. Even the head of marketing at Screen

Gems, a man named Ed Justin, pitched a series idea to him. In his cover letter Justin proudly announced to Bert that he had written the whole show — an outdoor adventure series that he called *The Big Beaver* — at home on a Saturday morning. Bert couldn't resist responding sarcastically, "Dear Ed, I think you're wasting your time as a merchandising man and that you should come out here and write the scripts."

The most unusual suggestions came from an aspiring writer named Warren Eugene Crane, who sent Bert a list of twenty prospective television series. Some were uninspired (*Quirks in the News, The Philatelists' Hour*) and others were wildly uncommercial (*I Love a Poem Each Day, Your Handwriting Tells a Story*). But a few stood out as the work of a man with a sort of prophetic genius: *Charge of the Lighter Brigade* was "a series I propose about weight reduction"; *Crane Family Recipes* would be "A Broadcast of Recipes of Delicious Foods concocted from Recipe Book of My Wife which contains some excellent dishes to tempt the palate of the epicure"; and the peak of Crane's creativity, *Paw 'n Maw,* which would be "a series of humorous telecasts based on a family of droll frontiersmen and women

who joke about danger as if it were a pas-
time."

12.

With the show's success, El Rancho Rin Tin
Tin became a destination: a place where
you could see, in real life, the miracle dog
of television. Lee had always kept old Rin
to himself, but now he welcomed visitors to
the ranch and encouraged them to play with
Rinty. He always brought them to the
Memory Room, urging them to sit a while
so he could unfurl his stories of the past.

The fact that this dog, Rin Tin Tin IV,
wasn't the dog that actually appeared on
television didn't make Lee uncomfortable.
If he worried, he wouldn't have welcomed
visitors who might have pointed out the
disparity. For one thing, the various dogs
used on the show looked enough alike, and
enough like his Rinty, that it would have
taken close examination to tell them apart.
But anyone could figure out that Rinty lived
in Riverside while the show was being
filmed sixty miles away, making it obvious
that the dog at El Rancho Rin Tin Tin
couldn't have been also on the set. But no
one complained.

Swept up in the rush of attention from

the television show, Carolyn and her mother tried to fit into the latest version of their domestic life. It had never been easy for them to live with the famous dog and the famous man behind the dog, but now it was even more difficult, especially for Carolyn, who once told me that she had "the weirdest childhood in the world." Every kid she knew watched the show and fantasized about living the life she was living, with Rin Tin Tin in the backyard, but she felt lost in that life, an odd afterthought — the little sister, awkward and unexceptional, to a dog. After her photograph appeared in an article about the Duncans in *Western Horseman,* for instance, she got three marriage proposals. Another teenage girl might have been flattered, but Carolyn felt demeaned by it, certain that the suitors just wanted a way to get closer to Rinty.

At least they now had some money, and Eva finally got the house Lee had been promising her since they moved to Riverside. A local architect designed a long structure with an elegant entrance, big jalousie windows, and the first kidney-shaped swimming pool in Riverside. Eva chose the interiors: metallic wallpaper and freestanding planters, all-electric appliances and foldaway bathroom scales. On the floors, she went for white carpeting. ("Brave woman," one reporter noted.)

It wasn't ostentatious the way a Hollywood house could be, but by Riverside standards it was a showplace. The local paper ran a two-part feature about it, and the Riverside City Panhellenic Society included it on its 1958 Home Tour. "Here is the house that Rinty built, complete on the anniversary of his beloved owner's 40th year in show business," the tour pamphlet stated. "Linen draperies . . . a fabulous bath . . . notice the custom-built furniture, the tanned-to-order leather, the hand-woven blinds . . ."

I spent long days in Riverside so I could read Lee's papers, which were stored in big cardboard file boxes in the annex of the Riverside Municipal Museum. I knew I was lucky. Lee was a saver and a carbon-copier and a newspaper clipper, so his life was documented and preserved. The index of the material alone was several inches thick.

I commuted to Riverside from Los Angeles, driving seventy miles almost directly east, across the San Jacinto fault, on highways that got emptier and straighter as I went along. I whipped past road signs for places you never visit in California, like

Avocado Heights and South San Jose Hills and Diamond Bar and the Phillips Ranch, which are lined with rows of identical houses that from a distance look like angry welts. I made the drive so often that I did it almost automatically, barely aware that I was driving, and I was often startled to find myself in Riverside when I felt like I had left Los Angeles just moments before. There was a big billboard saying we buy ugly houses a few miles outside of town, and if I wasn't lost in a reverie I noticed it and would realize I was almost there.

This was the drive Lee took when he left Hollywood. Back then, Interstate 60 wasn't a divided highway; it had just two lanes, and they were rough and rutted by flash floods. It was a long way, literally, and an even longer way, by every other measure, from the gloss of Hollywood to the dust of Riverside. By the time the television show was on the air, Lee had been away from Hollywood for twenty years, and even though he made the drive on occasion to visit the set of the show or attend to business with Screen Gems and Bert, he was never at home in Hollywood again.

Often, as I drove to the museum, I took a detour down Field Lane to look at the house that used to be called El Rancho Rin

368

Tin Tin. Field Lane was near the freeway entrance. It is a small road that runs along a park and a golf course at the northern edge of the city, where the Pomona, the Riverside, and the Moreno Valley freeways meet. Riverside is arid and open and hot as hell, and anything that isn't sheltered by the local oaks or ponderosa pines is so baked it seems radiant. Field Drive, though, is in the gully of the Santa Ana River, and it wanders in and out of the trees, so to drive along it was like driving through a strobe, a blast of sun followed by a wall of shade. If I left my car window open I could always hear the crack of golf swings coming from Fairmount Park.

The current owners of the house, a young family named Bradshaw, bought the place in 1997. Boyd Bradshaw told me he knew when they bought the house that there was a Rin Tin Tin connection to it, but he didn't know much about it. Since then, he and his wife, Lisa, have learned about the Duncans and decided to preserve the original house as best they could. They had modernized some of it, taking out the twin beds in the master bedroom and some of the boomerang room dividers, and adding a large family room for their kids, but otherwise, Boyd said, the house was almost exactly as it was when Lee and Eva and Carolyn had lived there.

I visited the house one afternoon after many hours in the archives, when my head was full of Lee Duncan. It was the day I came across the pamphlet for the Riverside Home Tour, and I was trying to imagine Lee's reaction to it. I wondered if he was pleased to be living in a house that was newsworthy or whether the house made him feel like a hayseed guest. He once told a reporter that he sometimes missed their rickety old house because he hadn't had to worry about putting his hat in the wrong place or tracking dirt on the white rugs.

He was probably glad to have finally made Eva happy, after keeping her waiting for her house for twenty years. But in truth, his life was with his dogs and his horses, and the new house was far removed from that. It wasn't a house that fit naturally on an old California property where you'd keep cattle and horses and dogs; it looked suburban, as though it belonged in Orange County. Field Lane had been a dirt road on the outskirts of town when Lee and Eva moved there, and the original house was just as unassuming. But then Field Lane was paved and landscaped, and split-levels with circular driveways were soon cropping up all around them. The old house probably began to look a little out of place by the time it was torn down; the new house better suited this revised version of the neighborhood. It is an attractive house, a place that would have been considered "artsy," and Eva, who had begun making clay sculptures and paintings, undoubtedly loved the modern feel of it and appreciated that she could display her art on all the built-in shelving. It was Lee who must have felt out of place.

Boyd Bradshaw showed me around, pointing out with pride the architect's innovative touches. We walked outside and circled around the blob-shaped swimming pool, and then crossed the yard to look at the kennel. It was an overgrown, cobwebby A-frame shed — not a miniature stucco palace at all, no matter how Wauhillau La-Hay's publicity had described it. But it looked like it had been a fine place for a real ranch dog to live.

When *The Adventures of Rin-Tin-Tin* became a hit, Bert also moved into a new house — the big Tudor on Los Feliz, with a swimming pool and a tennis court, just a block from Griffith Park. Bert was only thirty-three years old, but the success of the show gave him stature. He never lacked for self-confidence, but now he could afford to indulge himself a little. He liked to take meetings in a bathrobe, clenching the fattest cigar he could find between his teeth. He was an avid tennis player and could hold his own on his backyard court, even though he liked to smoke those fat cigars while he played. Sam Katzman wasn't paying for his gambling anymore, but he still had what appeared to be an inexhaustible credit line, which many people thought Screen Gems covered as a thank-you for bringing them Rin Tin Tin.

As a courtesy, Lee always offered Rin Tin Tin puppies to people involved with the show, and Bert took one of the puppies as a pet. I don't know the dog's name or anything about him other than the fact that he was from one of Lee's Rin Tin Tin litters. It was nice for Bert and Willetta's baby, Steven, who was then eighteen months old and toddling around, to have a pet.

At some point in this sparkly time, Bert's father, Morton, made one of his rare visits to Los Angeles. Morton was alone at the house one day, taking care of Steven — helping out, evidently, which was something Bert said he rarely did. At some point, Morton left Steven alone near the pool with the dog. After some time Morton returned to the yard, but he was too late. He found Steven in the pool: he had drowned.

I can imagine no experience worse than losing a child, and in this case the tragedy was compounded by the fact that Bert's own father, who had never been fatherly to him, was involved in it. What really happened can never be known, but as a rule, dogs don't push children into swimming pools out of malice; in fact, there are many stories of dogs saving people from drowning. If the baby and the dog were roughhousing, there is certainly a chance the dog accidentally knocked him in. Morton was said to have claimed that the dog had pushed the child in, as if to suggest that the dog's actions had been deliberate. It was like an eerie reprise of the Prince Llewellyn story and so many other Rin Tin Tin silent-film plots that involved misjudgment and accusation: it is possible that child fell in and the dog jumped in to save him, only to be accused of a terrible thing. It was an awful irony that the dog was related to Rin Tin Tin. Losing a child at the exact moment he was proving his talent for communicating to children made it that much more painful for Bert. The sadness of it wouldn't stop, and within a few years, Willetta and Bert separated. Soon after their separation, they divorced.

13.

Rin Tin Tin was being reborn in the middle of the biggest baby boom in history. It began in 1946 when veterans came home from the war and got married. Seventy-seven million babies were born in the United States between 1946 and 1964. My family was a typical product of that period: my father was in the service in World War II, where he had served in Army Intelligence and then returned home to Cleveland, his hometown. He and my mother got married in 1950. They moved from the city to a newly built house in the suburbs. My brother was born in 1951, and my sister and I followed in 1953 and 1955. In our suburban neighborhood, every house seemed to have at least two or three kids, and new elementary schools popped up like mushrooms. It was like living in a children's village. There were more of us than adults. After dinner, on most nights, all the children on my street came out to play for one last hour before bedtime. We poured out of our houses in our pajamas, and in that shimmery time just after sundown we rode our bikes up and down the sidewalk, caught fireflies, traded baseball cards, lit punks, and ran zigzagging across lawns with sparklers, leaving glittering trails in the fading light. Then we went home and watched TV.

The babies of the boom consumed all entertainment rapaciously, gobbling up movies and comic books and toys as well as TV. The effect of all these children, the mass of us, must have been bewildering to our parents, almost like witnessing an invasion of hungry aliens, and intriguing to sociologists and marketers. Children, and especially teenagers, had never been observed and measured and considered as a group before, but now sheer numbers made them a moving force. Beginning with the baby boom, anything manufactured or produced was evaluated for its potential to appeal to all these eager children. Not only did they have their own tastes, but they also seemed to dictate what the rest of their families, including their parents, watched and ate and bought. A 1955 issue of *TV Guide* carried a story titled "Who's Boss of Your TV Set?" The answer, according to the social scientists, was kids.

In December 1954, a five-part serial about the frontiersman Davy Crockett, starring a character actor named Fess Parker, ran on the ABC show *Disneyland.* The network was counting on it being a simple success. Instead it launched a frenzy — not just for the show but also for the 3,000 products that Disney licensed with the Davy Crockett name. Within a few months, Americans spent the equivalent of $800 million on Davy Crockett merchandise. They bought 14 million Davy Crockett books; 4 million recordings of the show's theme song, "The Ballad of Davy Crockett" ("Da-veee, Davy Crockett, king of the wild fronteeeer!"), and millions of other Davy Crockett–branded toys and clothes. Hopalong Cassidy had sold a good number of black cowboy shirts and white hats, but the scope of Davy Crockett sales was far bigger. Some observers wondered if the rage might continue until literally every child in America had a full complement of Davy Crockett paraphernalia — coonskin hat, rifle, powder horn, book, and record.

Merchandising was a new idea, but Davy Crockett made it clear that pairing up products with a television show could be overwhelmingly potent. Just five episodes made Davy Crockett the king of the toy department. Some producers were still skeptical of all these products, especially since much of the merchandise had nothing to do with the show or character itself except that it featured the image or name. It was one thing to sell a coonskin hat just like the one Davy Crockett wore, but what was the exact meaning of a Davy Crockett wristwatch? A Davy Crockett hot chocolate mug? Bert, however, believed that marketing was the future of television. In 1955 he told a reporter that he believed that merchandising of television shows might one day "be as economically important as television itself" — a radical idea at the time, but one that, at least in the case of children's television, turned out to be true.

Almost as soon as *The Adventures of Rin-Tin-Tin* was on the air, you could buy a Rin Tin Tin cavalry mess kit, uniform, hat, bugle, gun, and holster, as well as a recording of the 101st Cavalry bugle calls, cavalry belt-and-suspender sets, a Rin Tin Tin–branded pocket knife, a telescope, a walkie-talkie, a beanie, a pennant, a 3-D color viewer with viewer cards, a brass magic ring, a pinback button, a Wonder Scope, a lunch box, a thermos bottle, a wallet, slippers, jigsaw puzzles, and all sorts of mechanical games. Cheerios cereal included premiums for *The Adventures of Rin-Tin-Tin* plastic totem poles; Nabisco Wheat Honeys offered coupons for six different Rin Tin Tin masks. For a box top plus one dollar, you could have a Rin Tin Tin T-shirt; for more box tops and more dollars, you could get Rusty's uniform or a televiewer with twenty-four 3-D adventure slides. You could even buy a Chrysler that was endorsed by "the best mounted cavalry in the world" — namely, Lieutenant Masters, Sergeant O'Hara, and Corporal Boone, who appeared in uniform at Fort Apache beside the car in a 1956 Chrysler ad.

And then there were all the Rin Tin Tin products: dog brushes and leashes and collars and beds; plush-toy Rin Tin Tins; metal Rin Tin Tin coin banks, bookends, and doorstops; matchbook covers, letter openers, and paperweights featuring his picture; playing cards and wristwatches; Rin Tin Tin costumes, complete with rubber German shepherd face masks. The Breyer Molding Company in Chicago produced the eight-inch plastic Rin Tin Tin that my grandfather always kept on his desk, enticingly out of my reach. The Hartland toy company made another, smaller plastic Rin Tin Tin. Royal Doulton, Martindale, and Premier Porcelain made Rin Tin Tin figurines in fine materials, in a variety of poses, including Rinty in his signature stance on a rock ledge.

Companies' fortunes were made on Rin Tin Tin products. They were "presold to 13,750,000 kids" in a "once in a blue moon" opportunity, according to an ad in *Merchandising News* magazine for the Pekett Headwear Company, which owned the license to produce Rusty's official cavalry hat. Marx Toy Company sold millions of plastic Fort Apache models in the United States and Europe. Hermann Handkerchief, Gem-Dandy Accessories, Bradley Watch, Brewster Shirt Company, Spec-Toy, Craftint, Esquire Novelty, Yunker Manufacturing, puzzle makers Gabriel & Son — all were at their production limits by 1955, trying to satisfy the demand for Rin Tin Tin items.

A license to manufacture a Rin Tin Tin product was gold, and all manner of crackpots and con artists approached Lee and Bert with schemes. Proposals for Rin Tin Tin–branded dog training schools, jewelry, and canine horoscopes arrived almost every day. "Mr. Duncan, it is apparent that you are a person who is very much interested in dogs, and also one who isn't unwilling to make a great deal of money," a piano teacher named Francis Bloom wrote to Lee in 1955. Bloom hoped to get Rin Tin Tin's endorsement for a flushing dog toilet he'd patented, which was designed in such a way that the dog wouldn't get its foot caught in the drain nor be squirted by the flush water.

Everyone seemed to want to be part of the phenomenon. People offered to appear on the show, or allow their dogs to appear on the show, or write episodes of the show. In the 1950s, many major newspapers had a reporter covering dog shows and pets. Alice Scott, the "Blue Ribbon Dog" columnist for the *Los Angeles Examiner* and author of *How to Raise and Train a Pekinese,* proposed to Lee that she leave her job and start "The Rin Tin Tin Fan Club for the Children of America," which would hold meetings "each month, in each community of the United States." Other offers of help were less welcome. In 1955, a songwriter recorded a studio demo of his song "The Ballad of Rin Tin Tin." He sent it to Lee with a note saying, "Honestly, sir, I believe that another Davy Crockett hit is in the making. I feel certain, sir, you will go for the song. It has punch and personality. We should sell a million copies." Lee passed the song along to Bert, who listened to it and replied, "Dear Lee, I think the recording is pretty dreadful." (Lee wrote back to the man offering a kinder version of Bert's reaction, explaining, "Mr. Leonard . . . feels that it is not exactly what he is looking for.")

The companies that did make deals with Screen Gems wanted the show to help promote their products. The crayon and paint-by-number companies wanted an episode to include a scene of Rusty learning to paint and draw. The hat manufacturer wanted to be sure Rusty wore his hat in as many scenes as possible. Nabisco, which was using Sergeant O'Hara in many of its commercials, threatened legal action if O'Hara didn't appear prominently in enough episodes. Karastan knew it couldn't have its Rin Tin Tin rug actually appear in the show — Karastan rugs wouldn't have existed in 1870 — but the company's sales manager requested a publicity shot of Rin Tin Tin in a room with one of the rugs "looking at it with jealousy or love," or a shot of Rusty making Rinty jealous by pointing to the rug. When the toy gun company worried that Rusty wasn't shooting enough, Ed Justin, who handled merchandising for Screen Gems, sent a memo to Bert, urging him to appease the company. "Bert, if possible, work in an occasional bit in which Rusty uses his new guns," Justin pleaded. "We had better show him shooting at targets or shooting the heads off rattlesnakes, or doing something with those guns from time to time."

Many stores set up special Rin Tin Tin promotions. Bullock's, a luxury department store in Los Angeles, decorated its toy department to look like Fort Apache and stocked it with the full array of Rin Tin Tin merchandise. When Lee appeared there with Rinty and Lee Aaker, 3,000 people showed up and another 2,500 had to be turned away. Kresge's, a five-and-dime chain, set up larger-than-life Rusty and Rinty cardboard cutouts at the end of every aisle in a few of its stores to promote Rusty bugles and gun-and-holster sets. The promotion was so successful that Kresge decided to set up the same displays in every one of its 650 stores around the country.

Bert paid close attention to the merchandising; he considered Davy Crockett a benchmark they should meet and, he hoped, exceed. His exasperation with Screen Gems now had a new point of tension — he was convinced they were missing opportunities left and right. Bert wrote an angry note to Ralph Cohn about one event in Albuquerque, complaining that 17,000 people had showed up but the store had run out of all its Rin Tin Tin merchandise. When I first read the letter, I thought that number sounded improbably large, and that it might have been a typo, but given the excitement about Rin Tin Tin at the time, I'm not so sure.

14.

It must have been gratifying but also a little odd for Lee to see this happening, to see his dog on thermoses and bookends and mechanical games. He had experienced Rinty's fame before, but in the 1920s and 1930s fame meant selling lots of movie tickets and signing lots of autographs and perhaps endorsing a variety of dog food. Now it was no longer enough for fans to watch passively — people wanted celebrity in some form right in their pocket. Merchandise had made that possible. Just like that, you could own a piece of a star; you could own part of what seemed enchanted.

Lee visited the set on occasion and made a few merchandising suggestions. He liked the idea of manufacturing a "Do-It-Yourself rocking dog with a Rin Tin Tin head in place of the usual horse head," and he planned to write a book about dog training, which would expand on the article he wrote for *The American Magazine.* He even appeared again on television, overcoming his dread of being on camera enough to do a commercial with Rinty for Pal Tiny Bits dog food; it ran during *The Adventures of Rin-Tin-Tin.* But he spent most of his time in Riverside with his dogs.

He had always bred and sold puppies, relying on the sales for his income during the years when he didn't have movie work. German shepherds were now more popular than ever. According to one breeder, the Rin Tin Tin show had "set the country on fire and is making heads spin among shepherd breeders." Lee's German shepherd puppies were the most prized of all, and he had more requests than he could satisfy, even though he charged $250 for a puppy — equal to about $2,000 today.

Screen Gems liked giving Rin Tin Tin puppies to its most important accounts, so they often sent Lee requests to ship a puppy to someone like the president of Esquire Novelty or an important executive at Nabisco. Rinty was "procreating like mad," according to Ed Justin. At one point, Screen Gems sent a memo requesting five puppies to send as a gift to an advertiser. "Five puppies impossible," Justin replied. "Rin Tin Tin has slipped disk."

For many people, a Rin Tin Tin puppy was

an aspirational acquisition. "We are far from wealthy people," one woman wrote to Lee in 1958, "but I no longer can resist writing to ask you the price of one of Rin Tin Tin's female puppies. I just hope and pray it will be possible somehow for me to buy one of Rinty's dogs." One man hoping to get a Rin Tin Tin puppy wrote that his German shepherd had served with Dogs for Defense; unfortunately, after the war, the dog became overly protective of his son and too dangerous to keep. He said the boy still cried out in his sleep for the dog; could they possibly get one of Rinty's puppies? "Perhaps we are reaching too high for our pocket book, as we are working people," the letter continued. "But we feel if we can possibly manage to have one, we sure will try."

Occasionally, Lee was willing to barter. He once traded someone a male puppy for a pair of rare pheasants, and he frequently agreed to sell a puppy on credit. He was a soft touch for anyone passionate about Rin Tin Tin; he couldn't help himself. In 1957, he got a letter from four kids, which began, "Dear Mr. Duncan, we would just love to have a dog like Rin Tin Tin. Dawn has been babysitting to get money for the dog. Chris sells butter so we can get this dog. Michael saves all his money and puts in every penny he had. Gail babysits and sells butter for the dog. We have saved up $22.55. If this is not enough please write and tell us how much we have to save." Lee wrote back that if they could raise $25 by the end of the month, he would send them a puppy. A telegram, sent by their parents just after Thanksgiving, reported that the puppy had arrived safely, and that Dawn, Chris, Gail, and Michael were delighted.

Lee's files were filled with letters and telegrams from people who had failed to pay him for the puppy he'd sent them. It seemed as if everyone wanted a Rin Tin Tin puppy, but then they were struck with a hernia, they lost their job, their house was robbed, their spouse was in the hospital, they had terrible luck at the race track, or they hadn't yet recovered from the Great Depression. Their misfortune only made their need for a Rin Tin Tin puppy more acute. A Missouri woman named Dorothy Bishop asked Lee for a puppy on a layaway plan. "With Mr. Bishop a bed-bound invalid," she wrote, "and our boys all gone, and conditions changing all around us almost hourly . . . crime creeping slowly almost to our back door . . . my daughter and I do need a genuinely recognized and trained watchdog." Lee sent one. One telegram from a delinquent owner read HAVE NOT MEANT TO DODGE DEAL ON THE WONDERFUL PUPPY JUST HAVE NOT HAD THE MONEY PERHAPS WE COULD WORK OUT A TIME PAYMENT. A woman in Texas with two Rin Tin Tin puppies wrote, "I will send you the money for the dog as soon as possible. You'll just have to trust me I guess but I'm sure you do. . . . I will do my best to bring them up as a fine example of their famous father and a credit to you."

And still Lee couldn't resist. He was so proud of his dogs, and so dedicated to seeing Rinty's heritage preserved, and most of all, so moved each time he met someone who shared his devotion, that he saw nothing else beyond that.

The number of German shepherds in the United States had been growing even before the television show went on the air. In 1947, 4,921 German shepherds were registered with the American Kennel Club. In 1954, before *The Adventures of Rin-Tin-Tin* had its impact, the number had more than tripled, to 17,400. By the time the show finished its prime-time run in 1959, German shepherd registrations with the AKC had grown to 33,735.

German shepherds are known as "trotting

dogs," and they have a long, gliding gait. In a show ring, a German shepherd moving in a flying trot looks both powerful and weightless, as if it were on a cushion of air. To make that trot even more dynamic and long in reach, breeders started to look for dogs with hindquarters that were deeply angled, in a perpetual crouch, ready to spring forward. The line from the dogs' shoulders to their hips was no longer horizontal; it was an almost forty-five-degree slope. The inbreeding to produce dogs with such an unnatural pose also produced dogs with a tendency toward hip dysplasia, cataracts, hemophilia, and aggressiveness. Other popular dogs that were bred to exaggerate their show qualities suffered the same deterioration.

"Success, like a chicken bone, is bad for dogs," began a February 1958 story in *Life* magazine called "Sad Degeneration of Our Dogs." "The higher a dog rises in public favor, the more devastating its downfall. None has soared higher or fallen harder than the German shepherd." Blaming "assembly-line reproduction," the article included a chart of "the changing leaders in the canine derby, all heading for certain fall."

Lee, in a letter to the editor, wrote, "You

speak of the degeneration of the Shepherd dog — and quite rightly." He explained that his dogs were bred to work, not just to trot around looking showy. His dogs — and Frank Barnes's dogs — were big-boned (with the exception of the first Rin Tin Tin, who was much slighter than his descendants). They were solid and square, without the extreme crouch that was getting attention at shows. Even so, the trend for German shepherds with extreme angulation continued. Some of them looked almost deformed, unable to stand up straight. Among German shepherd fanciers, a rift developed between those who preferred the dog to be rectangular and those who wanted an angled dog with the big trot. Meanwhile, people seemed to want German shepherds of whatever shape they could get, and their numbers kept growing every year.

15.

In 1955, after what was described as "several weeks of delicate negotiation," Rin Tin Tin and Lassie, along with their costars, Lee Aaker and Tommy Rettig, appeared together on the cover of *TV Guide*. According to the *TV Guide* writer, the tension in the studio had everyone "verging on nervous prostration." This might have been dramatic license, but the two camps were indeed wary of each other. At the time, *The Adventures of Rin-Tin-Tin* still had higher ratings than *Lassie,* but Bert was always concerned about slipping. He nagged Screen Gems anytime he noticed a dip in the ratings. When Lassie's producers began to woo PTA groups around the country to ensure that the show was well liked by parents, Bert insisted they set up a series of counteroffensive screenings to push Rin Tin Tin ahead in their affections.

Lee paid even more attention to any challenge by Lassie. He was not a combative man, but he became testy about Lassie. When Roy Rogers advertised in both Lassie and Rin Tin Tin comic books — both produced by Western Publishing — Lee was furious and told the head of the company to reject any such ads in the future. No actors, including extras, that appeared on *The Adventures of Rin-Tin-Tin* were allowed to work on *Lassie.* When a reporter for the *Los Angeles Times* asked if the Hooker brothers, the show's regular stuntmen, ever worked with Lassie, Lee snapped, "The Hooker boys are under strict contract to be bitten exclusively by Rin Tin Tin." Were Lee's feelings about Lassie petty? Not if you consider how galling it would have been to him anytime he heard someone equate Rin Tin Tin, a real dog, with the pretty but imaginary Lassie. There was something deeper in Rin Tin Tin's story that Lee and Bert and, later, Daphne feared would be misunderstood or underestimated, something about it that needed protection. The fact is, Lassie and Rin Tin Tin aren't the same at all. Lassie was a popular character in a book that was then portrayed in film and on television by nine talented dog actors, beginning with Rudd Weatherwax's dog Pal. Rin Tin Tin was a dog who had a real life and ended up becoming an actor.

As is the case with human actors, the characters Rin Tin Tin played in films had other names: Scotty, Lobo, the Grey Ghost, the Wolf Dog, Buddy, King, and Satan, among many others. In some films, his character was called Rin Tin Tin or Rinty, even when the character and the story had nothing to do with his life; in other words, these were not cameos. It was as if Humphrey Bogart's characters in his movies were named "Humphrey Bogart," which of course never would have been the case. Why was he called "Rin Tin Tin" in those films? Dog names don't seem hard to think of.

His name was used because giving him a different name, even within the fictional world of a particular film, seemed to fritter away some of his star power. Rin Tin Tin was not just an actor, but also a kind of franchise, no matter what character he was playing. Whether he was playing a half-breed wild dog in Alaska, say, or a soldier dog in World War I or a borax miner's companion dog somewhere out west, he was always, foremost, Rin Tin Tin. Using his name also made it seem that Rin Tin Tin existed within the film and outside of the film at the same time. Within the film, he was a cinematic character in some cinematic predicament, existing in some other place or time. Outside the film, he was Rin Tin Tin, the famous actor dog. Fusing those two manifestations together highlighted the artifice of film and the self-referential nature of art, the fluid relationship we have with those things we imagine and create. With television, Rin Tin Tin underwent another conceptual transformation. The show was not set in Rinty IV's time period, nor in the time period of any of the other Rin Tin Tins: it was set in 1870, almost fifty years before the first Rin Tin Tin was born, in a place thousands of miles from where he was found, in circumstances he and his ancestors couldn't ever have experienced. German shepherds as a breed didn't even exist in 1870. The plotline of *The Adventures of Rin-Tin-Tin* was pure fiction. The character in the show named Rin Tin Tin was a creation, a type of character with a set of qualities that had come to be bundled up under the name "Rin Tin Tin" — steadfastness, bravery, toughness, heroism, and loyalty. And even though there was a real, living dog named Rin Tin Tin at the time the show was being made, that dog stayed behind on El Rancho Rin Tin Tin, while the dog in the show was played by another dog, JR, who just happened to be better at portraying on screen the things that Rin Tin Tin had come to mean.

16.

The cast of *The Adventures of Rin-Tin-Tin* often went on the road, performing a twenty-minute live show, which began with Lieutenant Masters — actor James Brown — singing in his big, warm baritone. After he finished, he introduced "the star of our show," Rin Tin Tin, who entered the arena riding in a covered wagon with Lee Duncan and Frank Barnes. As they climbed out of the wagon the announcer shouted, "Here he is! The fourth generation of a family that has entertained America for over thirty years! And his owner, and discoverer of the original Rin Tin Tin, Mr. Lee Duncan, and his co-trainer, Mr. Frank Barnes!"

The dog who made these appearances was almost certainly Barnes's dog JR, rather than Rin Tin Tin IV, especially since it was Barnes, not Lee, who put the dog through his paces. Lee took the role of the elder statesman, introducing Barnes to the audience as "my associate of many years" and stepping aside. After the dog performed, actors dressed as cavalry entered and did some horseback maneuvers, followed by a skit involving Apache braves sneaking up on Rusty as he sat around a campfire. At the end, Rin Tin Tin dashed in to set things straight.

The live show was very popular, selling out venues as large as Madison Square Garden. Screen Gems considered expanding the performance to two hours, although, as Ed Justin pointed out to Bert, "this would require us to hire some inexpensive cornball acts like hillbilly singers, etc." The longer show was never developed. It might have been harder to find cornball acts than Justin had imagined, or more likely the actors objected. They were already starting to grumble about being underpaid. James Brown, in particular, complained about his salary, his scripts, and even the requirement that anytime he flew somewhere to perform the live show, he had to disembark from the airplane in his Lieutenant Masters uniform.

Lee received 10 percent of the show's profits and also earned money from Rin Tin Tin books. This gave him enough income to have built the new house and some additional margin of comfort, but he wasn't wealthy. In 1958, when he received his first Social Security check, the newspaper in Riverside reported, "Although Duncan is anything but destitute, he said, 'We can use the money.'"

He felt tired much of the time but he kept working hard. In the first year the show was on the air, at LaHay's prompting, he traveled to New York several times, appearing on *The Ed Sullivan Show, What's My Line?* and the *Today* show. He also judged the *Adventures of Rin-Tin-Tin* Name the Puppy Contest, which drew almost a million entries. "My first entry is 'Nani Wahine I Leke Duncan von Rin Tin Tin,'" one of those entries read. "My second entry is 'Nani Kama'liivahine von Rin Tin Tin.' Would like to have your opinion on the choice."

He also often took on work that was surprising for someone of his stature and age. Even when his dog was once again the most famous dog in the world, when 2 million Rin Tin Tin comic books were sold each year, when 40 million Americans watched the dog on television, he agreed to appear at events like the Riverside Council Boy Scouts pet show, where he was asked to choose the pet "with the curliest tail; the one with the most expressive eyes; blackest nose; the noisiest pet; and the longest pet."

It seems preposterous, but he did it because he believed in the connection between a kid and a pet, and in the deep satisfaction of having your pet admired, and he never felt far away from his experience as a boy needing a pet to fill his heart.

He still wanted to go out with the dog, just the two of them — to perform, to meet the people who loved the dog, and to tell his stories. Being with Rin Tin Tin was still the thing that made him happiest. He was content whether they were in front of an audience or traveling alone together, just enjoying each other's companionship, as he had when the first Rin Tin Tin was an old dog and they had their last and most tender time together camping in the Sierras.

Lee's contract with Screen Gems stated

that he always had the option to be part of any *Adventures of Rin-Tin-Tin* personal appearances and live shows — but it apparently had not occurred to him that the studio might not want him appearing on his own. If a Scout troop or an orphanage asked Lee to come visit with Rinty, the studio insisted that Barnes, and perhaps another cast member as well, be present. This was expensive and sometimes difficult to coordinate with the show's filming schedule. Lee resented this, and the studio grew impatient with him. Memos between studio executives began referring to Lee as "eccentric" and "troublesome at times." His insistence on making these public appearances was "terribly embarrassing."

Screen Gems perceived any interference with its control of the show to be a nuisance. Lee — stubborn, single-minded, and old-fashioned — was becoming a nuisance. He was a dog man who had happened into Hollywood; the people at Screen Gems were Hollywood men who happened to be making a show about a dog. "Inasmuch as Lee Duncan is somewhat of an eccentric . . . and inasmuch as it is imperative that Bert maintain happy relationships with Duncan it is desirable that you get some action on this a.s.a.p.," Ralph Cohn commanded in a studio memo, adding that he thought Lee's publishing deals, which were in place before he signed on with Screen Gems and therefore out of the studio's control, were "idiotic."

When the relationship between Lee and the studio seemed particularly strained, Screen Gems hurried some royalty payments to him and sent him an advance of $15,000 when he found himself with a deluge of bills for the house construction. ("This was a god-send," Lee wrote to Bert, "and has eased our minds of worry considerably.") The truth was, the studio didn't need him and didn't need his dog; the appeasement was just a courtesy. While he and the dog had served to inspire the idea of the show, it ran independent of him; his connection to it had become only symbolic.

Bert, who cared about Lee and wanted to protect Lee's dignity, tried his best to mediate. He tried to explain to Screen Gems how Lee saw things. But Bert was always most concerned about what was best for the show. In the end, he just seemed uncomfortable. "Lee Duncan is a very peculiar man," he explained to Ralph Cohn. "Though he would hurt no one he lives by his own code."

Frank Barnes was probably in the most awkward position. He had Lee's job, and his dogs had the job Lee had hoped his dog would have. Whether it was on his own or at Bert's urging isn't clear, but Barnes always took great care to pay Lee respect whenever possible. Barnes often wrote to Lee when he was on the road with JR, who was of course being presented to the public as Rin Tin Tin. One of those letters was sent from Houston. It was written on hotel stationery, milky white and thin as silk, with a drawing of the hotel filling the upper quarter of the page. It was easy to imagine Barnes hunched over a desk, with the dog asleep at his feet, trying to think of what to say, understanding that he was an instrument in Lee's sense of loss, his fading significance. "Dear Lee, I have heard nothing but 'Lee Duncan' since we have been here," the letter began. "I believe you are better known than the President." After a few remarks about the weather, Barnes added one more sentence before signing off: "I can tell you that the name 'Lee Duncan and Rin Tin Tin' is nothing less than magic."

This was the first time I had ever spent so much time learning about one person's life, and it was a new experience for me to fall so deeply into it, and strangest of all, to feel, as I did sometimes, that I knew more about Lee than he might have known about himself, and more than I would have known if I had met him and talked to him and learned about him in that more usual way. Before I spent these hours in Bert's storage room and Lee's file boxes in Riverside, I had never realized how crackling and alive someone's papers could be. I always assumed that archives would be as dull as an accountant's ledger. But instead, they made me feel as though I had drilled my way inside a still-humming life. It was all there — the details and the ordinariness, the asides and incidentals, and even the misfires and failures that might otherwise have gone unmentioned. These are the things that make up an actual existence, the things a person wouldn't think to share because they seemed inconsequential, or wouldn't be willing to share because they seemed too intimate, but they are at the heart of who we are. I am sure that Lee, interviewed in person, would have been interesting but frustrating. He was a talker but not someone who was anxious to be revealed. He was desperate for you to know the legend that his life seemed to be, and he wanted you to

know about his dogs, but really nothing
more.

I had been in a funk for a while because
as I worked my way through his papers I
could feel him receding. I knew the inevitable end of the story — this was 2010, after
all, and Lee had been born in 1893, so it
was no mystery that his story would soon
be fulfilled. But over the year I had spent
learning about him, he had come to life for
me, and as I worked my way toward the end
of his papers in Riverside, some of those
afternoons felt very gray, even as the building was baking in the harsh desert sun.

17.

By the fourth season the show was falter-
ing. Bert had always expected that it would
need, in time, what he called "a shot in the
arm." He replaced Douglas Heyes as the
head writer and considered leaving Corriganville for a location in Oregon. He knew
there were limits to the show's basic setup,
especially because there was only one possible outcome to all of the episodes: triumph
over adversity, aided by the dog. Repetition
was inevitable. The characters themselves
didn't offer a great deal of variety. Women
occasionally appeared as guest stars in

episodes like "Boone's Wedding Day" and "Hubert's Niece," but none appeared regularly. The rest of the cast, except for Rinty, were white male military personnel.

Rin Tin Tin wasn't the only iconic animal star beginning to age. *Lassie* was adding celebrity guest stars, such as Brooklyn Dodgers catcher Roy Campanella, to attract new viewers. *The Adventures of Champion,* starring Gene Autry's horse, was canceled in 1956 after one season, and its replacement, *My Friend Flicka,* another horse show, lasted only until 1957. Television wasn't getting rid of animals, but they were no longer cast as creatures that were omniscient and heroic. They were talking horses like Mr. Ed or an absurdist pig like Arnold Ziffel on *Green Acres.* Just as the heroic animals in silent film became comedians in talkies, animals on television were becoming jesters, something Rin Tin Tin had never been.

By this time, Bert also had much more on his mind than Rin Tin Tin. He had launched his two new shows, *Circus Boy* and *Tales of the 77th Bengal Lancers,* and then introduced his most ambitious television project, a brooding police drama called *Naked City,* starring James Franciscus and John Mc-

Intire. Bert loved *Naked City* as social commentary; while he wasn't active in politics, he was a committed liberal, and he encouraged the show's writers, Stirling Silliphant and Howard Rodman, to focus as much on the criminals' stories as on the police.

It was a writer's show, and Bert was quickly developing a reputation in Hollywood as a writer's producer, siding with them against the studios even when it cost him. He seemed, as always, to enjoy taunting executives. "I find they are pedestrian people," he told a reporter from *Variety*. "Their consensus is cliché. Something is good because they've seen it before."

He didn't always win his battles. For the first season of *Naked City,* Silliphant wrote an episode in which James Franciscus's character watches an inmate being executed. ABC was outraged, but Bert insisted he wanted to use the episode; the network responded by canceling the show. (The following year, *Naked City* was brought back for four more seasons, at the urging of the show's principal sponsor, the tobacco company Brown & Williamson.)

Bert was also developing a moody, existential series with Silliphant as the chief writer. The show, *Route 66,* was almost plotless; it followed two young men and their experiences as they roam across the country in a Corvette. To add to the show's realism, Bert wanted to film entirely on the road, rather than on a set or at a studio; this had never been done for a television show. "The studios weren't interested in it because they felt nobody would sponsor a show about two bums on the road," Bert explained in a *Variety* interview. "So I put my own dough in it and got it made."

Route 66 debuted in 1960 to good ratings and even better reviews, and for that moment, Bert, who still looked so young that he often got carded when he ordered drinks, was one of the most successful producers in Hollywood, with three acclaimed shows on the air. "Television has few success stories to match that of Herbert B. Leonard, the cherubic proprietor-producer of 'Naked City' and 'Route 66,'" the *Los Angeles Examiner* reported in 1961. "Seven years ago, at the age of 30, Leonard borrowed a thousand dollars to launch the Rin Tin Tin series. . . ." As Bert himself once put it, "I don't know how I got to be so good."

But in the meantime, he was having less luck with *The Adventures of Rin-Tin-Tin.* The ratings were slipping. With so many new projects, he couldn't have had as much time to spend on it. Besides, the show was no longer new. The excitement of the early seasons was missing. Screen Gems' publicity department decided to try making Lee Aaker more of a star. "Nothing is more modern than modern youths," one of its press releases declared. It continued:

They are up on nuclear weapons, stratosphere ships, moon rockets. . . . Eleven-year-old Lee Aaker is no exception. "Sure I get a kick out of rocket ships and everything like that," says Lee, "and I bet kids playing in that kind of TV show must have a lot of fun. But, well, maybe you'd call me old-fashioned, but I get more fun out of playing with Rinty and riding my horse." Although Lee does keep up to date as all modern kids are doing, he still does prefer the things which interested boys years ago, animals, Indians, etc. "I get a big kick out of being in a cavalry troop and riding hard with all the soldiers," Lee says.

The press release inadvertently pointed out the show's greatest liability. It was, in fact, very old-fashioned, built on a belief in gallantry and an innocent affection for a dog. There was also an unwavering respect for official power — as Rip Masters said, in more than one episode, "It never pays to defy the authority of the U.S. government!" In the beginning, the show fit the tone of the time, but it began to seem out of step. The world was shifting. Defiance was in the air. The first of the baby boomers were growing up; they were teenagers. As their attitudes began to take shape, and especially as they began to pull away from their parents, they became a new and potent force, and popular culture reflected it. In came Marlon Brando and Elvis Presley and *American Bandstand,* Allen Ginsberg's *Howl* in 1956, Jack Kerouac's *On the Road* in 1957, and William S. Burroughs's *Naked Lunch* in 1959. In 1955, *Rebel Without a Cause,* starring James Dean as a disaffected teenager, was celebrated as a definitive portrait of American suburbia, and *Blackboard Jungle,* with its cast of sneering punks and the first rock-and-roll sound track in film, made city teenagers seem predatory and cruel. The prospect of comfortable postwar affluence in bedroom communities filled with pliant, pink-cheeked babies was curdling. Affluent bedroom communities were dull and deadening, and the babies had become bored adolescents. A dog hero and a cavalry troop began to seem like an artifact from another time.

In the spring of 1959, the 164th episode of *The Adventures of Rin-Tin-Tin* was broadcast. It was an unusually bleak story about a poor farm family, the Barkers. As the episode begins, the head of the family, Manley Barker, has disappeared, stirring suspicion that he is responsible for a string of robberies in the area. He has left a cryptic farewell note for his wife that says, "I have to face it. I'm a failure. Please try to understand." The banker in town swoops in to foreclose on the Barkers' house, and the wife of the banker, a gloating crone named Emma Crabtree, announces that the Barkers' two children will be taken away from their mother and put in an orphanage.

Rin Tin Tin has only a small role in the proceedings, helping Lieutenant Masters track down Manley Barker. Once they find him, it becomes clear that Barker has nothing to do with the robberies; he left his family because he believes he's a disappointment to them. "I reckon I'm just a failure," he tells Lieutenant Masters, gloomily. He agrees to come home, and even though his name has been cleared, nothing has improved: the family is still broke. The threat of the foreclosure and the orphanage is brandished once again by Emma Crabtree, until her husband, the banker, has had enough of his horrible wife; he steps in and declares he is going to buy the house and let the Barkers live in it together for free. The Barker children and their friend Rusty celebrate; the orphanage — always a theme, overtly or otherwise, in *The Adventures of Rin-Tin-Tin* — has been narrowly avoided.

This episode was called "The Failure," and it was the last episode of *The Adventures of Rin-Tin-Tin* ever shot. After its glorious start and wide success, the show was over. Nabisco had informed Screen Gems that because of the falling ratings, it was canceling its sponsorship. It was the end of a relationship between Nabisco and Rin Tin Tin that had spanned decades. "Being a sucker for nostalgia, it set me thinking about some of the fun we have had during our association with you," Nabisco's advertising manager wrote to Lee when the decision was announced. "It is going to be rather strange not seeing the publicity releases about you and Rinny, such as the one which is in front of me now entitled 'Ten tricks to teach your dog' by Lee Duncan. I am sure you are aware of the fact that everyone here at NABISCO knows how much you and Rinny have meant to us."

ABC began broadcasting the show in

reruns twice a week, and CBS picked it up for Saturday mornings. Screen Gems reported the good news about the bad news. "As if we didn't have trouble enough counting all that Hanna-Barbera loot; and the Dennis the Menace shekels," the memo, titled "Rin-Tin-Tin Re-Runs Wild!" said. "We dusted off Ol' Rinty and Rusty and Rip and turned them loose on the CBS Network Saturdays at 11 a.m. If ratings mean anything at all, EVERY kid in the United States is watching the RIN TIN TIN show — WITH TWO HEADS!!"

18.

All this time, Bert and Lee never stopped thinking about the movies. Lee, in particular, always held out hope that the story of his life would be made into a film. The television series didn't quell that desire; in fact, now that another generation was embracing Rin Tin Tin, he seemed more determined to explain that the dog was not merely a fictional character on TV. He also wanted it known that he had a story, one that even now seemed to astonish him, as if his whole life had come to him as a surprise.

Back in 1953, when they first met, Bert had told Lee that he was eager to make the movie based on Lee's life. He had convinced Columbia Pictures to back the project, and he hired Douglas Heyes to write the screenplay. According to the contract, the movie "shall star the dog Rin Tin Tin who is used in the television series of pictures . . . or another German shepherd of similar appearance." Bert hoped Jimmy Stewart would play Lee; if Stewart wasn't available, then perhaps James Brown would take the role. Bert told a friend that he pictured the movie being about "how Lee got the dog, the dog's love life, Lee's love life, and how it affected their relationship." It seemed like a sure thing, especially once the television show took off and gave Bert the credentials of a viable producer. " 'Lin Tin Tin' Vidpix Series Prompts Theatrical Biopic of Famed Film Dog," *Daily Variety* reported, saying the film would be released in early 1955.

Then nothing. Lee referred to the film in a letter to Bert in 1958, saying, "Our greatest hope is that we will have a fortune to share and that we can make the RIN TIN TIN story before too late," but that was it. The next public mention of the film didn't come until a year later, when the *New York Times* ran a story headlined "Rin Tin Tin Script Posing Problems." By then, Stirling Silliphant, who was the head writer on *Na-*

410

ked City, had replaced Douglas Heyes as the screenwriter on *Rin Tin Tin and Me,* as the script was being called; Silliphant confessed to the *Times* reporter that the project wasn't going well. He was confounded by the challenge of writing for a dog. "The approach I'm following is the same as you would if you were writing a movie in which the central character were a deaf-mute," Silliphant explained.

And then, once more, nothing. It ate at Lee that the movie wasn't getting made. This wasn't just another project to him: it seemed like he thought it would sum up everything his life had been. And what an unusual, funny life it had been, full of serendipity and myth, acclaim and reversal; the sweep was cinematic in its improbability. As much as Lee wanted other people to know the story, it was as if he needed to see it on the screen to understand it for himself. He talked about the movie often, to everyone. An article in the newsletter from the Fred Finch home, where Lee had spent those hard years as a little boy, noted, "One of the unfulfilled dreams which Lee had talked to us about in recent years was the making of a full-length movie of the story of Rin Tin Tin, to be actually the story of his own life and including significantly the Fred Finch Children's Home."

19.

In 1957, while he was in Minneapolis doing an appearance with Rinty, Lee had a mild heart attack. He came home to Riverside and recovered, but he was discouraged. Eva confided to a friend that Lee thought he might never be "active" again — that is, he would not be strong enough to do a lot of travel. Later that year he developed diabetes. From that point on he sounded different — valedictory, reflective, as if he were looking back from a distant place. "That's what made it a real full life, my dogs and my cattle," he told a newspaper in 1958. He told another, "It's nice to have lived a real story."

He then had a stroke. He had always been fit — lean, strong, rugged, athletic even at sixty, his cowboy build little changed from his twenties. But this series of illnesses, one after another, overwhelmed him, and after the stroke he was housebound — not even able to wander out to the barn to see the animals on his own; this must have felt like death to him.

I had come to feel that I knew Lee Duncan. He had become as familiar to me as a family member, and, as is often the case with a family member, he also remained a mystery. He was at once ingenuous and impenetrable. In some ways his life seemed so simple, but that simplicity made it hard not to wonder if there was more hidden beneath it. Lee's devotion to Rin Tin Tin was so absolute that everything else, even his identity, seemed withered by comparison. He would have been difficult to have as a friend or a husband or a father, because he wasn't really entirely there, except in connection to Rin Tin Tin. But I had grown to feel real affection for him. He seemed so guileless, forever the boy left at the front door of the Fred Finch home or the man in that last newsreel with old Rin, his face lit with joy as the dog leaped and landed in his arms, the prize of a lifetime.

So why was Rin Tin Tin so important to him? Vanity would not have been enough to drive him this hard, especially because most of his vanity pertained to Rinty. Whatever attention Lee was paid he deflected back toward the dog. Making money mattered, but it was never the single principle that shaped him; Lee was a sloppy deal-maker, an indifferent bargainer, and even though in Hollywood he briefly developed a taste for cars and clothes, he lived most of his life unassumingly, splurging only on more countrified luxuries like nice saddles and purebred cattle.

Lee simply believed in what he found in Rin Tin Tin. He believed in the good luck that visited him when he first came upon the puppy, and in the solace and friendship he had with him, and in the epic story told through the dog, a story of valor and loyalty and strength and truth. And he believed that those qualities would always matter and always prevail, and as part of that epic story they would transcend time, always compelling and forever unknowable. He believed in the dog, and that was what his life was about.

As I was coming to understand Lee, I was inching along right behind him — doubting that any one thing could mean so much, while all along believing that understanding Rin Tin Tin and his story would explain something important about how we make sense of the strangeness and solitude of existence. It was what I believed in, just as Lee believed in Rinty.

I had finished reading through almost all of Lee's papers at the Riverside Museum, starting every morning before the sun became so punishing that shades had to be drawn and the parking lot pavement got tacky. I began noticing letters that Eva had sent canceling some of Lee's travel plans, and notes from Wauhillau LaHay and Screen Gems executives asking after Lee's health. Then I came across letters Eva had written to people who owed money for their puppies, asking, with a new urgency, when they were going to pay. I knew that I was edging toward the inevitable. My perspective was one that the people involved could have never had: a bird's-eye view of a road and its end point that a traveler on that road could never have seen. No matter how I had prepared myself for it, I gasped when I came to the last note in the box, written by Eva and addressed to the American Kennel Club in September 1960, informing the club that her husband, Lee Duncan, had just died and that she needed the ownership of the dogs transferred to her name.

THE LEAP

1.

Lee never stopped saying "There will always be a Rin Tin Tin," but he never followed that statement with another sentence or two addressing all the questions such a statement raised. To him, the permanence of Rin Tin Tin was plain truth and needed no embellishment; he never saw the need to explain how this immortality would be achieved or whom he pictured taking over as the dog's custodian when he was gone. I don't mean arrangements for the actual dogs living at El Rancho Rin Tin Tin: after Lee's death, those dogs obviously belonged to Eva and Carolyn. What he never specified, and what remains a puzzle, is whom he pictured as the steward of everything the dog had come to mean — the whole range of it, from the puppies he was breeding, to

417

the character on the television show, to the dog he hoped would be portrayed in the movie about his life, to the image of the dog, the iconic Rin Tin Tin, that was now spread around the world through merchandise and performances as well as movies and TV.

In interviews Lee often complimented Carolyn's talents as a dog trainer and more than once said that he expected her to be in charge of Rin Tin Tin "one of these days." After Rin Tin Tin IV died, she was given the honor of choosing Rin Tin Tin V from among the many Rin Tin Tin puppies being whelped at the ranch. This designation was a serious matter to Lee, like choosing the next Dalai Lama or an heir to a throne. The publicists at Kenyon & Eckhardt always made sure to note that Carolyn was the only person besides Lee who did any of the dogs' training.

But Carolyn stopped thinking of herself as her father's successor the moment Bert turned up at the ranch. She felt shunted aside, and her attention shifted from dogs to horses, and then from horses to a boyfriend. She got married when she was just nineteen. "My father was going to leave Rin Tin Tin to me. That's what I had always heard, my whole life," Carolyn told me.

418

"But it was just talk. He believed Bert was his true heir and he gave him everything."

Lee did give Bert the rights to the dog as a cinematic character, but not the training and breeding of the dogs themselves. It is hard to know what Lee thought would happen with it all after he was gone. He couldn't have expected Bert to take over the kennel — Bert was a producer, not a breeder, not a dog lover. Lee liked and respected Frank Barnes, and Barnes might have been a logical person to step in if Carolyn didn't take that role. But Barnes never got more involved than working as the trainer for the show. The truth is, there was no one else at all. For someone who believed he had created something sweeping, permanent, and everlasting, Lee never seemed to have a picture of the future in his mind.

2.

In 1956, in his usual pile of fan mail and puppy requests, Lee had received a letter from a woman named Jannettia Propps Brodsgaard, a German shepherd breeder from Texas. She explained to Lee that she'd been trying to track him down for years, and that she had wanted a Rin Tin Tin dog ever since seeing *Where the North Begins,* in

1923. "Two years ago I decided I would get one," she wrote. "Then I got cold feet, afraid you might not talk to me. I am not one of those rich Texans you hear about. Just a plain old country girl."

Like Lee, Brodsgaard had grown up in a lonely place. Sinewy and tall, with a long jaw and a hard gaze, she was born and raised on the plains of West Texas at the Matador Ranch, where her mother was a cook and her father was a ranch hand. The ranch comprised almost a million acres of open range. As a child, her closest companion was a timber wolf she managed to tame. Brodsgaard didn't get her first German shepherd until she was in her twenties, when she and her husband were living in Houston and happened on a stray. Even in pitiful condition, the stray reminded Brodsgaard of her old pet timber wolf — and of the pleasure she felt when she first saw Rin Tin Tin on screen. She took the stray home, fattened her up, and started breeding her. Then she began looking for Rin Tin Tin.

She learned from a magazine story that Lee lived in Riverside; like a lot of people trying to reach him, she simply addressed her letter to "Lee Duncan, Owner of Rin Tin Tin, Riverside, California," and it was delivered to him. They began corresponding. They agreed on their feelings about dogs; they preferred a shepherd with a light-colored coat, for instance, rather than a dark gray coat like the first Rin Tin Tin's. Lee, in fact, was dedicated to breeding for that paler color because he believed that the harsh lighting needed to make old Rin visible on film had damaged the dog's eyes. Brodsgaard was just as particular. "I guess you think I am crazy," Brodsgaard wrote in a letter to Duncan, "[but] a dog just HAS to be a certain color." They had both grown up in so much vacant space, and both seemed to have the habit of mind that focused on a single purpose, as if to make up for not having a talent for connecting with other people.

In 1957, Lee sold Brodsgaard a male puppy he considered the pick of his current litter. When the puppy arrived in Texas, Brodsgaard telegrammed to say she had named him Rinty Tin Tin Brodsgaard and that he was perfect. The arrival of the first Rin Tin Tin puppy in Texas was newsworthy — this was, after all, the zenith of the television show's popularity — and a writer from the *Houston Press* was stationed at Brodsgaard's house to report on the event.

This puppy was only the first of four dogs Brodsgaard bought from Lee, and they became the foundation of what Brodsgaard's granddaughter, Daphne Hereford, now calls "the living legacy of Rin Tin Tin dogs in Texas." Daphne framed a copy of Lee's letter to her grandmother confirming the sale of that first puppy and has it hanging on a wall in her house in Texas. I noticed it the first time I visited her there, and when I went back to see her a second time, I made sure to look at the letter closely. Lee could never master a typewriter; he either dictated all his correspondence or wrote a draft in longhand, and then Eva typed it and presented it to him for his spider scrawl of a signature. Their typewriter had a few hiccupy keys and a smudgy ribbon. The stationery was their ranch letterhead: EL RANCHO RIN TIN TIN was displayed in large block letters across the top of the page; beneath it was a pencil drawing of the Duncans' house on Field Lane, with two riders on horseback next to the house. Suspended over the whole scene, peering out from a gigantic lucky horseshoe, bigger than the house, the horses, and even the people, was the handsome head of Rin Tin Tin.

3.

After Lee's death, Eva was alone at the ranch. "The dogs are my salvation," she wrote to a friend. "I don't know what I would have done without them. I'll always keep the dogs, they mean so much to me and I plan to keep on going the way Lee would want us to." But with Lee gone and Carolyn living too far away to help, Eva's plan quickly proved unworkable. She never was a dog person. What she loved was art, and she spent all her free time taking classes and painting. The ranch had been Lee's, the dogs had been Lee's, and she hardly had a place in it.

After a few months, she decided she really didn't want to stay on the ranch, and, in fact, she didn't even want to stay in Riverside. Instead, she wanted to travel around the world with a friend of hers, the Australian pop singer Helen Reddy, and then move to a condominium somewhere close to a beach. She put the ranch on the market and sold it for $80,000 to the first person who looked at it, a local banker who wanted to move in as soon as possible. She needed to dismantle the place before she left on her trip — to pack everything and find homes for all the animals. She was keeping only one dog, a young sable male she had named Vincent Van Gogh.

By then, there was only a small number of dogs left at the ranch. Screen Gems wanted one of them to give to a Rin Tin Tin merchandise licensee. Eva sold a few of the others, and she gave the rest of the animals, including the one-eyed fighting dog Hey You and Lee's palomino horse Deputy-Master, to a family named Crawford who lived nearby in Riverside.

She still had to deal with the Memory Room — all those clippings and pictures and mementos and letters gathered over decades, worn now from being held and handled and remembered. This had been Lee's private room. It was the repository of a life Eva hadn't really shared and had often resented. Still, she couldn't quite bring herself to throw the contents away. She realized that it was the record of something significant. She also still hoped that Lee's story would be made into a film. She had caught Lee's yearning for it, and asked Bert about it frequently; he had assured her that it would happen sometime soon. Everything in the Memory Room was part of that.

In the end, what she did seemed to express her ambivalence toward Rin Tin Tin and all he had meant in her life. She didn't empty the room and throw the contents away, nor did she make sure they were protected. All she could bring herself to do was to gather everything hurriedly and ask her neighbors, the Crawfords, if she could leave it in their shed. The way she left things made it seem as if she expected to come back for it someday.

But she never came back: she moved to a condominium south of Riverside and never sent for the papers, never traveled to Riverside to collect them, never left instructions for how she wished them to be disposed of or archived, and they were still in the Crawfords' shed when she passed away. They sat untouched in the shed for a decade, the acid of the paper slowly eating up the clippings, the photographs fading, seeming to belong to no one. At some point the Crawfords decided to move, and they asked one of Dr. Crawford's employees, Freeda Carter, to help them pack. After she finished in the house, Carter decided to look inside the shed, in case they had left something behind. And there she found what she always calls "the treasure."

When Carter told Dr. Crawford about the papers, he told her not to worry — he would arrange for someone to haul them away. But throwing the Duncan papers away felt wrong to her. "I grew up with Rin Tin Tin, and so did my children," Carter explained when we talked some time ago. "I just didn't want to do that." So she asked Dr. Crawford to wait, and the next day, with a borrowed pickup truck, she took it all home.

Carter spent the next year sorting it out — smoothing the creases in the pages and the dog-show ribbons, brushing the dirt off the booties Rin Tin Tin wore as part of his army-issued uniform. She spread everything out around her house while she fussed over it, reassembling and restoring the Memory Room. It took over her house and her life. Every surface was covered with some clipping or picture: "I was constantly saying, don't sit on that! That's 1937!" she explained. In the end, she donated it to the Riverside Municipal Museum, where it was boxed and filed and indexed and recorded — permanent and preserved at last.

4.

For Bert, the idea of Rin Tin Tin "going on forever" meant something different than it did to Lee. They shared an ambition, but the two men came to their relationship with Rin Tin Tin from opposite directions. Bert was passionate about stories; Lee was passionate about his dogs. Bert wasn't on the field in Flirey, didn't scramble to get the puppy home on a troop ship, didn't knock on doors along Poverty Row with the notion that his clever dog might have a place in the movies. Bert grew up knowing Rin Tin Tin not as a dog you might hike with through the Sierras but as an actor and a character — as a story. He loved stories; in fact, he sometimes choked up when he told a story because he was so moved by the power of a narrative, the way it could lift you and carry you along. He loved the Rin Tin Tin story, and he devoted himself to doing whatever he could to keep it going.

The dogs themselves were fungible; in Bert's opinion, Rin Tin Tin was now an acting meritocracy, not a hereditary monarchy. But in the end, Bert and Lee cared about the same thing. They both believed the dog was immortal — that there would always be a Rin Tin Tin, whatever that might mean. As Bert wrote to Eva, in 1962, "For all of us, Rin Tin Tin seems to go on forever."

El Rancho Rin Tin Tin was now a banker's home, and Lee's dogs were scattered. In Texas, though, Brodsgaard was raising Rin Tin Tin puppies with the idea that she was carrying on the line. Since the momentous arrival of Rinty Tin Tin Brodsgaard, several other kennels in Texas had gotten puppies from Lee, so Brodsgaard was no longer the only breeder in Texas to have some of Duncan's dogs. But she was the most single-minded, just as Duncan had been.

In 1965, when she was well into middle age, Brodsgaard unexpectedly found herself raising two toddlers — her granddaughters, who had been left by their mother in the Brodsgaards' care. Eventually the younger of the two girls went back to California to be with her mother, but Daphne, who was five when she was deposited with her grandmother in Houston, never lived with her mother again. When I first met Daphne and learned this about her, I couldn't help noting the similarity between her childhood and Lee Duncan's.

Daphne practically grew up in the Brodsgaards' kennel. "Dogs were all that Daphne knew, they were her life," Daphne wrote in her self-published memoir, which is told in the third person, as if she viewed her personal history as a kind of saga. "When it came time in school to learn fractions in the 5th grade, the only way it made sense was when her teacher compared the pie pieces of fractions to a litter of puppies." Daphne was a natural with the dogs, and at a very young age she felt a passion for Rin Tin Tin that was as thorough as her grandmother's.

In 1965, Carl and Jannettia Brodsgaard divorced. Jannettia was left with nothing except her dogs; she had no marketable skills. Then by chance she was contacted by a construction company looking for dogs to guard worksites. Brodsgaard's dogs had never been trained for security work, but what happened next, according to Daphne's book, was remarkable: Brodsgaard went into her kennel, picked out the dog she thought might have a chance at passing as a security guard, and gently told him "that if he wanted to continue to eat, he had to act like a guard dog. Amazingly enough that is exactly what he did." And just like that, Brodsgaard had a successful guard dog company.

Of course it couldn't have been just like that, but by the time I met Daphne, I was used to the idea that everything connected to Rin Tin Tin was full of happenstance and charm, lightning strikes of fortune and hairpin turns of luck; from a standstill, life around Rin Tin Tin always seemed to accelerate out of the depths of disappointment to a new place filled with possibility. Just like that, wonderful things happened to someone who otherwise would have been luckless, friendless, abandoned. This is what the story of Rin Tin Tin had become in my mind — a myth — and why it had drawn me in, as it had drawn in all these other people. The facts were all interesting, but they were mere armature; the rest was like an ancient legend, wondrous, lifting everything around it, as buoyant as a dream.

5.

Everything changed for German shepherds on May 17, 1963. That day, *Life* published a photo essay by Charles Moore titled "They Fight a Fire That Won't Go Out," about the violent police response to civil rights protests in Birmingham, Alabama. The text that accompanied the photos began, "ATTACK DOGS. With vicious guard dogs, the police attacked the marchers — and thus rewarded them with an outrage that would win support all over the world for Birmingham's Negroes." The story reported that Birmingham's police commissioner, Eugene "Bull" Connor, had allowed white spectators near the police action on purpose. "I want 'em to see the dogs work," Connors was quoted as saying. "Look at those niggers run."

No one who has seen these photographs

could easily forget them: shot in rich, silky black-and-white, they capture a horrifying moment on a Birmingham street. Three of the pictures show a thin, elderly man in a porkpie hat being bitten by two German shepherds. The fourth is a shot of a Birmingham officer with his dog, a black-and-cream shepherd, standing up on its back legs, its teeth bared, straining at the leash.

German shepherds had always been popular service dogs, from the very beginnings of the breed, when Max von Stephanitz gave some of the first of his dogs to the German police to demonstrate their responsiveness and courage. During war, German shepherds' strength and intelligence made them ideal military dogs, and they became the breed most often used by police. Even though they were bred to work herding livestock, they became associated around the world with war.

Because German shepherds looked like wolves, they were sometimes assumed to be more closely related to them than other breeds of dogs even though they are not. Many early Rin Tin Tin movies played on that misperception, and so did Hitler's celebration of the German shepherd as "wolflike." In the 1920s, a sheep farmers' association in Australia began a campaign against German shepherds, asserting that they were part wolf and likely to breed with wild dingoes. In response, the Australian government banned the import of German shepherds to the country that wasn't repealed until 1974.

In the United States, German shepherds came to be viewed as an extension of the police, representing order and authority; during the 1960s, when those qualities were being questioned, everything associated with them was questioned, too. Dozens of other photographs documented police violence, but Charles Moore's pictures of the attacking dogs were the most searing, because they made the police seem like animals themselves, and because they made the scene look like a war. They brought to mind the image of Nazi guards patrolling World War II concentration camps with their slinking German shepherds, and sometimes the association was not only conceptual. A 1961 article in the Jackson, Mississippi, newspaper reported that two German shepherds, Happy and Rebel, were making the Jackson police department's "orders to racial demonstrators more meaningful." The writer then added, "Harry Nawroth of Springfield, the former Nazi storm trooper who trained killer Dobermans to guard Hitler's airports, trained both Happy and Rebel."

According to historian Arthur Schlesinger Jr., the photographs of Bull Connor's police dogs lunging at the marchers in Birmingham "did as much as anything to transform the national mood and make legislation not just necessary . . . but possible." Jacob Javits, the former Republican senator from New York, said the pictures "helped to spur passage of the Civil Rights Act of 1964."

For German shepherds, the taint lingered. Beginning in 1969, the popularity of the breed went into decline, even while other large breeds like Rottweilers and Doberman pinschers gained. There were more dogs in the United States than ever, but the breeds that were becoming most popular were golden retrievers and Labrador retrievers, always smiling, and cocker spaniels, always quivering.

I was eight years old when the Charles Moore pictures were published. I was devoted to *Life* as a kid, and fought my brother and sister for dibs on each new issue, so I saw this issue as soon as it arrived. At that age, I don't think I understood what civil rights were, but that wasn't required in order to understand that something terrible was happening in those pictures. Because I loved dogs and suffered from the unrequited desire for one, and especially because I wanted a German shepherd, Moore's images of those snarling German shepherds hit me hard. And yet I still loved Rin Tin Tin — I watched the reruns on Saturday mornings, and when my family visited my grandparents, my brother and sister and I drifted upstairs to my grandfather's office, where he kept the untouchable plastic Rin Tin Tin figurine. It was so noble, with its smart, beautiful face and little waves of plastic etched fur, always standing at attention between my grandfather's Paymaster 8000 Check Printer and his manual adding machine.

This is what finally happened. One day, my grandfather gave in, or grew tired of us gazing at the dog, or suddenly thought better of his strictness about it, and he agreed to let us take the Rin Tin Tin home and play with it for a day. We didn't dream that we would be keeping it, but being allowed to even touch it was amazing, a crack in the invisible wall around my grandfather's world. And what I remember is that we took the figurine home, and in our excitement, as we fought over it, the dog's right leg broke off, leaving a hole in the bottom of the hollow body.

I don't remember how my grandfather reacted when we brought back the broken
dog, but I do remember that it was not put
back in its usual place on the desk, where
we could still look at it, but in a high cabinet
with a door that was shut tight. We never
saw it again. I've never asked my brother or
sister whether they recall the incident or
think it happened this way, because I'm not
sure I want to know if I'm remembering it
correctly or not. What matters is that it's
the story I've always told myself. I have
come to believe that I've been looking for
that dog ever since that day.

6.

Eva once told a friend that Bert was "planning to run the present TV pictures for two
or three years and then make an entirely
new series with Rin." That may have been
Bert's plan, but it wasn't working out that
way. The show was in reruns on CBS from
October 1959 until September 1964, and
then the network decided it had reached its
limit. *The Adventures of Rin-Tin-Tin* had been
on television for a total of ten years: it was
starting to look old. Television shows in the
1960s were more designed, more stylish,
more movielike, than *The Adventures of Rin-*

Tin-Tin, with its switch-hitting cast and Corriganville setting, and in 1964, everything on TV was in color.

The declaration that "television has few success stories to match that of Herbert B. Leonard, the cherubic proprietor-producer" might have been published just a short time earlier, but the success that had inspired that newspaper story about Bert now felt far away. Coming so soon after his quick, starry start, the stalling of his career was abrupt, even in Hollywood, famous for meteoric rises and falls. His three big shows, which at one point were all on the air simultaneously, tailed off one by one. *Naked City* was canceled in 1963. The re-runs of *The Adventures of Rin-Tin-Tin* went off the air in 1964. *Route 66* was canceled, also in 1964. Bert had launched a show in 1958 called *Rescue 8,* about a team of Los Angeles Fire Department rescue specialists, which had the makings of a hit — it was the first "emergency" show on television, predating the popularity of the genre by a decade. But it ran for only two seasons and was canceled in 1960.

He was the kid with the quick fists, a fighter, and even with this run of disappointment, Bert got to work on new shows. He developed a series called *The Freeboo-*

ters, based on an Isaac Bashevis Singer novel, and a western, *Kingfisher's Road,* but wasn't able to sell either one. In 1967, he made a pilot for a campy TV comedy called *The Perils of Pauline.* When he wasn't able to attract a sponsor or a network, he wove together the three episodes he had made and released it as a film, to little notice.

The next year, he seemed to right the ship: he produced a successful movie called *Popi,* starring Alan Arkin as a Puerto Rican widower trying to find a better life for his two young sons by having them pretend to be orphans. The movie got some attention, and Arkin was cited for his performance. For that moment, it must have felt to Bert that he was once again the man who was marveled over in the *Los Angeles Examiner.*

But one fairly successful movie couldn't fix everything that was going wrong. He had probably been spending too freely since *The Adventures of Rin-Tin-Tin* became a hit. He and his third wife, Jenny, had four daughters. He was also helping care for the children of his brother Roger, who had worked for Bert as a location manager. In 1962, Roger was indicted on murder and conspiracy charges in a mob shooting in a Sherman Oaks restaurant. The charges were later dropped, but Roger was then indicted on federal perjury charges. His case never came to trial because he died from a brain hemorrhage shortly after being released on bail. He left no money for his wife and children, and Bert worried about them — he adored Roger's widow, Blanca, and was especially attached to his niece Patty, among Roger's four kids, so he bought a house and motel for Blanca, to provide her with a source of income and a place to live.

He and Jenny divorced, so he was paying child support and alimony, and then there was his expensive affection for gambling. In spite of having produced three hit television shows in quick succession, he admitted to a friend that he'd "never made real money." His financial situation was like a stage set, an elegant facade propped up by spindles of lumber with no actual foundation. He started to fall behind on payments to his lawyers and accountants and credit cards. When the flow of income from his television series slowed and then stopped, he was almost broke.

Through all this, he never stopped thinking about Rin Tin Tin. He believed there was still some life in the character. He told Sam Manners that he believed Rin Tin Tin was "a magic name that would go on and on."

He sketched out a score of new story ideas in which Rinty would star. One was a series starring Rin Tin Tin as a seeing-eye dog. Most guide dogs for the blind were German shepherds, and the series would highlight the dog's intelligence and intuition. Bert started researching details. "Call Braille Institute. Who teaches recent blind people?" he wrote in a note to himself. "Are the teachers also blind people? If a blind person dies can the dog be used by other blind person or does family of dead blind person adopt the dog?" In the margins of this note there was tiny, barely legible handwriting. After studying it, I figured out that he had been calculating the amount of money he was going to leave each of his daughters in his will. This same calculation appeared in the margins of many of his memos and scripts, and even on scraps of paper in his files, as if he was always measuring and reconsidering what he would leave behind.

He had more ideas for Rin Tin Tin: he was never short of those. After he read a newspaper article about the illicit trade in endangered species, he wrote a script called *Rin Tin Tin the Tracker,* in which the dog worked with a team of Fish and Wildlife agents. He described another idea, *Rin Tin*

Tin the Ultimate Weapon, as a canine version of Spider-Man. In a note describing it to his agent, he wrote, "Instead of an intern reporter being bitten by a spider, Rin Tin Tin's body is invaded by a horde of fleas from a lab chimp who thinks Rin Tin Tin is a chimp."

There was also *Rin Tin Tin Private Investigator, Rin Tin Tin the Wonder Dog,* and *Rin Tin Tin, Secret Agent,* about a fourteen-year-old computer whiz who owns the smartest dog in the world, a German shepherd named Rin Tin Tin 10th. "You see, Luke's great-great-great-grandmother loved the original Rin Tin Tin, a great Warner Brothers movie star dog so much she somehow found out where Lee Duncan, the owner and trainer of that famous dog lived," Bert wrote. "And on a Sunday afternoon in 1931 [she] traveled by car on a very rough road all the way to Riverside and bought a Rin Tin Tin puppy from Mr. Duncan for seventy-five dollars. . . ." This particular story proposal intrigued and also unnerved me. Bert had no way of knowing Jannettia Brodsgaard, but this perfectly summarized her pursuit of Lee and Rin Tin Tin. That rough road out to Riverside was familiar to Bert as well, although it may have begun to seem like something that had happened a very long time ago.

7.

Bert always toyed with the idea of somehow reviving the original show — a crazy notion, maybe, but it stuck in his mind. There was precedent for the idea. *The Mickey Mouse Club* had begun just one season after *The Adventures of Rin-Tin-Tin* on ABC and was canceled in 1959. But in 1974, Walt Disney and Stanley Moger, a media syndication executive, thought it might be time to bring back the show. After all, in 1974, baby boomers were in their twenties and early thirties, and many of them had young children of their own. They might be feeling the first twinges of nostalgia for their youth. Moger traveled around the country, offering the show to local stations. To his delight, he discovered that his hunch was right — more than half the television stations in the country bought *The Mickey Mouse Club* reruns, and the show had a huge audience when it ran.

Moger is an intense, chatty man with a thatch of thinning brown hair and a rumbling, gravelly voice, like a radio announcer's. I visited him in his New York office,

441

which is lined with pictures of himself shaking hands with or hugging or standing close to dozens of actors and politicians, a mosaic of Moger's face beside a celebrity face, shining in the silvery spray of camera flash. The first thing Moger did when I arrived was to wordlessly point to a cardboard box on his desk. Then he pulled off the lid and held it out so that I could admire the contents, like a waiter in a fancy restaurant serving duck à l'orange. Inside the box were the costume and gun Lee Aaker had worn in *The Adventures of Rin-Tin-Tin.* The gun looked real. The boy-sized cavalry uniform, faded now to a pale blue-gray, had a name tag in the pants on which someone had written, incorrectly, "Lee Acker."

"I was in the Beverly Hills Hotel in 1975 and got a call from this fellow, Herbert B. Leonard," Moger said, leaning back in his desk chair. "He had a high-pitched little voice, just a tiny voice. He said how impressed he was with what we'd done with *The Mickey Mouse Club,* and he said that he wanted to do the same thing with Rin Tin Tin." Moger put the costume and gun back in the box and replaced the lid. Then he told me that after they had gone into business together, he and Bert fought over money. Moger got hold of the costume —

he never quite explained how — and held it hostage, telling Bert he wouldn't give it back unless they settled their disagreement. Apparently, Bert's reluctance to settle was stronger than his desire to get the costume back, so the strategy didn't work. Now Bert was dead and Moger had Rusty's uniform. Their relationship ended the way many of Bert's relationships did — with a few unpaid bills and a comingling of admiration and exasperation. "He was a charming guy, but there was always an angle with Bert," Moger said. "He had a real habit for self-destructing."

At their first meeting, Bert explained that he had a chance to get the rights to the show from Screen Gems if he acted quickly. Moger was interested, so he watched a few episodes of the show. Afterward he called Bert and said he thought syndicating the show would be impossible. "I told him it was crazy," Moger said. "I said, Bert, you've got snarling dogs, you refer to Indians as 'redskins,' there are no black kids or Hispanic kids, it's a lily-white show. How are you going to sell this in today's world?"

Moger's complaint was more about the trappings of the show than its content. Bert was proud of the "moral lessons" that were woven into *The Adventures of Rin-Tin-Tin,* which reflected his own progressive ideas. For instance, the episode called "The Legend of the White Buffalo" — Bert's personal favorite — is pointedly egalitarian. The episode begins with white hooligans shooting buffalo on an Apache hunting preserve. Apache braves and Rin Tin Tin apprehend them, and the cavalry is called in to mediate. The buffalo poachers expect to be let off because they are white and the cavalry soldiers are white. But Lieutenant Masters takes them into custody, prompting one of the poachers to sneer, "Whose side are you on, soldier?"

"Whichever side is right," Masters tells him.

"He's an Injun, ain't he?" the poacher says. "I'm a white man! That makes me right."

"Right or wrong," Masters says, "isn't a matter of the color of a man's skin."

The white buffalo of the episode's title is a mystical creature that appears only once in a lifetime to avert disaster, but it will appear only to someone whose heart is "brave and true." An Apache elder tells Rusty the legend, saying, "If it is real or just a dream, I cannot say."

The poachers' friends decide to set off a buffalo stampede for revenge. Thousands of the animals bear down on Rusty and Rinty. Just as they are about to be crushed, the white buffalo appears before them, like a cumulus cloud; the stampeding herd sees the white buffalo and halts in place, and the boy and the dog are saved. When Rusty gets back to camp, he tells the story of the stampede and the white buffalo to Kemali, one of the young Apaches, who accepts the story for what it is — something that no one will ever completely understand. "Who can explain it?" Kemali says. "Who can say?"

Bert knew that the format and some of the content of the show needed to be changed. He told Moger he would edit out the offensive language, the outdated scenes and the dog fights. Then he proposed shooting three-minute "wraparounds" — short scenes that would introduce each episode. The wraparounds would feature Rip Masters — actor James Brown — sitting in a barn, describing his days with the cavalry and Rin Tin Tin to a multicultural group of children. Then the scene would fade and the old show would begin, as if it were part of Masters' recollection. The show would end by fading in once again to Lieutenant Masters talking to the kids. The original episodes would be tinted sepia, to make them look far away, to emphasize that they were being remembered. Bert had already been in touch with James Brown. Even though Bert said he had become "most uncooperative and bitter" by the end of the original series, Brown was willing to do the new openings for the show.

Bert cleared space in the dining room of his house on Los Feliz and summoned the writers from the early days of the show. At his dining room table, they edited all the episodes, snipping out anything that could be considered offensive. Bert wanted to shoot the new scenes at Fort Apache, in Corriganville, but the Los Angeles Police Department had already dismantled it in order to use the area as a firing range. Instead, Bert sent James Brown, the crew, and the cast of children, made up of boys and girls and including an African American, a Jew, and a Hispanic, to a film location in Kanab, Utah, next to where Clint Eastwood was shooting *The Outlaw Josey Wales.* Eastwood loaned them the wagon Brown leaned against while he talked to the kids.

Stanley Moger's company, SFM Entertainment, agreed to finance the wraparounds, and Bert budgeted $3,600 for each one. But a weather delay in Utah and a hiatus while Brown recovered from pneumonia drove the cost to ten times what had been planned. After Bert had run through close to $800,000 to shoot just twenty-two of the wraparounds, Moger decided he'd spent enough. The remaining episodes were edited and tinted, but they wouldn't have the modern-day bookends.

This scrubbed-up version of *The Adventures of Rin-Tin-Tin* was announced with a triumphant press release. "After Coca-Cola and IBM, Rin Tin Tin is probably the most widely known and immediately identifiable name in the world today. Astoundingly, this is despite the fact that millions of children and their parents (and perhaps their grandparents) have never seen the heroic dog on television," the press release began. "This universal awareness can be accounted for only by the realization that the television series and the value it projects and espouses — bravery, loyalty, and morality — have become as much a part of the American tradition of fairness, fraternity and freedom as baseball, Sunday afternoon football and hamburger with all the fixings."

There was a huge press party at the Waldorf Astoria in New York to celebrate the first episode on the air. In a story headlined

"Old Dog, New Tricks," the *New York Times* remarked on Bert's clever fix, noting "the rerunning of 'Rinny,' the heroic German shepherd who actually had his origins in pre-television movies, involves quite an unusual recycling job." By the end of 1976, the show was airing five days a week in more than 85 percent of the country.

The Adventures of Rin-Tin-Tin was no longer in prime time; stations could schedule it whenever they wanted, and many ran it early in the day, when the audience consisted of children too young to go to school. This annoyed James Brown, who complained to a newspaper about the new viewers. "All they know is 'Doggy, doggy,' " he said. "They wouldn't know an Indian from a schmindian." But the fact is that they had managed to make Bert Leonard a success once again.

8.

Almost sixty years after the first Rin Tin Tin was born, half a century since he'd starred in *The Man from Hell's River,* Rin Tin Tin was still alive. In this incarnation, though, there was no longer a dog on a set learning to bark on cue. For the moment, the actual dog seemed to have dematerialized — to have melted away from real life, only to live as a character on screen.

The tinted, edited episodes ran in syndication from 1976 until 1978. Then stations stopped renewing their contracts. As much as the editing and wraparounds had helped, television was changing once again. After decades monopolizing home entertainment, network television was suddenly upended by cable television. In 1975, Home Box Office was founded, and Showtime began the following year. The first videocassette recorders for home use were also being introduced. In the middle of the 1970s, there wasn't a single video rental store in the United States, but by 1978 there were 3,500, and by 1979 there were 10,000. The most popular early rentals were children's movies. It was stiff competition for the shows that were on the air, particularly an old children's show like *The Adventures of Rin-Tin-Tin.*

Bert drew out yet another idea for Rin Tin Tin from what seemed to be his inexhaustible supply of ideas for extending the life of the character. The wraparounds and tinting had been refreshing, but they hadn't really renewed the show. He thought what the show needed was color — full color, not just the tawny tinge of sepia that had, in fact, made the show look even older, preserved in amber. If only Screen Gems had spent $5,000 more to film in color when the show was first being made — but they hadn't. However, Canadian engineers had just invented a method for adding color to black-and-white footage. Computer technicians could undo Screen Gems' mistake, reviewing every frame and applying red or blue or yellow or green onto every bit of gray.

It cost a fortune to add color to black-and-white film, and it's hard to determine where Bert found the money. He was always good at charming people, inflaming potential investors with the same excitement he felt for his projects. People trusted him. In 1978, for instance, Eva Duncan turned over all the copyrights to Rin Tin Tin that were in her name. "I never doubted Bert for a moment," she explained in a deposition. "That's what I said all these years that we've worked with him."

Bert must have borrowed against everything he owned or seduced an investor. On his own, he couldn't have afforded the nearly $3 million he spent to have sixty-five episodes of the show colorized in a lab in India. The moment the first episodes were finished and sent back to him, he screened them for television executives. They did look different; the colorization brightened everything. But the effect was more like a watercolor paint-by-number version of *The Adventures of Rin-Tin-Tin* than a film shot in color the first time around. Still, Bert was optimistic.

Unlike the eager reception he and Moger had gotten for the edited, modernized version of the show, however, the colorized *Adventures of Rin-Tin-Tin* didn't find any takers. What was popular at the time was *Mork & Mindy* and *Battlestar Galactica,* and *Buck Rogers in the 25th Century* and Nickelodeon, a new cable channel, the first to be especially programmed for children. Even scrubbed of anachronisms and infused with color, *The Adventures of Rin-Tin-Tin* still seemed out of place. "Evidently, the Western is not where kids' heads are today," Bert wrote to his agent. "Space and special effects, car chases . . . are in vogue. And so Rinty hasn't happened yet." Bert's use of the word "yet" is particularly striking in this context. He was still sure that Rin Tin Tin would live another day. "Eventually, the quality of the show will make it once it gets on the air," he added in his letter to his agent. "When that happens, the success will come from the original quality of the program and the greatness of the star, Rin Tin Tin, and NOT from colorization."

9.

Bert became as adamant as Lee had been in protecting the dignity of Rin Tin Tin, even at a cost. In 1976, a producer named David Picker began work on a film that spoofed early Hollywood and Rin Tin Tin's career. The film's original title was *A Bark Is Born,* but Picker renamed it *Won Ton Ton: The Dog Who Saved Hollywood* and offered Bert a fee for permission to base the story on Rinty. Bert needed the money, but he refused Picker's offer and then sued him for infringing on Rin Tin Tin's name and character. Both Picker and the film's director, Michael Winner, thought Bert's reaction was ridiculous. Winner, speaking to an audience of film students in New York before the film's release, said, "It's absurd to be sued by a dog, especially a dog who's been dead for the past twenty years."

Bert lost the lawsuit, but he felt he'd made an important point: the movie was insulting to the character of Rin Tin Tin and exploitative of the years he'd devoted to cultivating him as a familiar name. As his friend Max

Kleven explained to me, "Rin Tin Tin was like religion to Bert. It was serious. It was not something you poked fun at." You certainly didn't make a film like *Won Ton Ton* that, according to *Variety,* left "no stone unturned in straining for broad, low laughs in the worst possible way." It was so bad that the reviewer speculated that it might actually have been designed to lose money for its investors to provide them with tax write-offs. Before the fight over *Won Ton Ton,* Bert had had business dealings with David Picker, and at one time even talked to him about producing his films, including the movie of Lee Duncan's life story that Bert and Lee were so anxious to make. Picker could have been useful to him, especially when Bert's circumstances went from difficult to hopeless, but *Won Ton Ton* was something Bert never forgave.

At what point does devotion become a form of willful blindness? It would be impossible to commit to anything or anyone if you didn't have a certain capacity for self-delusion and obliviousness. After all, there is nothing in the world that's perfect — nothing that doesn't require, on occasion, the averted glance or the moment of selective deafness or the carefully calibrated memory lapse in order to remain lovable.

To be passionate about something requires the ability to forget what's wrong with it. But how much forgetting is the right amount? When is loyalty more about forgetting, and the love of being in love, than about the truth of what's at hand? Knowing how to gauge the nature of devotion — that is, knowing the difference between those instances when your glance has been averted too many times and those when you gave up on something far too fast — seems a life skill, a talent. Just to realize when enough is enough would be a gift. But it seems we are forever weighing things with a finger on the scale, always too quick to give up or too ardent by half.

Lee devoted his whole life to Rinty, at a cost of never seeming to get a hold on anything else that mattered, like his family or his friends, and never to have found a sense of his own existence except through the experience of the dog; and there were moments in Bert's life, like this one, when it would have been easier and perhaps more sensible to move on. He was still young enough. But he didn't make that choice. What is it about Rin Tin Tin that was so compelling? What made this one character outlast everything around him, leaving in his wake Strongheart and dozens of others no one remembers; finding generation after generation to admire him; engaging one person after another to devote their lives to him? And how could I marvel at Lee and Bert and later Daphne when I had stepped in line right behind them, just as beguiled by the story of this real and not-real dog, while the rest of my life ticked away? What could account for the perfect irony that I was now telling the story of that story, doing exactly what Lee and Bert and Daphne had done, advancing the story yet again?

Nothing would last if we all gave up quickly, or even gave up when it was logical to do so. Even ideas wouldn't last, because they, too, become frayed and worn without their defenders. Bert's fierceness about Rin Tin Tin might have been a terrible mistake for him personally, but he ended up as a steward in a remarkable episode that has outlasted every expectation. Being forgotten, washed away — that is what is typical in human experience. Anything that can withstand that inevitable decline is fascinating because it has managed to do what none of us can do: it has lived on when everything else is destined to die.

We want things to last because life without them would be bewildering, an endless question of why anything has value or feels familiar and how any of us could be connected to anything outside ourselves. Those lasting things have been floated through time on someone's ferocious devotion and the will to remember only what was shiny and promising, even when that person is sometimes sunk in the process. The rest of us get the benefit of what comes of that — those things that stretch past a vanishing point, that we can follow through life's scattering of moments and emotions, so we can experience something that feels whole and everlasting, the mark that is indelible.

10.

There were still real Rin Tin Tins being born all this time, in Texas, where Jannettia Brodsgaard and Daphne continued to breed the dogs descended from the four puppies Brodsgaard had gotten from Lee. Brodsgaard still operated her guard dog business, Bodyguard Kennels, and Daphne, who married a deputy sheriff and had two children, launched her own, called Super Dogs, Inc. In 1979, Brodsgaard decided to retire. She wanted to keep breeding German shepherds, but she was more involved with her new hobby, raising exotic birds. Daphne, in the meantime, expanded Super Dogs.

Daphne's interest in Rin Tin Tin had come to her almost automatically, since she'd grown up with Brodsgaard's Rintys; now Rin Tin Tin was her passion. "Most people devote themselves to family and home," she told me once. "Any man who was with me would have to know they would never be anything to me other than second to Rin Tin Tin." She ran Super Dogs for a few more years but then decided she wanted to get out of the guard dog business and open a pet shop instead.

She found a space in Houston's Town and Country Center mall. "She designed a magnificent pet shop with vignettes of an old western town, complete with carpeted floors, and all the foo-foo associated with a plush shop," Daphne wrote in her memoir. By any description, it was a highly unconventional pet shop. Except on Saturdays, when breeders sometimes brought in puppies for display, there weren't any animals in the shop. Instead, Daphne saw it as a referral source for anyone interested in pedigreed dogs, horses, and cattle, which could be viewed at the shop on videotapes supplied by breeders. It was like a salon for an online dating service. Eccentric as it was, Daphne says it was a "tremendous success" until the recession rolled through Houston in 1984, wiping out scores of businesses, including Daphne's shop, which for the year it operated was called El Rancho Rin Tin Tin.

When I first got interested in the story of Rin Tin Tin, Daphne emerged immediately as the present-day custodian of the dog's legacy. Even though, at the time, Bert was still alive and working on Rin Tin Tin scripts, he was not in the public eye. Eva Duncan died in 2000, and Carolyn had little connection to Rin Tin Tin, other than the few pictures in her dining room and Bert's phone number on a memo pad next to her kitchen sink. Daphne, on the other hand, had registered ten Rin Tin Tin trademarks, reserving the use of the name on, among other things, "dog clothing, dog collars, dog leashes, dog shoes," magazines and pamphlets, posters, stickers, the Rin Tin Tin Fan Club, the Rin Tin Tin Canine Ambassador Club, dog food, live puppies, and "entertainment services in the nature of an ongoing television series in the field of variety and motion pictures featuring a German shepherd dog as a live or animated character." She also registered the Internet domains Rintintin.com and Rintintin.net. If you went looking for something related to Rin Tin Tin, Daphne is who you would find.

Daphne is compact and sturdy-looking and has an upturned nose and crinkly reddish brown hair that she usually yanks back in a ponytail. She has a voice that comes only from a lifetime of dedication to cigarettes. Her manner is brisk and commanding and at the same time engaging. She has the air of a grudge-holder and someone who might keep very close track of whether you agree with her or not. Her personal history is littered with friendships and partnerships that came apart. She is what some people would call controversial or maybe, more simply, plainspoken. Once when I was with her, I wondered out loud what the *B* in "Herbert B. Leonard" stood for, and she shot back, "That's easy! Butthead." At the time we met, she was living in Latexo, a speck of a town outside the slightly bigger speck of Crockett, Texas. At that moment, she happened to be the mayor of Latexo, which consisted of approximately 250 residents. She was also the managing editor of the local paper, the *Houston County Courier;* she was preparing to open the first ever Rin Tin Tin museum in her garage to display her eight thousand pieces of Rin Tin Tin memorabilia; and she was the founder and chief executive officer of ARFkids, a nonprofit organization that provided German shepherd service dogs to autistic children. The name ARFkids was an acronym for "A Rinty For Kids."

Daphne is divorced and her two children are grown; at the time of my visit she was living in a narrow brown house on a featureless state highway outside of town, with her dogs Miss Piggy, Xanada, Little Rin, and the Old Man, Rin Tin Tin VIII. That weekend, she was matching some puppies with their new ARFkids families, who had gathered at her house to get acquainted with their dogs. Two other families at her house that weekend were picking up puppies they'd bought as pets.

It was a humid day and so hot that the air seemed to be buzzing. There was a bit of a riot at Daphne's house, puppies tumbling and yipping and the autistic kids careering from parent to puppy and back again, while some of Daphne's dogs, kenneled in her backyard, watched the crowd with excitement and then hurled themselves at the chain-link doors of their runs every minute or two, making a metallic crash. Daphne didn't seem to notice the chaos; she went about her business, occasionally hollering at someone to do this or that or at one of the dogs to be quiet and then picking up whatever conversation she had just dropped as if there had been no interruption at all.

She led me inside her house, which was almost more chaotic than the backyard because there were animals everywhere and several visitors and neighbors milling around. She wanted to show me some material about her grandmother and introduce me to a few of her dogs — especially the Old Man, a huge, slow-moving German shepherd with a blocky head and a coat as thick as mink. The Old Man was Daphne's special dog; this was when I learned that she was thinking of having him stuffed when he died. She obviously adored her dogs, but she introduced them to me with a dismissive sweep of her hand, saying, "Here they are, my bacon-stealing flea circus." Then she grabbed one of the dogs by the nose. "Hey," she scolded, "quit your countersurfing."

At first the story of Rin Tin Tin had seemed touching and a little mournful, like an old folk song. This was because of the dark presence of war in the early years of the story, and also because of Lee's difficult childhood, and his vulnerability: the more I came to know him, the more he seemed almost lost in the world except for his connection with the dog. It pained me to follow Lee along, watching him attach ever more deeply with old Rin, as if he believed he had willed away the hard fact that our dogs will die before we do.

And then at some point the story took a turn. I was in Texas and in Los Angeles on and off for several years, and I began to feel like everyone I met or heard about in connection to Rin Tin Tin was a little crazy — even the side players and background people and definitely the main characters in the narrative. Every one of them had a facet that glinted with just a bit of madness. A singular passion helps you slice through the mess of the world, but I had also come to believe that cutting such a narrow path plays tricks with proportion and balance and pushes everything that much closer to the edge. It's not that passionate people are crazy: it's that by necessity, they have traded the sweep of a big view for one that's contracted and focused, which can give their world a peculiar shape. I remember sitting with Sam Manners and hearing his stories about the cast of the television show — which stuntman had been murdered by his wife, which one had hired a private eye to spy on Bert — and all the while I was thinking, boy, this is all starting to sound a little nuts. It seemed that the narrative had begun to curlicue and twist into a slightly cracked comedy.

I myself began to feel like I was getting a little unhinged, launching into arguments whenever anyone made a comment equating Rin Tin Tin with Lassie, or asked me, as they always did, whether there was just one Rin Tin Tin, or — even more simply — why I had spent years writing a book about a dog. One afternoon, I went to interview a man in Los Angeles who collected merchandise from television shows. His apartment was dim and stuffy, and nearly every surface was hidden under a *Leave It to Beaver* lunchbox or a Smurf figurine. He had a collection of Rin Tin Tin memorabilia that I was excited to see, and I had skipped doing something more conventional, like going to the beach, in order to see his Fort Apache play set and Rin Tin Tin thermoses. He was a sweet, odd man who lived alone and could recite where and when he had gotten each of his television collectibles. My first thought was that he was weird to have such a rarefied pursuit and I couldn't imagine fixating so completely on anything. And then I looked around the room and took note of the fact that the only people in it were this sweet, odd man and me.

It was inevitable that at some point, Herbert B. Leonard and Daphne Hereford would collide, and they did. It didn't happen all at once. For ten years or so, they pursued their individual and passionate relationships to Rin Tin Tin, more or less unknown to each other, essentially out of each other's way. Bert was still casting around in Hollywood for a project, while Daphne's interest was in the real dogs — breeding them, promoting them, keeping the Rin Tin Tin name alive.

11.

In 1984, Bert edited together five of the colorized *Adventures of Rin-Tin-Tin* episodes to distribute as a movie-length feature, but he never managed to get it released in theaters. Just a year later, however, a new cable channel, the Christian Broadcasting Network, approached him with the idea of remaking the show with a new cast but with the original story of the orphan, the dog, and the cavalry. Surprisingly, Bert said no. He wanted Rin Tin Tin to star in a television show, but he now thought that the story of the cavalry was past its prime. Instead, he told CBN he wanted to develop an idea he had for a show he called *Rin Tin Tin K-9 Cop*, about a police officer, Hank Katts, and his unusually gifted German shepherd police dog. Katts lives with his nephew Stevie, whose policeman father — Katts's brother — had been killed in the line of duty. The boy's mother had moved in with Katts in order to provide her son with a surrogate father.

Evangelist Pat Robertson, who had founded CBN, loved the idea and ordered twenty-two episodes. The series, which was called *Katts and Dog* in Canada, and *Rin Tin Tin K-9 Cop* everywhere else, was going to be shot in Canada rather than on location in California. As happy as he was to have a project finally get under way, this presented a problem for Bert. He had just gotten married for the fourth time. He was fifty-nine, his new wife, Betty, was twenty-five, and he was so infatuated with her that he couldn't bear to be away from home; he later described his relationship to her as an addiction. He decided to stay in Los Angeles and left the show in the hands of his assistant producers in Canada, who resented his absence and began scheming to elbow him off the show.

Then another problem arose: in the middle of the first season, Pat Robertson called to say a handful of viewers had complained that the show was "salacious" because it portrayed an unmarried man and woman living together, even though their relationship was platonic. Bert asked Robertson what he expected him to do. "Kill her off," Robertson told him. Bert pointed out that the show was a hit, but Robertson insisted. Bert never responded well to executive authority. "Bottom line," Bert wrote in a note to a friend, "I left the show before the end of the second year." The character of the mother *was* subsequently killed off, as Robertson had requested, and the show ran for more than one hundred episodes, but Bert had little to do with it except for getting a small amount of money for the right to use Rin Tin Tin's name.

He was never very good at picking his battles. "Bert could never face the fact that he had goofed," Sam Manners told me. "He couldn't even watch the show. For him, it was too heartbreaking to see."

He churned out more television ideas: *Lady and Jo,* about a female trucker who takes her daughter with her on the road; a revival of *Route 66* called *On the Road Again.* Others were just wisps of concepts, sometimes just a title written on a page: "New York City or Bust"; "The Nazi Olympics"; "The Slumbercoach Murders." In one of his bulging file boxes, I found a few pages of a script he had worked on with veteran screenwriter Walter Bernstein, titled *Rin Tin Tin — The Dog Who Saved Bert Leonard,* written by hand on a yellow legal pad. The title might have been the result of a night spent joking around with Bernstein, but the content seemed genuine. It began:

1. Night. Boy & Dog asleep. Noise. Dog out. Fights grizzly. Boy & Dad w/guns, kill bear. Dog wounded. Take care of him.
2. Town. Wagons into town to sell wheat. No good. Rained. Finds out in gen. store about Cal. Gold strike. Ends with beat 35) who knows what may happen?
3. End notes: ONE CAN'T GIVE UP. Message of the movie: The kid ready to give up but the dog won't let him quit.

Even as he was writing this, the temptation to quit must have been powerful. Bert was now living on borrowed money because he had no income and nothing in the bank. To make matters worse, one of his employees was caught embezzling from him, but not before she had made off with close to $100,000 of his savings, which he never

recovered. He also made a disastrous investment in a Mexican beauty products franchise; when it failed, he owed a fortune to
his lawyer, James Tierney, who had lent him
the investment money. Because he had no
cash, he gave Tierney his ownership shares
of *Naked City* and *Route 66* to settle part of
his debt. It must have hurt to give away
things he was so proud of — two-thirds of
the work product that had made him such a
notable Hollywood success. For the moment, at least, he held on to Rin Tin Tin.

Tierney, a former federal prosecutor who
had gone into private practice as an entertainment lawyer in Los Angeles, now was in
control of *Naked City* and *Route 66,* but this
cinematic windfall couldn't distract him
from his own troubles. A year earlier, in
1992, one of his clients told him he needed
some cash. The client owned a number of
valuable paintings, including a Monet and a
Picasso, and, he explained, if the paintings
disappeared, he could file a $17 million
insurance claim for them. Tierney agreed to
help him out. By their arrangement, Tierney
broke into the client's house and stole the
paintings. Then he gave the paintings to a
young lawyer in his firm for safekeeping.
The young lawyer decided to stash the
paintings in a warehouse in Cleveland.

Unfortunately, the young lawyer also had some problems, including a volatile ex-wife, who also happened to be the first California highway patrolwoman to pose for *Playboy;* a jealous girlfriend; and a crack cocaine addiction. He was also, evidently, unable to keep a secret and ended up telling both his ex-wife and his girlfriend about the stolen paintings; they, in turn, both informed on him to the police, each hoping to beat the other to the $250,000 reward being offered for information on the case. When the young lawyer was arrested, he immediately pointed the police back to Tierney. Before long, Tierney ended up in prison and lost his law license, his house, and his marriage. When I interviewed him, shortly after he was released from prison, he was shuffling around, a little adrift, in a dreary apartment in Santa Monica, miles from the house he had once owned in Beverly Hills. He told me, with no apparent self-consciousness, that one of the jurors who voted to convict him had said that Tierney struck him as a man who would screw his grandmother "if he could make a buck on it." Until his downfall, Tierney continued to represent Bert while at the same time lending him spending money.

Bert's income had dwindled to nothing

and his debts had escalated, but he didn't seem to understand the direness of his circumstances. An independent studio offered him $400,000 to produce a series of low-budget direct-to-DVD Rin Tin Tin films. But, just like *Won Ton Ton,* the project didn't suit his idea of Rin Tin Tin's dignity, so even though he was desperate he turned it down. Then he asked that same studio for $25 million to finance a film based on one of his favorite Rin Tin Tin screenplays — a western epic he called *River of Gold.*

12.

In 1993, Daphne sent a letter to Bert. It was the first time they'd been in contact. "Your dedication to Rin Tin Tin over the years is to be commended," she wrote. "Like you, my dedication has lasted for many years. . . . I am very interested in a revitalization of Rin Tin Tin and would like to discuss with you the possibilities. I understand that both Lassie and Benji are presently working on feature films and a Rin Tin Tin film would certainly attract a larger audience." She described her grandmother's relationship with Lee Duncan, and said she felt she was now one of two families — her own and the Duncans — dedicated to preserving Rin Tin Tin's legacy. She liked the possibility of teaming up with Bert to restart Rin Tin Tin's movie or television career. Moreover, she thought the Old Man — Rin Tin Tin VIII — was a "mirror image" of the dog that appeared on *The Adventures of Rin-Tin-Tin* and would be a great movie dog. She could work with the dog on the film. She could step into the void that Lee had left, that Carolyn had never been offered, and that Frank Barnes, who had since died, had never taken.

Bert interpreted Daphne's letter as more ominous than a friendly suggestion for co-operation, and he replied a few weeks later with a six-page cease-and-desist letter, drafted and signed by his lawyer, James Tierney. Rin Tin Tin, Tierney explained, "has a very strong, widely recognized, and vivid secondary meaning," which Bert owned as part of his copyright, and any unauthorized use of the name was a violation of Bert's ownership. Daphne, though, owned the only Rin Tin Tin trademarks the U.S. Patent and Trademark Office had issued, so she felt she had nothing to worry about. When Bert didn't reply to her lawyer's response, she put the whole matter out of her mind and continued to do what she felt was her right and duty. She was busy breeding puppies and collecting as much Rin Tin Tin material as she could in preparation for opening the world's first Rin Tin Tin Museum.

A few months after Bert's cease-and-desist letter, Lee Aaker contacted Daphne. This was unusual, because Aaker had rarely been seen since *The Adventures of Rin-Tin-Tin* ended its original run in 1959. Aaker was sixteen at the time the show ended, an awkward age for a child actor, and he had no luck landing adult roles. For one season, he worked as an assistant to Bert on *Route 66,* and then he decided to get out of the movie business entirely. He had only $20,000 left of the money he'd earned working on *The Adventures of Rin-Tin-Tin;* when his mother was asked, she said she "didn't know" what happened to the rest. Aaker worked as a carpenter and then left Los Angeles and moved seven hours north, to Mammoth Lakes, a ski resort in California near the Nevada border, where he got a job as an instructor specializing in teaching children with special needs to ski.

Ever since the show ended, there had been rumors about what happened to Aaker, as there often are about child actors. There were stories alleging that he'd become a drug addict and trafficker or been institutionalized after a nervous breakdown. It was hard to figure out what was true. One thing was certain: he was no longer working as an actor in Hollywood. He did, however, make occasional appearances at film festivals and memorabilia shows. He rode on a Celebrity Wagon Train at a rodeo in Newhall, California. He signed autographs at a Memphis film collectibles show. It wasn't uncommon for retired actors to show up at these kinds of events, to sign a few autographs and greet fans. Many of the other *Adventures of Rin-Tin-Tin* cast members, including Rand Brooks, Joe Sawyer, and James Brown, made the circuit, too.

Sometimes Aaker's behavior was strange, although not so strange that anyone thought to wonder about it. Lots of child actors seem different when they grow up, and look totally different from when they were first in the public eye. Aaker was just a little more so. He didn't always remember details about the show. He frequently seemed to go missing and then suddenly reappear. His phone number was unlisted and he was impossible to find, but then he would crop up in something like the *All-American Cowboy Cookbook,* contributing a recipe for Rusty's Pork Chops (alongside such other recipes as Hoss Cartwright's Nevada Nutty Slaw Salad and Clint Eastwood's Spaghetti Western).

Other times he made surprising efforts to get in touch with fans. Once, out of the blue, he called a Rin Tin Tin collector I know, a man named Scotland McFall, and suggested they go to an antiques show together. McFall was shocked but also thrilled. At the antiques show, McFall and Aaker stopped at a booth selling a Rin Tin Tin board game, and Aaker offered to sign it. The dealer immediately doubled the price on the game and sold it to a very happy buyer who'd watched Aaker sign it. A few minutes later, McFall and Aaker bumped into Rand Brooks, who had retired from acting and started a successful ambulance business in Los Angeles. Brooks and Aaker exchanged pleasantries.

Aaker also came down from Mammoth Lakes when James Brown died in 1992. He gave the eulogy at Brown's funeral. It was a sentimental reunion for the remaining cast members, even though in his last years Brown had been on a campaign against Rin Tin Tin, telling reporters that the dogs on the television show were unmanageable and vicious, and that his part in *The Adventures of Rin-Tin-Tin* had kept him from getting any other significant acting roles. He also told people that the original Rin Tin Tin, whom he'd never actually had contact with, was not in any of the early Warner Bros. films: Brown claimed that the dog in those movies was some no-name from the San Fernando Valley. But back in the days of the show, Brown had been close to everyone in the cast, and especially to Aaker. The truth was, the whole cast had a great time together, scrambling to shoot back-to-back episodes out on the dusty rocks of Corriganville; Aaker's eulogy reminded them all of those old, happy days.

Aaker's call to Daphne, then, was remarkable, but it appeared that he did keep track of what had become of Rin Tin Tin, so it wasn't surpassingly peculiar. He told Daphne that he would love to meet the current Rin Tin Tin. He said he was planning to make an appearance at an upcoming Hollywood collectibles show at the Beverly Hilton Hotel; perhaps they could meet there. Daphne, delighted by this, convinced a friend to pay for her flight from Texas to Los Angeles with a selection of her best Rin Tin Tin memorabilia and two of her dogs, the Old Man and his mate, Joanne.

It all would have been so perfect — the reuniting of Rusty and Rin Tin Tin — and for Daphne, it would seem to demonstrate her legitimacy as the new keeper of the legacy. There was just one hitch: Lee Aaker wasn't Lee Aaker. He was a middle-aged man named Paul Klein, roughly the same age as Lee Aaker and vaguely resembling him, if you squinted your eyes. Klein was a resident of Reseda, California, who hung out at a bar called the Cowboy Palace and sometimes pretended to be a police officer. He'd also been posing as Lee Aaker for years, riding Celebrity Wagon Trains, signing autographs, and even, in the case of James Brown's funeral, eulogizing cast members of the show.

The fraud was finally exposed in 1993, the same year Klein contacted Daphne, when the actor Paul Petersen, a star of *The Donna Reed Show* and a close friend of the real Lee Aaker, caught Klein pretending to be Aaker at an autograph show. After that, the real Lee Aaker came forward and agreed to an interview with *The Globe,* a tabloid magazine. He said that he had indeed been a drug addict and a dealer, and had suffered from paralyzing panic attacks, but that he'd been sober since 1980. He lived quietly, but, according to the magazine, the imposter was "making Lee's life hell!"

When I saw this story, I read it with a

skeptic's eye. Was this really Lee Aaker or was it a double-cross, another imposter posing as Lee Aaker complaining about an imposter? I had learned from several sources that Aaker lived in California; why did the article say he lived in Arizona? I was sure he taught special-needs kids how to snow ski; why did the article say he was a waterskiing instructor? Why would he give such a seemingly important interview to a tabloid magazine? And if this wasn't the real Lee Aaker, did it really matter? The story of Rin Tin Tin, after all, was rife with moments when identity became murky, starting with Lee Duncan's father, whose identity was molded to fit the story Hollywood wanted to tell. Cinema and theater spring from the idea that identity can be assumed — that an individual can choose a persona and wriggle into it as if it were a snakeskin. Whether this version of Lee Aaker was the real one or not was less interesting to me than the amazing fact that someone had gone to such lengths to pretend to be him.

In a book about film and television westerns called *White Hats and Silver Spurs,* Aaker — presumably the real one — told the author Herb Fagen that what bothered him the most about the Paul Klein situation was that the other Rin Tin Tin cast members accepted Klein as real. "They told me they didn't know [that he was an imposter], but I was upset," Aaker told Fagen. "I had a grand relationship with these people. I choose to think they were fooled, too."

I found a photograph of some celebrities attending a western film festival in Atlanta. There were cast members from *Buffalo Bill Jr.* and someone from *Maverick,* and, smiling into the camera with their arms around each other, James Brown and Paul Klein. The caption described Klein as Lee Aaker. If I were Lee Aaker and saw the picture of my former costar, someone I'd worked closely with for four years, who had been a sort of father figure to me, standing with his arm around the shoulder of an impersonator, I would be devastated. At one point the real Lee Aaker was actually sued for impersonating himself and had to produce his Screen Gems contract, pay stubs, and Social Security card to prove his identity.

Paul Klein died in 2007 after abdominal surgery. Someone who knew him "fairly well" left a post on a website describing him as "a good decent guy," but then added, "I know 100's of people who thought he was the kid on Rin Tin Tin. It is funny the two of them do look similar but sure not the same. So I don't know what the real story is." But another former friend of Klein's told me that he actually wasn't such a decent guy. He always played the angles and had gotten in trouble many times for petty theft and pretending to be a police officer.

I have never been able to figure out what motivated Klein to engage in this fantasy or what he got out of it. It certainly wasn't money, because most of the events he did were free, and most of the value he brought to things by signing them, like the Rin Tin Tin board game, accrued to someone else's benefit. The payoff certainly wasn't fame in the largest, glittering sense of the word. By the time Klein was impersonating Lee Aaker, decades had passed since Aaker had been a Hollywood star, and even at his most celebrated, Aaker was always that sort of demi-star, known by association; he was always "the little boy in the Rin Tin Tin show." He would have been lucky to draw a middling crowd at a Hollywood autograph meet.

A former friend of Klein's told me that Klein used the assumed identity to pick up women at bars. But there must have been something more to it; Klein could have pretended to be Lee Aaker at bars and skipped the film festivals and the eulogies and the collectibles shows. Maybe Klein enjoyed seeing a few fans light up when he signed the back of their Rin Tin Tin comic books. Maybe having that power to thrill someone made him feel important; maybe he liked the idea that he was attaching himself to history, and that it just might bring him some small measure of immortality.

After the fake Lee Aaker contacted Daphne, she saw the *Globe* article and realized she'd nearly been duped. Then the real Lee Aaker contacted her. Just like the fake Lee Aaker, the real Lee Aaker told her he was planning to attend the April 1994 Hollywood Collectors Show at the Beverly Hilton Hotel and would like to meet her there and have a chance to see the current Rin Tin Tin. According to Daphne, she flew to Los Angeles with the dogs and met with Aaker — the real Lee Aaker — and then worked for hours to set up her memorabilia display. The next day, the show opened. The whole episode of almost being suckered might have been redeemed by the good experience of meeting the real Lee Aaker. However, the first person to approach Daphne's booth was a process server, who handed her papers notifying her of a federal lawsuit filed against her by Herbert B. Leonard for interfering with his ownership of Rin Tin Tin.

How Lee Aaker came to contact Daphne is astonishing. According to Bert, Aaker had been in an airport in Texas and overheard someone talking about how she owned the descendants of Rin Tin Tin. Without telling her who he was, Aaker approached the woman — Daphne — and asked about the dogs. She gave him her business card, which indicated that she was the CEO of Rin Tin Tin Incorporated, and they had lunch. "In fact," Daphne told me recently, "I *paid.*"

Because he knew Bert, Aaker was puzzled by Daphne's claims of being the owner of the Rin Tin Tin dynasty, so after the encounter he called Bert and told him about it. Bert was outraged. He and Lee Duncan had never signed a lot of formal papers; they made their agreements Lee's way, with handshakes, but Bert's lawyer assured him that his ongoing use of the Rin Tin Tin character was all he needed to protect his rights. Bert decided to press the matter in court. He asked Aaker to call Daphne and identify himself as the boy from *The Adventures of Rin-Tin-Tin* — without letting on that he'd met her in the airport. He wanted Aaker to encourage her to come to California so she could be served with the lawsuit within state lines. The strategy worked. In spite of the disagreeable surprise of her first visitor at the show, Daphne stayed in California so she could display her dogs and her memorabilia and tell visitors her version of the story of Rin Tin Tin.

13.

Over the next two years, *Leonard v. Hereford* "raged on," as Daphne says. The central question had to do with money — who had spent money to build the Rin Tin Tin name and who deserved to profit from his celebrity. On another level it was a dispute over the more emotional question of who was the true custodian of the Rin Tin Tin legacy. What did Lee Duncan, the founding father, intend for the dog? Eva and Carolyn Duncan were both deposed in an effort to figure that out, and both of them suggested that Lee had seen Bert as his heir.

By the time Bert gave testimony, he was seething. Throughout his deposition, which was on videotapes that I found in his storage unit, he tapped the table impatiently, rolled his eyes, and looked like someone who felt sorely put upon. At one point Daphne's attorney asked Bert: "Would you say keeping the name 'Rin Tin Tin' in the limelight so all little boys and girls could love him as much as you and Lee Duncan did would be a good idea or a bad idea?" Bert replied:

I am so outraged by this whole situation that I can't tell you. But I have to explode and tell you that this woman is out of her bloody mind; that I and Lee Duncan for the last seventy years have given up a good deal of our lives to perpetuate, to spend millions and millions of dollars . . . to create the name, title and likeness and character, interior character, exterior look of this dog. And for some woman from Peoria, Texas, to come here and claim that she has any right to use the name "Rin Tin Tin" in . . . the commercial manner she has is the most absurd and ridiculous piece of thievery. She must be related to Jesse James.

The prickly exchange continued. The attorney once again asked Bert if he thought keeping Rin Tin Tin "in the limelight" for little boys and girls was a good idea, and Bert snapped, "I have done that for the last forty years. Duncan did that previous to that."

"So you would say it's a good idea?" the attorney asked.

"We have lived with that idea," Bert snapped.

"Why?"

"Because," Bert said slowly, "we . . . thought that — I personally thought that it was a great way to tell little morality stories. And that's why Rin Tin Tin was a great hit for all these years and has carried on little positive experiences in life that express the most genuine reward for good deeds, love, the relationship with the dog and the boy and the cavalry and all the things that represent the good aspects of American life. And we did that not only — it wasn't just a matter of making money. I always believed if you do something worthwhile, you'd make a lot of money. And that was the goal, to do something absolutely marvelous that people would identify with and love, and then out of that would come success and whatever the rewards were, emotional and financial. And that's how I've lived with Rin Tin Tin."

I have sorted out the many chapters of the Rin Tin Tin story in my mind and even thought of them with titles — the World War I Finding the Puppy period, the Breaking into Hollywood period, the Move to River-side period, and so forth. The moment Daphne and Bert faced off in court began what I thought of as the Endless Lawsuit period. At the time, Bert was suing the producers of *Rin Tin Tin K-9 Cop* for cutting him out of the show; the City of Pearland, Texas, where Daphne was then living, was suing her to reduce the number of dogs she had on her property; soon, Bert would sue Daphne again over her trademark for Rin Tin Tin dog food, and Columbia Pictures would oppose her trademark on Rin Tin Tin "entertainment services." Sony Pictures, for arcane reasons having to do with copyright and the fact that Bert owed them a fortune, was suing him for attempting to release the five colorized episodes of the television show as a film. The lawsuits came so thick and fast that I gave up trying to keep track of them: they seemed to boil down to one simple question — who owned Rin Tin Tin? — and one complicated one — what was Rin Tin Tin now that this one dog, born in 1918, had expanded exponentially into so many different forms?

What was Rin Tin Tin in 1923? What was he in 1983? In 2003? What about today, and what about tomorrow? Was Rin Tin Tin simply one dog found on a battlefield in

France? Was he the qualities one particular dog was good at projecting as a film star? Was he the army's mascot dog in World War II? A character in comic books, children's books, and coloring books? A fictional dog of the 1890s that lived with a cavalry troop? Puppies that were related to the real dog found on the battlefield? Merchandise decorated with German shepherd imagery? A sweeping idea, like Hero Dog or Loyalty Personified? Was it, as Bert said once in an attempt to define what he believed he owned, "the actual dog and the look of the animal or some aspect of his ability translated into merchandising and publicity and the subtext of what the dog represented"? Was it all of these things, and more, and could that wide, wide range of manifestations really belong to anyone?

Sometimes it seemed fitting, though disheartening, that the Rin Tin Tin narrative made this detour into the courtroom. The United States had become, in the last twenty years, a little litigation-crazy. Every dispute that once might have been settled by the application of common sense or ideas of fairness and ethics now seemed to require a squadron of lawyers and multiple court filings. Lee Duncan never had a lawyer. He never had an agent. He was loath to sign contracts, feeling that his handshake was his word. He was one man with one dog and one idea, and he never saw it as more complicated than that. The world he belonged to was, in many ways, equally uncomplicated.

But Rin Tin Tin had become a compound entity at the same moment that entertainment was swelling into something gigantic and corporate: characters were becoming brands, movies were becoming franchises, and lawyers were stepping in to choreograph the structure and content of it all, adding the particular obfuscation of lawyering to something already tangled and confused. At any one time, Daphne seems to have been engaged in a royal flush of lawsuits. In Bert's storage unit, I found boxes bursting with depositions, briefs, motions, and trial material. I often wondered what Lee Duncan would have thought of the fight between Daphne and Bert, and how dumbfounded he might have been, had he been in the deposition room, to hear one of the many lawyers say, in an attempt to summarize what was going on with Rin Tin Tin: "Let us stipulate that we have a stipulation."

14.

The initial lawsuit between Bert and Daphne was finally settled in 1996. The two parties struck an odd compromise: Daphne agreed to assign the trademark for the Rin Tin Tin Fan Club to Bert. I don't understand why he accepted this settlement, since he had no interest in running a fan club, but maybe wresting at least one of the trademarks from her made him feel he had made a point about his control.

The more meaningful outcome was that the lawsuit seemed to bring Bert's attention back to Rin Tin Tin. That year, he drew up an extensive, detailed investment proposal for "Rin Tin Tin — The Motion Picture." This movie was not the Lee Duncan story — he was still determined to make that as well — but instead his western masterpiece, *River of Gold.*

He had developed the script for *River of Gold* with writer Stephen Harrigan; it was about a farm family in the late 1860s and their struggles and adventures along with their dog, Rin Tin Tin. Bert wanted it to be his *Gone with the Wind,* according to Max Kleven. "He wanted it to be a big, sweeping movie," Kleven said. "Farmers in Kansas, famine — something epic."

In Bert's mind, the movie was about loyalty. Rin Tin Tin's role in it was as the "great American dog Hero . . . that stands for bravery, loyalty, and courage against evil of all kind. This movie . . . will encompass all the human and moral values." He believed the movie would revive the Rin Tin Tin franchise for "aging baby boomers that are now between 40 and 50 years old and their children and grandchildren with whom they will want to share their favorite dog hero, Rin Tin Tin. We cannot let this movie fail them."

In 1994, Disney Studios paid him $100,000 for a "first look" at his script, with the promise of $1 million if the studio decided to buy it. The deal was a great boost. It suddenly felt like the early days, when Bert was wooing Screen Gems with *The Adventures of Rin-Tin-Tin* — the same excitement and the same friction. In fact, before he went into one of his meetings with Disney, Bert jotted a note to himself: "Tone & attitude cannot be defensive in story meetings with Disney! Sit back and LISTEN." It all seemed to be going well, but in April of that year, Frank Wells, a former Warner Bros. executive who was Disney's president and had championed the Rin Tin Tin project, was killed in a helicopter crash.

Many scripts at the studio, including *River of Gold,* stalled while Disney CEO Michael Eisner and studio head Jeffrey Katzenberg fought over filling Wells's job. Finally, Disney decided to let its option lapse on *River of Gold.*

Bert took his script around Hollywood, knocking on doors the way Lee Duncan had more than seventy years earlier, offering his story the way Lee had offered his dog, hoping someone would see the same thing he saw in it, how it was electric with possibility, vivid and alive.

Warner Bros., Paramount, and Fox all politely declined *River of Gold.* One of their concerns was that a recent Lassie movie had flopped, leading them to assume that in 1994 there was little interest in dog movies. "The Lassie movie deserved to die. It was bad," Bert wrote in his investment proposal by way of counterargument. He kept swinging. To a private investor, he wrote, "I would not like to guess but . . . I do instinctively feel we could achieve well up in the multimillion dollar figures. When one realizes Rin Tin Tin was as big a star in both silent films and the early talkies as many of his two-legged co-stars — why shouldn't history repeat itself?"

An executive at New Line Cinema thought *River of Gold* would conflict with a script in development called *Snow Dogs.* Bert responded, with evident exasperation, " 'Snow Dogs' has a group of no-personality Huskies. 'River of Gold' has an American — and world — icon, Rin Tin Tin." British investors were tempted ("Bert, this movie project sounds so marvelous"); small studios liked it ("Script is a very pleasant surprise . . . would make a fun Alcon film"). But no one offered to buy it.

At one time Disney had proposed buying Rin Tin Tin from Bert. Not a script; it wanted to buy everything Bert owned that related to the dog: the rights to the character of the dog; scripts for four Rin Tin Tin movies that were already written; the rights to James English's book *The Rin Tin Tin Story,* which Bert held; all the Rin Tin Tin comics and children's books; the colorized television episodes and those that were in sepia or black-and-white; Bert's small ownership position in 106 episodes of *Rin Tin Tin K9 Cop;* and the rights to develop more Rin Tin Tin television shows and movies.

Bert needed the money, but he refused to let go, even though his former lawyer, Tierney, told me that the Disney offer was generous — he remembers it as being close to $5 million. Even if he paid off his debts, Bert would have enough left to be comfortable. He wasn't interested. "I'm not ready to retire," he told his niece Patty. "I think I can make a couple of hit movies and at least one hit series on behalf of the Rin Tin Tin franchise."

His debts mounted while his scripts sat in a box, untouched. By 2003, he owed one of his lawyers $600,000 and another $100,000; he owed producer Irvin Kershner, who had agreed to direct *River of Gold,* more than $100,000 that Kershner had loaned him to help with living expenses. He owed Stephen Harrigan $50,000 for writing *River of Gold.* Max Kleven, who had loaned him $350,000 and now wanted it back, was suing him. The judge in Kleven's suit imposed a deadline of December 1, 2003. If Bert failed to make the payment, Kleven would take over the rights to all future projects based on Rin Tin Tin. To Bert, this would be like giving up all hope. He had an easier time releasing the rights on old projects, but giving up the rights to all future Rin Tin Tin projects was too hard. As he told his lawyer, "All I have left of my life's work is Rin Tin Tin."

He decided he could bear to give up a half ownership in Rin Tin Tin. The prospect of selling even that much was torture, but he was beginning to understand it was a necessity. He went back to Disney, hoping to reignite interest there, offering the half share to them for $5 million. "Rin Tin Tin is a great American icon waiting to be reborn in all its glory for the kids and families of the 21st century," he wrote to Michael Eisner, the head of Disney, with his usual trumpeting confidence. Then the tone of his letter changed, almost as though he were stripping off a costume of bravery and standing naked on a stage. "Rin Tin Tin is like a family heirloom," he wrote, "a first child, hard to give up, but maybe it is time. But like a good parent you want the best home for your first child, and that's the reason for my writing you this letter."

In the end, Disney's interest was not reignited, and Bert's agent contacted twenty other media companies to offer them the half share. He summarized the meetings to Bert in a bluntly worded memo. "It is important to note that in the twenty meetings to date, the unanimous opinion was that the $5 million is much too high. Classic Media" — the company that owned the rights to *Lassie* and *The Lone Ranger* and seemed like a likely taker — "thought the Rin Tin Tin properties were grossly overvalued and wouldn't have gone over

$500,000."

This must have fallen on Bert with a thud. Time had whipped past him, and maybe past Rin Tin Tin. Bert still had that bright, boyish face and crinkled-up, smiling eyes; he could have passed for fifty-five or sixty, but he was now in his seventies, no longer the young success, the "cherubic proprietor-producer" who had just landed in Holly-wood. He and Betty had two young daughters, so he now had six daughters to support. Bert sold the house on Los Feliz, losing money on the transaction, and moved with Betty and their daughters to Reno because it was more affordable.

The move might also have been an effort to restore their marriage. It was a tumultu-ous, broken-crockery sort of relationship, and Bert complained to friends that Betty was more attached to her young friends than to him, but he was hopelessly smitten with her. In the Rin Tin Tin movie proposal, amid hundreds of pages of spreadsheets and financial projections, he devoted a page to pictures of Betty snuggling him, the glaring camera making her blond hair look white. They finally divorced. It didn't last: they soon got remarried. But nothing changed, and they separated again. Betty kept the Reno house. Bert couldn't afford a place of his own; he was reduced to staying with friends and relatives. He would wear out his welcome on one couch and then pack his little Mazda coupe with his clothes and boxes of business papers and move to someone else's couch every couple of days.

15.

By coincidence, at that same moment, Daphne was on the road, too. After she left Pearland, where the city had complained about the number of dogs on her property, she had moved to a thoroughbred farm owned by a friend. But then she left after she and the owner had, in her words, "a difference of opinion on the importance of continuing the Rin Tin Tin legacy."

She had her El Dorado convertible, and all the time in the world, and most of all, the ambition to bring attention to her Rin Tin Tins. So along with her cat and her three favorite dogs — Rin Tin Tin VIII, Joanne, and Gayle — she set off on her ten-month road tour, appearing at pet stores, dog shows, children's hospitals, parades, anywhere there was an interest in Rin Tin Tin.

If you could see the whole story of Rin Tin Tin at one glance, you would see that finally, at this moment, she and Bert and Lee were moving to the same beat, an accidental harmony that had begun in 1922 and kept pulsing more than seven decades later. Each of them had become a messenger trying to deliver the same story — by foot, along the sidewalks of Hollywood, or by Mazda coupe or El Dorado convertible, with the dog heeling alongside, or springing to life on a typewritten script, or sprawled on the backseat, along for the ride.

Everybody liked Bert; I heard this time and time again. He made "the best first impression of anyone in the world," according to Tierney. He was a "charming rogue," according to another business associate, an "immensely appealing man." There "wasn't anyone in the world that didn't like him." I had come to like him, too, even though I knew him only by way of other people's recollections, and by reading through the scraps of his life in boxes stacked ceiling-high in storage unit 3482. He was sharp and funny; even his contentiousness had a certain honor. He loved writers, hated bureaucracy. He stiffed people out of money, owed something to everyone, but it wasn't out of malice — he was always a hair's breadth away from the next opportunity, which would set him right and allow him to make good on his debts. He believed in principle. He wanted to succeed but he cared about making it matter. He wanted Rin Tin Tin to tell stories that had a moral point and would entertain kids as they learned something important about life. He used *Naked City* to examine ordinary people who had fallen away from society and *Route 66* to capture the real feel of the United States in 1960 rather than a set-directed soundstage version of it; he wasn't afraid of making a television show that had a drifty, uncentered center that captured in its aimlessness something true about young people at that time. He didn't love dogs so much as the ideas and stories that Rin Tin Tin could carry inside him.

Even in his humbling circumstances of homelessness he kept working. Back in 1986, he had teamed up with a writer, Chris Canaan, and they wrote a script called *Calexico,* which director Bob Fosse was planning to make as his next film at the time of his death. The main character in *Calexico* was Sam Maclaine, "a vibrant but rumpled man" who had fallen far down the well of Hollywood. But Maclaine was trying his best to clamber back. "Don't call me history, kid!" Maclaine shouts in one scene.

"Dead people are history!" Later, Maclaine adds, "Listen, punk, I ended up in the toilet because no-talent young cretins like you opened up shit factories all over Hollywood."

Part of Bert's appeal was that kind of belligerent optimism — it drove his brashness and his certainty that everything he touched would be fine. "I've survived the film and television business for forty-six years, enduring many dry periods," he wrote to his lawyer in 2002, sounding as if this low point were just a difficult phase he would pass through, even though he had been reduced to borrowing money for food and gas. His third wife, Jenny Cobb, "came to the rescue," as he put it, giving him a place to stay for stretches at a time. But there were moments when he couldn't rally, when he was beginning to sound uncharacteristically defeated. "For a man who was a very rich and successful man, it is very tough," he again wrote to his lawyer. "It's hard to get any job when you're 79; in my profession it's impossible. I am really disgustingly broke. Nada income. Big talent in old body. Maybe I'll make it back, maybe I won't."

16.

Bert hadn't forgotten his promise to Eva that he would get the story of Lee's life on the screen. In one of the last letters they exchanged, Bert wrote to Eva, "I have tried to sell the Rin Tin Tin story. . . . I have not yet been successful but I do think that it is still a possibility." On couches and at coffee shops, he continued to work on *Rin Tin Tin and Me,* a script he'd been working on for almost fifty years. He was now writing it himself in the form of a treatment that could be expanded into a script. He began it by describing the bond between the man and the dog "nurtured in the simplicity and loneliness of Duncan's early background" and how finally "the career which had skyrocketed Lee to fame has come to an ignominious end."

The outline of the story followed the outline of Lee's life, but the character was not quite Lee. In the script, the character of Lee was bolder and cockier than Lee had been in real life, and he was also, in Bert's words, "incredibly weak and impressionable with women; even more so if they [were] beautiful." It was as if Bert was grafting some of his personality onto the cinematic version of the Lee Duncan he was creating.

He was perhaps beginning to feel the urge that Lee had had for so long — to put his life into a story, and then on screen, to give it some order and logic, and also expand it so it took on the shimmering, vast scope of a myth. It was his version of a Memory Room, in the form of a movie, where he had always felt most at home.

One of his drafts began, "In 1921, Lee Duncan was an unemployed veteran of WWI. He had no experience in training dogs. But he had dreams and he had Rin Tin Tin. And he had an imagination. So, we begin with a fable . . ."

In late 2002, during a routine trip to the dentist, Bert was told that something was amiss. Further examination revealed that he had a malignant growth in his throat. The first doctor he consulted told him there was nothing to be done and he had only a few months to live, but a second doctor agreed with what Bert felt: he wasn't ready to die. He had surgery and a course of chemo-therapy, and it seemed like he was cured. He wanted to get back to work on *River of Gold* and *Rin Tin Tin and Me,* even as he was convalescing. He spent hours with his niece Patty and his friend Rob Stone, trying to figure out how to create something out of his remaining rights to Rin Tin Tin. He wanted to work, to make a deal, but he also began to sound like a man who was taking final stock of his life. "I've made a lot of mistakes," he told Stone. "But I had a good ride. I stood on principle. I want it all but I still want to do what I want to do. I haven't given up. I haven't got a complaint in the world. I'm one of the lucky guys who did what he believed. I've made some stupid, stupid decisions, but you know, it was a lot of fun."

The cancer recurred in 2005. This time the surgery included the removal of his voice box. He wrote a note to Patty saying, "I'm tough but at 83, I'm scared." He moved in with Max Kleven for a time, and even though he had dropped to a skeletal 136 pounds, he wanted to work on his scripts. It kept him going, just imagining the movies getting made.

At night, Kleven read him sections of *River of Gold* or *Rin Tin Tin and Me* out loud. As Bert listened, tears rolled down his face. Patty paid to have a nurse, Maria Briseno, move out to Kleven's to help take care of Bert. He wrote notes to his daughters, saying Briseno was his angel, that he didn't know what he would have done without her. One afternoon, Patty drove to Kleven's house to pay Bert a surprise visit. She walked into the living room and came upon Bert and Maria dancing to a Frank Sinatra record, cheek to cheek.

He got sicker; he left Kleven's house and moved in with his daughter Victoria. He wanted to work on his scripts and also re-edit episodes of *The Adventures of Rin-Tin-Tin.* Through hand gestures and notes, he indicated what he wanted changed; a friend who had access to an editing room worked on them. When they were completed he brought them back for Bert to screen.

He died on October 14, 2006, in the living room of the house his ex-wife Jenny shared with their daughter Gina. Several of his daughters were there. Sam Manners went to Bert's funeral expecting to see thousands of people; after all, Bert Leonard had been such a big figure in town. But only a few people attended the service. Mourners were given a card with a picture of a young Bert standing in front of a plane. So many of the people who knew him when he had a golden touch in Hollywood had died before him, or turned against him, or simply forgotten him. But his work had been bigger than that. Millions of people around the world had been affected by the story of a boy and a dog that he had concocted on his lunch break that day in Corriganville.

In his will, besides leaving money to his daughters and his ex-wife Jenny, he specified that 10 percent of his estate go to Lee Duncan's family and another small portion to the estate of Douglas Heyes, who had written most of the episodes of *The Adventures of Rin-Tin-Tin.* Of course, there was no money; there wasn't even enough money in his bank account to cover his funeral expenses. It was a purely symbolic gesture; he knew exactly what he had and didn't have: in the margins of his notes and papers, he had time and again tallied up how much he owed and to whom. But in his mind he never gave up the hope that things were about to straighten out, that his luck would change. Maybe he just wanted to make a final gesture to the two men who had been right beside him when everything in his life was in its place, when the world was listening to the story he was telling.

"This sounds like a fairy tale, doesn't it?" Bert asked Rob Stone in a long talk they had shortly before the surgery that took his voice away. "But it's all true. My life has been something built on more than money. I think — I think it was built on dreams. I cared about these things. I cared about all of these things."

On the day when I was in Texas, the ARFkids families, the puppy buyers, and I left Daphne's house, piled into our cars, and drove to the local agricultural arena to watch an agility demonstration by two dogs and their trainers. The arena was an open-air building with high rafters and a sloping roof, the sort of place that birds seem to view as a ready-made housing development for birds, so there was peeping and fluttering and nervous preening going on just overhead. A sign in the grandstands noted that the arena was "The Resting Place of Wimpy — #1 Grand Champion Stallion at the 1941 Southwest Exposition and Fat Stock Show in Fort Worth." Wimpy, according to the plaque, possessed a good temperament, endurance, and intelligence. The plaque seemed to imply that Wimpy was buried under the dirt floor in front of us, a disconcerting image, but I couldn't think of another way to interpret it. In the arena, the dogs bounded over obstacles and dropped their fetched toys on command, eyes locked on their trainers the entire time. The ARFkids — some silent and withdrawn and others, including a pair of towheaded twin girls, twirling like tops — watched the dogs and bounced and fidgeted and didn't watch the dogs and pointed at the birds in the rafters and the ones taking dust baths beneath the stands.

The man sitting next to me was one of the puppy buyers. His name was Herbert Molina; he lived in Florida but had grown up in Peru watching *The Adventures of Rin-Tin-Tin* on television. I remembered seeing the spreadsheets showing international sales of the show, and Peru was up near the top. Molina was about my age, and I realized that probably the only thing our childhoods had in common — his in Lima, Peru, and mine in Cleveland, Ohio — was that we had spent hours of them watching *The Adventures of Rin-Tin-Tin.* Molina was wearing an oxford shirt, which he unbuttoned while we were talking to show me a German shepherd T-shirt he had on underneath. He said he'd been waiting to get a Rin Tin Tin dog his entire life, and he couldn't believe he was finally going to bring one home. "I think," he said, raising his eyebrows, "I was a German shepherd in my previous life."

Reincarnation and transubstantiation were everywhere I looked, or so it seemed. When Eva Duncan was deposed in the matter of *Leonard v. Hereford,* she was asked if she knew of people who had large collections of

Rin Tin Tin memorabilia. "There was one girl, yes, that I knew but I can't remember her name," Eva responded. "She claims that her dog was — how would you say it — was reincarnated, a Rin Tin Tin reincarnation."

"So the original Rin Tin Tin was reincarnated into this dog?" asked Daphne's attorney.

"Into her dog, yes," Eva replied. "She used to write us letters, reams of letters telling us about this dog. And she would collect all the Rin Tin Tin memorabilia that she could find."

"Oh, my goodness," the attorney said. "So then we're not talking about bloodlines anymore. We're talking about something else. We're talking about spiritual succession?"

"Right, reincarnation," Eva said. After a moment, she added, "You get a lot of goofy people in this business."

Over the years that I'd been in contact with Daphne, there were times when she seemed to appreciate my interest in preserving and extending, in my own way, the legacy of Rin Tin Tin. But there were other times when I suffered what many people around her have suffered, namely, her indignation and sense of insult over something I did or a perceived threat to her dominion over Rin Tin Tin. During one of the periods when she was mad at me, she wrote me a letter reproaching me for something I had said to someone. She ended the letter in high dudgeon, with the simple electrifying statement: "I am Rin Tin Tin."

At the time of this particular visit, though, we were on good terms, and after the obedience demonstration, we came back to her house for the official opening of the museum. Some of its contents were things Daphne had collected, and another significant portion came from two collectors, Edythe Shepard and her husband, Shep, who had gathered German shepherd figures of every sort and style after a chance encounter with a German shepherd statue they liked at a garage sale. After a short ceremony on her lawn, Daphne opened the doors to the museum and everyone filed in. There were shelves of German shepherd objects made of porcelain, ceramic, iron, bronze, and glass; German shepherd plush toys in every possible size; carnival clays and Royal Doultons; Rin Tin Tin books and posters and pictures; oil paintings, needlework portraits, and pedigree cards. I wandered through, pausing every few feet to examine a new version of Rin Tin Tin I had never before seen.

On a shelf near a dark corner in the back of the garage I spotted something familiar, and I hurried over. There it was, leaning against the back of the shelf: the Breyer plastic Rin Tin Tin figurine, with its ridges of fur, its alert stance — my grandfather's toy, the Rin Tin Tin that enraptured me and frustrated me and finally came to such a bad end. I almost hesitated to look at it too closely because I knew that in real life it could never be as big as it was in my memory, nor as wonderful and desirable, because only something remembered can stay intact and perfect and never fade or fail.

But I reconsidered, and a few weeks after I came back from Texas I looked around on the Internet and found one of those Breyer Rin Tin Tins and bought it — and it sits on my desk to this day. There was something gratifying about being able to do that, and disappointing. It finally summed up a certain open equation in my life, but it also reduced a persistent memory, and even a persistent melancholy, into an eight-inch plastic figurine. I was happy to have it, but I sometimes missed the bittersweet weight of my memory, of recalling those days at my grandfather's desk, of feeling so sharply the aches and joys of childhood and the mystery of my family, of realizing that my hunger for that toy had led me to spend these years of my life learning the story of Rin Tin Tin.

There were moments, like the day my Breyer toy arrived, when I began to wonder if the legacy of Rin Tin Tin was finally contracting — whether the big sweep of his story, the international acclaim, the century of prominence, might shrink to the size of an eBay listing. I had haunted the website since starting to trace the story of Rin Tin Tin, and there were never fewer than several hundred Rin Tin Tin items listed — packets of View-Master slides for ten dollars; dexterity puzzles for a couple of bucks; Fort Apache play sets for $149. With the television show off the air, the movie rights tied up in knots, Lee and Bert both gone, it sometimes felt as if Lee's promise that there always would be a Rin Tin Tin had been reduced to some toys and comic books for sale. It seemed like such a compacted version of what Rin Tin Tin had been. A more optimistic viewpoint might be that, these days, living forever means having been enough of a material presence in the world to win a permanent place on eBay. But Rin Tin Tin felt bigger than that; at least that was what I had made myself believe.

As it happened, Daphne's entire Rin Tin Tin museum ended up on eBay just two years after its grand opening. I was browsing through the usual offerings of cereal premiums and Rin Tin Tin beanies when I saw it, listed with a starting bid of $75,000 and a "Buy It Now" price of $100,000 — the entire contents of the world's only Rin Tin Tin museum, "the chance of a lifetime for one lucky bidder." According to the ad, the museum was "conservatively valued at $100,000–$200,000 but due to circumstances beyond our control we MUST part with it. Immediately!" It seems that in the two years that had passed since the opening, Daphne's legal bills had continued to grow. Max Kleven, who now owned many of the rights to any new projects involving Rin Tin Tin, had sued Daphne over the issue of her trademarks. In addition, she had begun a lawsuit against First Look Studios, the production company to which James Tierney sold his portion of the Rin Tin Tin rights, after the studio announced plans to make a movie based on "the true-life story of Rin Tin Tin." Daphne argued that the film violated her rights to the Rin Tin Tin name. Even as the lawsuit was filed, the production got under way and the head of First Look announced, "We are very excited

about being able to have such a property."
The film was shot in Bulgaria and featured
a Bulgarian cast, including one young actor
who told a reporter, "I never actually
learned English. Most of the things I know
came from The Cartoon Network."

There were other lawsuits, too, for infrac-
tions real or theoretical, and then Daphne's
health began to decline and she decided that
selling the museum was the only sensible
option. She said she wasn't going to give it
to her son or daughter. "My kids aren't getting anything from me and they know it,"
she said. As much as she hated Bert Leonard — and the feeling was certainly mutual
— at that moment she would have found a
lot to discuss with him. They both had come
to know well the pain of parting with
something you believed was priceless,
especially when it was, ironically enough, to
cover the cost of protecting it. And of course
they shared the persistent, fundamental
belief in Rin Tin Tin, even when that belief
threatened to ruin them. "I used to joke that
Bert and I should have gotten married,"
Daphne said to me recently. "After all, we
really had a lot in common."

The eBay listing for the museum didn't
draw any bidders, but Daphne eventually
sold the contents to a German shepherd

aficionado, Debra Hnath, who lives in Oklahoma. The official Rin Tin Tin of the moment, Rin Tin Tin XI, whose pedigree name is the oddly repetitive Rin Tin Tins Rin-Tin-Tin, was also sent to Oklahoma to live with Hnath in order to continue breeding more Rin Tin Tin puppies, under an agreement between Hnath and Daphne that eventually became deeply disputed and, finally, formed the basis of another lawsuit. Maybe this final piece of litigation changed Daphne's mind about choosing an heir apparent. Maybe family took on a new importance in her life, because she recently told me that when she retires she intends for her son and daughter to jointly take over the position of chief executive officer of Rin Tin Tin Incorporated.

At the end of that hot, hot day at Daphne's house in Texas, when the celebration of the museum opening was over and the puppies had been paired up with their new families, I got ready to drive to the Houston airport for my flight back to Boston, where I was living at the time. I noticed that there was one puppy — a tiny, dark, wide-eyed female — still sitting on Daphne's lawn, her head resting on her paws. She had been sold to a family in Boston and was going to be shipped to them the next day. As I said goodbye, Daphne realized I was heading to Boston myself, and she asked if I could take the puppy with me as hand luggage, saving her the shipping fee.

I was happy to do it — she was an adorable puppy, a bit shy and worried-looking, with a wrinkly brow and a whip of a tail and feet like little black paddles. She sat in a heap on my backseat during the drive from Crockett to Houston, glancing out the window and then quickly looking away. I realized that she probably had never been in a car before. After thirty miles or so she started to look a little peaked, and when I stopped to let her amble around on a patch of grass behind a fast-food joint, she promptly threw up and then fell asleep.

On the flight home, she sat at my feet, and when she wasn't napping she gave me a melting look that had the terrible effect of making me hope the people who had bought her had changed their minds and that the puppy would end up staying with me. Just like that, the German shepherd I had dreamed of as a kid, the dog I had wanted from the beginning of time, would finally, at last, belong to me.

But when we landed and I carried her out to the baggage claim the whole family was there, as of course I knew they would be, and they squealed and shrieked with excitement when they spotted me — when they spotted the puppy, that is — and they raced up and pried her out of my arms, and within a moment, they were gone and she was gone and I was left without her, standing by the baggage carousel. I had no right to cry about it, but I couldn't help it. For that moment, at least, after a lifetime of imagining it, that shy, worried, tender, heroic, brave, loyal, gallant puppy had been mine.

18.

For me, the narrative of Rin Tin Tin is extraordinary because it has lasted. He is that rare thing that endures when so much else rushes past; he is the repeating mark in our memory, the line that dips and rises without breaking. It is the continuity of an idea that makes life seem like it has a pattern that is wise and beautiful and indelible, one thing leading to the next; the individual beads of our lives, rather than scattering and spilling, are gathered up and strung along that endless line.

I believe there will always be a Rin Tin Tin because there will always be stories. He began as a story about surprise and wonder, a stroke of luck in a luckless time, and he became a fulfilled promise of perfect friendship; then he became a way to tell stories that soared for years. He made people feel complete. I had started my own story by thinking that Lee and Bert and Daphne were curious specimens for their stubborn devotion, and then I realized that I was no different, elbowing my way into the chorus of narrators to advance the tale that much further, to become a part of what "always" means.

I, too, had set out to be remembered. I had wanted to create something permanent in my life — some proof that everything in its way mattered, that working hard mattered, that feeling things mattered, that even sadness and loss mattered, because it was all part of something that would live on. But I had also come to recognize that not everything needs to be so durable. The lesson we have yet to learn from dogs, that could sustain us, is that having no apprehension of the past or future is not limiting but liberating. Rin Tin Tin did not need to be remembered in order to be happy; for him, it was always enough to have that instant when the sun was soft, when the ball was tossed and caught, when the beloved rubber doll was squeaked. Such a moment was complete in itself, pure and sufficient.

The final scene of Bert's treatment for *Rin Tin Tin and Me* takes place on a movie set, on location in Corriganville, where a movie with Rin Tin Tin is being made, and Lee and Eva are there with the dog to film the movie's climactic action sequence. They are all there, in a way: the real dog, who was always the adored companion, and the movie dog, who was the figure of inspiration, and Lee, always alone but here, in this scene, appearing to at last connect with his family, and the unnamed producer, making it all happen, just as Bert pictured himself: all of them in a movie together, in a story about a movie, the endless circle that the Rin Tin Tin story always managed to be. In this rendering, everyone is happy, everything is, at last, complete. Before the scene begins, the producer stops and asks Lee if he might be interested someday in having Rin Tin Tin star in a television show — just as, long ago, in real life, Bert had once asked Lee. Lee shakes his head and says that after this movie he is getting out of show business, and he has everything he could want or need at home, at El Rancho Rin Tin Tin.

"Besides," Lee says to the producer, "what do I know about television?"

The producer smiles and says, "Let me worry about that."

The director calls for everyone to take his place. The shot he's trying to get is challenging; Rin Tin Tin has to run into the fort, climb a flight of steps to a balcony, run across the roof, and then leap to the roof of a nearby building. They all take their places. Lee says the dog is ready, and the camera begins to roll.

But the first take is no good: the dog runs and climbs, but he hesitates before he leaps. The director stops the camera. He asks Lee if he wants to rehearse again, but Lee says no, the dog will get it right this time. Lee puts his hand on the dog's head, a light touch; he glances at Eva and then says they are ready. The director calls for action, and the dog begins. He runs into the fort, climbs the steps, dashes across the balcony, and this time, without hesitation, he soars, defying time and gravity, across the break.

"The dog is brilliant," Bert wrote, at the very end of the story he had tried so many times to tell. "It is like the old days. Lee's eyes are damp." And then Bert added one final beat: "Lee feels a slight tug at his pant leg and finds himself looking down into the grubby little face of one of the many youngsters who live in the neighborhood and

517

come to watch them shoot. The five-year-old asks Lee, 'What's your dog's name?' Lee turns to the boy. 'Rin-Tin-Tin, son.'

"The camera starts back; the director's voice is heard: 'Okay, bring the camera over here.' Eva is alongside Lee and so is Rin-Tin-Tin. The crew is moving and the camera reveals the whole scene. The End."

ACKNOWLEDGMENTS

I have many people — and many, many dogs — to thank for their help in getting this book out of my head and into the world.

Most of all, I want to thank the Duncan family, especially Carolyn McHenry and Kimberlee Duncan Demers; the Leonard family, especially Gina Leonard, Patty Leonard, and Victoria Leonard; and Daphne Hereford. They generously gave me their stories and their time, and bore with me through the years the book was in the making. The Riverside Metropolitan Museum was my home away from home for months, and I owe much of this book to having been given unlimited access to their Lee Duncan collection. My tireless guide there was Kevin Hallaran. Thank you, Kevin, for help above and beyond the call of duty. Allan Shields and Ann Elwood, who have written their own wonderful Rin Tin Tin books, were incredibly generous in helping me with my particular version of this story. Thanks, Ashley Van Buren, for research and encouragement, and for producing the ebook. Thanks, Rob Stone, for giving me so much insight into Bert Leonard. Alice Truax worked on these pages from the beginning, and with her extraordinary eye and ear she helped shape this into a finished product. I am lucky to have her insight and friendship.

The team at Simon & Schuster has been extraordinary. Jofie Ferrari-Adler, my editor, is remarkable in every way, on the page and in person. Thanks, Jofie. Jackie Seow deserves all the credit for this gorgeous, perfect book cover. Alexis Welby made the wheels turn with the press. As for my wonderful publisher, Jon Karp, how great to be back together again.

Richard Pine, who has been there for me ever since I first started thinking that maybe someday I'd write a book, thank you. Thank you!

My everlasting thanks to Ravi Mirchandani, my longtime British editor and friend.

Thanks, in this instance and always, to David Remnick and Virginia Cannon at *The New Yorker,* for inspiring me and for encouragement and forbearance.

To the Nieman Foundation for Journalism at Harvard University, the Corporation of Yaddo, and the MacDowell Colony — places where I blasted through huge sections of the work and in some cases improved my Ping-Pong game — I am so grateful to have been given the chance to immerse myself in this project. Without those residencies, I don't know if I would have ever finished.

Thanks to the librarians and research helpers and press people who were accommodating, generous, and enthusiastic, especially Lauren Buisson at UCLA and Lisa Peterson at the AKC.

My friends and family provided cheerleading and were kind enough not to ask too frequently when I was *finally* going to be done. There are too many to thank, but here's to Jeff Conti, Sally Sampson, Janet Tashjian, Lisa Klausner, Karen Brooks, Richard McCann, Chip McGrath, Celia and Henry McGee, Tricia and Foster Reed, Patricia Marx, Emma Daly, Santiago Lyon, Gail Gregg, Annette Osher, Ann Leary, Susan Casey, Jenny Martinez, Larry Riff, and Deb Thompson. Ann Patchett, you are the best. David and Steffie Orlean, Debra Orlean, and Dave Gross, thank you. Bill and Nez Gillespie, thank you. Jay Gillespie, thank you! Mom, I love you. Dad, I so wish you were here to see the book — I think you would have liked it, even though, true to your character, you asked me, when I began to work on this, why anyone would want to write a book about a dog. (See pages 1 through 518 for my answer.)

Here's a modern moment: I want to thank my Twitter followers, who really did root for me on those long days in my writing studio when I would post my word count and ramble about procrastinating, and who shouted when I declared that I was finally done. Thank you, one and all, for helping me finish #RTT.

My amazing husband, John Gillespie, read every word, held my hand, and made me feel it was worth it, even when it was at great cost to him; there are no words that would suffice to express my love and thanks.

And my son Austin, who was just wishful thinking when I first considered writing this book, and now can actually read it to me, and who just told me that he has always, always dreamed of having a German shepherd just like Rin Tin Tin: you are my very favorite story.

NOTES ON SOURCES

This book covers a period of almost one hundred years and took me nearly a decade to write, and the sources I drew from were many and various, ranging from raggedy archived copies of *Physical Culture* magazine to meticulously detailed sourcebooks of animals on film. In addition to what I've listed here, I combed through newspapers from around the country, countless websites and blogs, scraps of paper, leaflets, flyers, and brochures. This is a selected list of those resources.

Books

Baker, Steve. *The Postmodern Animal.* London: Reaktion Books, 2000.

Basinger, Janine. *Silent Stars.* Middletown, Conn.: Wesleyan University Press, 2000.

Berger, John. *About Looking.* New York: Vintage Books, 1980.

Boone, J. Allen. *Kinship with All Life* (San

Francisco: Harper, 1954).

————— . *Letters to Strongheart.* Harrington Park, N.J.: Robert H. Sommer, 1977.

Brownlow, Kevin. *The Parade's Gone By . . .* Berkeley, Los Angeles: University of California Press, 1968.

Burt, Jonathan. *Animals in Film.* London: Reaktion Books, 2002.

Canaan, Christopher. "Calexico," unproduced screenplay, story by Herbert Leonard and Christopher Canaan.

Derr, Mark. *A Dog's History of America: How Our Best Friend Explored, Conquered, and Settled a Continent.* New York: North Point Press, 2004.

Dodge, Geraldine and Josephine Rine. *The German Shepherd Dog in America.* New York: Orange Judd, 1956.

Duncan, Lee. "Mr. Duncan's Notes," unpublished manuscript (June 21, 1933), Rin Tin Tin /Lee Duncan Collection [A719]. Courtesy of the Riverside Metropolitan Museum, Riverside, California.

————— . *The Rin-Tin-Tin Book of Dog Care.* Englewood Cliffs, N.J.: Prentice-Hall, 1958.

Elwood, Ann. *Rin-Tin-Tin: The Movie Star.* Copyright Ann Elwood, 2010.

English, James W. *The Rin Tin Tin Story.* New York: Dodd, Mead & Company, 1950.

Fagen, Herb. *White Hats and Silver Spurs: Interviews with 24 Stars of Film and Television Westerns of the Thirties Through the Sixties.* New York: McFarland & Co., 1996.

Fetherling, Dale and Doug (eds). *Carl Sandburg at the Movies: A Poet in the Silent Era 1920–1927* Metuchen, N.J., and London: The Scarecrow Press, 1985.

Foglesong, Clara M. *Peter.* Hollywood, Calif.: Myne Publishing Co., 1945.

Frank, Anne. *Anne Frank: The Diary of a Young Girl.* New York: Doubleday, 1967.

Franklin, Jon. *The Wolf in the Parlor: The Eternal Connection Between Humans and Dogs.* New York: Henry Holt, 2009.

Grier, Katherine. *Pets in America: A History.* Chapel Hill: University of North Carolina Press, 2006.

Hereford, Daphne. *Rin Tin Tin's Legacy.* Daphne Hereford, Publisher, 1998.

Kete, Kathleen. *The Beast in the Boudoir: Petkeeping in Nineteenth-Century Paris.* Berkeley, Los Angeles: University of California Press, 1994.

Lee, Raymond. *Not So Dumb: Animals in the Movies.* New York: Castle Books, 1970.

Lemish, Michael G. *War Dogs: A History of Loyalty and Heroism.* Washington, D.C.:

Brassey's, 1996.

Little Folks' Story of Rin-Tin-Tin. Racine, Wis.: Whitman Publishing Company, 1927.

MacDonald, J. Fred. *Who Shot the Sheriff? The Rise and Fall of the Television Western.* New York: Praeger, 1987.

Mitman, Greg. *Reel Nature: America's Romance with Wildlife on Film.* Cambridge, Mass.: Harvard University Press, 1999.

Paietta, Ann C., and Jean Kauppila. *Animals on Screen and Radio: An Annotated Sourcebook.* Metuchen, N.J.: The Scarecrow Press, 1994.

Rothel, David. *The Great Show Business Animals.* San Diego, New York: A.S. Barnes & Co., 1980.

Rothfels, Nigel, ed. *Representing Animals.* Bloomington and Indianapolis: Indiana University Press, 2002.

Sax, Boria. *Animals in the Third Reich: Pets, Scapegoats, and the Holocaust.* New York: Continuum International Publishing, 2000.

Shields, Allan. *The Spirit of Rin-Tin-Tin.* Copyright Allan Shields, 2001.

Simmon, Scott, and Martin Marks. *More Treasures from American Film Archives 1894–1931.* San Francisco: National Film Preservation Foundation, 2004.

Stuart, Reginald Ray, and Grace Dell Stuart. *A History of the Fred Finch Children's Home: Oldest Methodist Home for Children in California, 1891–1955.* Oakland, Calif.: Fred Finch Children's Home, 1955.

Taylor, Jordan. *Wonder Dogs: 101 German Shepherd Dog Films.* Bainbridge Island, Wash.: Reel Dogs Press, 2009.

Tuska, Jon. *The Vanishing Legion: A History of Mascot Pictures 1927–1935.* Jefferson, N.C., and London: McFarland & Company, Publishers, 1982.

Von Stephanitz, Max. *The German Shepherd Dog in Word and Picture.* Jena, Germany: Anton Kämpfe, 1925.

Wallmann, Jeffrey. *The Western: Parables of the American Dream.* Lubbock: Texas Tech University Press, 1999.

Warner Sperling, Cass, and Cork Miller with Jack Warner Jr. *Hollywood Be Thy Name: The Warner Brothers Story.* Lexington: The University Press of Kentucky, 1998.

Weatherwax, Rudd, and John Rothwell. *The Story of LASSIE: His Discovery and Training from Puppyhood to Stardom.* New York: Duell, Sloan and Pearce, 1950.

Willis, Malcolm B. *The German Shepherd Dog: Its History, Development and Genet-*

ics. New York: Arco Publishing Company, 1977.

Archives and Libraries

The Academy of Motion Picture Arts and Sciences, Margaret Herrick Library, Los Angeles, California.

American Kennel Club, New York City, New York.

Herbert Leonard Collection of Scripts and Production Materials for Television and Motion Pictures (Collection 29). Performing Arts Special Collections, University Research Library, University of California, Los Angeles.

Imperial War Museum, London, United Kingdom.

The Paley Center for Media, New York, New York.

Rin Tin Tin /Lee Duncan Collection [A719]. Courtesy of the Riverside Metropolitan Museum, Riverside, California.

University of Southern California, School of Cinematic Arts, Warner Bros. Archives.

Website Resources

Condon, Dan: http://home.metrocast.net/~buggartt/bugga/

http://www.angelfire.com/film/horsefame/saddlebag2.html

www.pedigreedatabase.com
www.olive-drab.com
Hereford, Daphne: http://www.rintintin.com
U. S. Army Quartermaster Foundation:
   www.qmfound.com/War_Dogs.htm
www.uswardogs.org
www.silentera.com
www.lassiecomehome.info
http://www.b-westerns.com/corvlle.htm
www.tv.com
www.silent-movies.com
www.firstworldwar.com
www.london.iwm.org.uk
www.naiaonline.org
www.poodlehistory.org
www.imdb.com

ABOUT THE AUTHOR

Susan Orlean has been a staff writer for *The New Yorker* since 1992. Her subjects have included chickens, surf girls, and origami. She previously worked as a contributing editor at *Rolling Stone* and *Vogue* and as a columnist for the *Boston Phoenix* and the *Boston Globe,* and her work has appeared in *The New York Times Magazine, Spy, Esquire,* and *Outside.* Orlean is the author of several books, including *Saturday Night, The Bullfighter Checks Her Makeup,* and *The Orchid Thief,* a *New York Times* bestseller that inspired the movie *Adaptation,* written by Charlie Kaufman and directed by Spike Jonze. She lives with her family and her animals in Columbia County, New York. For more information, visit www.susanorlean.com or www.rintintinthebook.com.